NAZI PRINCESS

Nazi Princess

Hitler, Lord Rothermere and Princess Stephanie von Hohenlohe

Jim Wilson

In memory of my Father and Mother, James & Winifred Wilson
and their friends
Jack & Annabel Kruse

First published 2011

The History Press
The Mill, Brimscombe Port
Stroud, Gloucestershire, GL5 2QG
www.thehistorypress.co.uk

© Jim Wilson, 2011

The right of Jim Wilson to be identified as the Author
of this work has been asserted in accordance with the
Copyrights, Designs and Patents Act 1988.

British Library Cataloguing in Publication Data.
A catalogue record for this book is available from the British Library.

ISBN 978 0 7524 6114 4

Typesetting and origination by The History Press
Printed in the EU for The History Press.

CONTENTS

INTRODUCTION

I strongly believe in the motto: Never explain; never complain Princess.

Stephanie von Hohenlohe

The populace get angry with fervent admirers of the arch-villain.

Collin Brooks, on Lord Rothermere

I learned to admire the excellence of British propaganda. I am convinced that propaganda is an essential means to achieve one's aims.

Adolf Hitler

I felt compelled to write this book for a number of reasons.

First, by any standards, and whatever view one takes of her motives or her actions, Her Serene Highness Princess Stephanie von Hohenlohe-Waldenburg-Schillingsfürst was a fascinating character. The so-called 'personal ambassador' for Lord Rothermere, one of Britain's foremost newspaper owners, yet at the same time Hitler's '*lieber Prinzessin*', 'dear Princess'. As the world moved inexorably towards world war, hers is a story of intrigue, manipulation, espionage and duplicity in Britain, the United States and Europe. She carried this off with charm, intelligence and undoubted political skill. If it suited her cause, and it frequently did, she exercised the attributes of temptress and seducer.

Second, her exploits during the 1930s encompass an absorbing cast of characters at a crucial time in history, when the policies of influential people in Europe and America were being played out against the receding shadow of one terrible world war, and in the gathering storm of another; in a climate of misunderstanding, appeasement and the dangerous blooming of fascist dictatorship.

Third, an intriguing thread runs through the narrative of links to my own family. Indeed, much of this story might never have happened had my Great-Aunt Annabel not made the fatal introduction that threw Lord Rothermere and the princess together, which led to her passionate love affair with Adolf Hitler's closest adjutant, and made Stephanie, born a Jewess, the Führer's 'dear Princess'.

Without access to secret British intelligence files, only derestricted and released to The National Archives in 2005, and a large collection of Princess Stephanie's own papers now held in the Hoover Institution Archives at Stanford University in California, it would not have been possible to tell her story.

Finally, my thanks to my wife Judith for her loving support and her patient forbearance.

Jim Wilson OBE
Norfolk

1

TWICE WED IN NEW YORK

The British secret service described her as 'the only woman who can exercise any influence on Hitler'.[1] The FBI called her 'dangerous and clever', and as a spy 'worse than ten thousand men'.[2] Hitler referred to her as his 'dear Princess'. Lord Rothermere, newspaper magnate and owner of the *Daily Mail*, employed her as his go-between with Hitler and his henchmen. She was courted in British, American and European high society, and she had access to most of the royal families of Europe. But others, particularly those who knew of her deception, regarded her as a temptress, manipulative and immoral, and prepared to use any means to gain her ends.

She was Princess Stephanie von Hohenlohe-Waldenburg-Schillingsfürst, mistress of Hitler's closest adjutant and a political intriguer of extraordinary ingenuity and skill. Duplicitous, intelligent and charming, as the 1920s and '30s drifted from the horror of one world war to the unknown terrors of the next, she wormed her way into British society, spreading Nazi propaganda at the highest levels. With her lover Fritz Wiedemann, Hitler's commanding officer in the First World War and then his personal adjutant, she pursued Hitler's mission in the United States fostering Nazi sympathies and working in the Nazi interest to keep America out of the war. The story of the princess and the newspaper proprietor is one of double-dealing and irony. What began as a genuine attempt to foster a closer understanding between Britain and the new dictatorships in Europe, ended in the most devastating war in history. Yet post-Second World War, Princess Stephanie emerged from internment in the United States to move in some of the highest circles in Washington as the guest of Presidents.

Many in influential positions in Britain, who might have been expected to show greater foresight, pursued a path of appeasement with Nazi Germany as Hitler inflamed tensions on the path to Europe's second disastrous world war. None did so with more tangled motives than one of the most powerful propagandists of his time, a genuine visionary and friend of Churchill. The story of Lord Rothermere, co-founder of the *Daily Mail*, and his dangerous flirtation with Hitler through the machinations of the Führer's Nazi princess, might stretch the imagination were it not true, as indeed would the extraordinary cast of characters who feature in it. One who played a pivotal part was Annabel Kruse, my great-aunt. She and her wealthy husband, owner of one of the most iconic collections of classic touring and rally cars between the wars, were close friends of both the princess and Lord Rothermere. Together they were the catalyst for this story of espionage and propaganda which, until secret MI5 files were declassified and released to The National Archives in 2005, could not be fully told. It is what these files contain, together with records and memoranda from America's Federal Bureau of Investigation, which prove how seriously the authorities in both countries regarded the princess' activities. They also point to the fact that although it was the press baron Lord Rothermere who employed her, it was the Führer to whom she gave her loyalty. Princess Stephanie spent half a lifetime denying what was obvious to those who knew her story, but with nerve and force of will she overcame all the suspicions and accusations to carve out a distinguished career in the 1950s and '60s as a 'fixer' for some of the most prominent publishers and newspaper owners in Europe and the United States.

My great-aunt was American, born Annabel Adora Belita Maria Colt in Georgia, Alabama, in 1893. Her father, George R. Kane, was owner of a chain of hotels. Her mother, Alma, was Spanish. With that clear Spanish blood in her family background she possessed the personality and temperament that came with it. She was petite, slim and full of fun, an intriguing girl with the ability to electrify any company. When she married my father's uncle, George Wilson, Annabel was only 21 but she had experienced the highs and lows of emotion in her life, having already been married and widowed. George brought her the companionship she was seeking. He was a ships' purser on a liner plying the North Atlantic passage between Liverpool and New York, and an on-board romance blossomed between them. They were married on 13 April 1914 in the grand surroundings of New York's City Hall. Annabel's address at the time was 610 West 127th Street, New York. On the impressive marriage certificate, now lodged in The National Archives at Kew and signed personally by an alderman of New York City Council, George gave his

rank as ship's officer from Hartlepool, England.[3] The marriage lasted through
the horrors of the First World War, but for whatever reason the relationship
broke down and in 1923 Annabel was granted a decree nisi. The marriage was
over when Annabel again crossed the Atlantic in 1924. She may have been
contemplating moving back to the United States permanently, but a chance
meeting in New York changed her life entirely. The man Annabel met and fell
for in New York was Jack Frederick Conrad Kruse, a flamboyant, extremely
handsome, 30-year-old eldest son of a banker. Kruse was not only physically
attractive, he was a man with a distinguished war record, a captain in the
Royal Navy Reserve, and seriously rich.

Jack Kruse was born in South Weald, Essex, on 20 September 1892. His
father, Herman Conrad Kruse, was from a family that had originated from
Germany and subsequently migrated to Holland. Before Jack was born, the
family uprooted again, this time to settle in England. Jack was educated at a
series of public schools and by the age of 20 he was managing an 800-acre fruit
farm at Salehurst in Kent, owned by Sir Harold Harmsworth. Harmsworth
was one of two remarkable brothers, Alfred and Harold, who together in May
1896 had founded the *Daily Mail*. Alfred was in many respects the inven-
tor of the modern newspaper. He was a Fleet Street genius, whose brilliant
news direction and unrivalled understanding of what would sell newspapers in quantities never before achieved, alerted readers of the *Daily Mail* to
events that would change their lives. His flair was to produce a newspaper that
grabbed its readers' attention and held their loyalty in a way previous publications had never been able to achieve. He invented the banner headline and
put emphasis on human interest stories, as well as introducing a much wider
coverage of sport. Within three years of the Harmsworths founding the *Daily
Mail*, it was selling over a million copies daily.

Alfred and Harold were the proprietors who ensured modern journalism
came of age. The Harmsworths followed their ambitious expansion of the
popular press by founding the *Daily Mirror* in November 1902. Their newspapers' campaigns during the First World War arguably changed the course of
the war and influenced the policies of the politicians who were prosecuting
it. They owned the most popular newspapers on the Western Front. The soldiers in the trenches found the *Mail* and the *Mirror* reminded them of home.
They enjoyed the way they carried so many pictures of life back in Blighty.
The *Daily Mail* and the other Harmsworth publications also set the pace
for the introduction of new technology. A year after the *Mail* was founded
a telegraphic link was established between London and New York, the first
transatlantic connection in Fleet Street. Through Alfred's uncanny grasp of

the headlines, features and competitions that would appeal to a mass audience, the *Mail* became the biggest success story in Fleet Street. Three years after the founding of the *Mirror*, Alfred was elevated to the peerage with the title Lord Northcliffe.

Harold's genius was in finance. He understood the stock markets; he had a reputation for successful investment; he excelled in projections of profit and loss and he controlled costs robustly. His task was to make his brother's prowess at journalism pay, and he did it so successfully that the two brothers came to own the largest magazine empire in Britain, and two-thirds of the newspaper titles on Fleet Street. Harold, like his brother, was also elevated to the peerage from the Baronetcy he had held since 1910, associated with his then estate at Horsey in Norfolk. In 1919 he took the title of Lord Rothermere. When Northcliffe died, three years later in 1922, Rothermere inherited all the publications and became reputedly the third richest man in Britain, with an estimated fortune worth £780 million in today's money.[4] By 1926 he had driven the *Daily Mail* to a daily sale of two million.

Like his brother, Rothermere exercised considerable power and influence, not only through the newspapers and magazines he controlled and owned, but also through his wide contacts in political circles. While he could be remarkably prescient in some of his judgements and predictions, he could also be ill-advised in the way he placed his influence behind causes and ideas others might hesitate to become identified with. Unlike his brother Northcliffe, who was inventive, outgoing, impetuous and personable, Rothermere's personality was more reserved, some said shy and ponderous. His introspective personality was emphasised by his physical stature and the walrus moustache he wore as a younger man. As he grew older he trimmed the moustache but not his manner, which as one writer described it was that 'of the proud gruff captain of industry'. He could be exceedingly forthright and blunt – even demanding and rude. Princess Stephanie later went on record as calling him 'erratic, a creature of rapidly changing moods, able to back the idlest of impulses with his millions, open to any suggestion and perfectly ruthless in carrying out any scheme that might bring him journalistic fame or personal prestige'.[5]

With his two favourite sons killed in the Great War and unhappily estranged from his wife Lilian, whom he never divorced, Rothermere, despite his riches and his influence, was a somewhat retiring and lonely figure who was inclined to take associates who he liked and respected under his wing. When he befriended someone, Rothermere had the money and the inclination to be immensely generous to them. Jack Kruse was just such a person. Rothermere had been impressed by Jack's management of his fruit farm in Kent before the First World War. He also admired Jack's war service in Gallipoli. After the war he asked Jack to be his private secretary, and subsequently promoted him rapidly through the ranks of his company; by 1924 Jack was a director of the Continental edition of the *Daily Mail*, published in Paris to cater for the needs of British expatriates in Europe.

In March 1924 Lord Rothermere, Kruse, his lordship's valet and a *Daily Mail* journalist called Arthur Fuller sailed from Monaco, a favourite playground of the rich where Rothermere had a private villa, to New York. Rothermere always travelled first class and stayed in the best hotels. In New York they were booked into the Plaza. It was Jack Kruse's first time in the United States and it is clear he was impressed, not just by the pace and vigour of life in the vibrant city, but also by the people he met. One of those people was Annabel Wilson. Whatever the circumstances that brought Annabel and Jack Kruse together, it must have been special enough for her to make an immediate impression on Jack, and incidentally on Lord Rothermere, too. The romance was whirlwind by any standards. Within a few weeks of meeting Jack, and a year after her divorce from George Wilson, Annabel, at the age of 31, entered her third marriage. In May the party were back on a transatlantic liner bound for Southampton. This time the passenger list recorded Jack and Annabel Kruse as husband and wife, together with Winifred R. Butcher, described as Annabel's personal maid. The speed of the courtship and of their marriage in New York was swift by any standards, even by those of the era they were living in, the carefree 'Roaring Twenties'.

2

ROTHERMERE AND
CHURCHILL

Wealthy and handsome with a distinguished war record, Jack Kruse was one of those young men who 'had it all'. After returning from the torment of action in one of the harshest theatres of the First World War, the ill-fated Gallipoli Campaign, he sought to put behind him the stress and horror of war by becoming involved in the world of fast sports cars. In the 1920s, motoring was coming of age. Famous marques like Rolls-Royce and Bentley in Great Britain were competing with Continental manufacturers Alfa Romeo, Bugatti and Lancia in Italy, and Mercedes-Benz in Germany. Each company was endeavouring to outdo the others in developing the cream of touring and sporting models. The roads were comparatively traffic free. Speed restrictions and speed cameras were a long way in the future. The open road enticed those with the money, a taste for excitement, and a pioneering spirit. Major sporting competitions, like the Monte Carlo Rally, the Alpine and Le Mans, were magnets to those looking for high-profile thrills. Kruse, with his money and his flamboyance, was well placed to gain pole position in this highly competitive and expensive world.

He had served with distinction in the war. Initially, when the call to arms came, he had signed up to join one of the most select and fashionable units in the British Army, the Queen's Westminster Volunteers. But once in khaki he was not as enthralled by the army as he thought he would be, and he opted for a transfer to the senior service, the Royal Naval Division, as a second lieutenant. The Royal Naval Division was a creation of Winston Churchill, then First Lord of the Admiralty. In most previous wars a naval brigade had fought alongside the army, and because there was a surplus of officers and men left over from service in the Fleet, Churchill decided they, together with a large part of the Royal Naval Volunteer Reserve, should be formed into one single fighting unit similar to an army division. Probably because Churchill was behind the Dardanelles venture, the Royal Naval Division was among the units sent to Gallipoli. Once appointed to the division, Kruse found that rapid promotion followed, greatly assisted, it would seem, by his friendship with Rothermere.

Lord Rothermere was a close associate and friend of Winston Churchill. Indeed, Churchill frequently wrote for the *Daily Mail*. In his 'wilderness years', when he felt rejected by the mainstream of British politics, Churchill knew he could always turn to Rothermere and the *Mail* to boost his income and give wide currency to his views. In the 1930s he was writing as passionately as Rothermere himself about the need for Britain to build up its air force. In the First World War Rothermere served briefly as Britain's first Secretary of State for Air. Appointed by David Lloyd George, he gave loyal support to the British government. He took the post with the ambition of creating the Royal Air Force, hoping to give a modernising boost to Britain's capability to prosecute war in the air. At the time, military flying was in the hands of the Royal Flying Corps, aligned to the army, and the Royal Naval Air Service, rather than a separate military organisation. It was Rothermere who, in December 1917, appointed General Sir Hugh Trenchard as his Chief of Air Staff. Trenchard of course went on to become, in the eyes of most people, the father of the RAF. But a share in that glory must also go to Rothermere, though the RAF did not emerge until after Rothermere left his ministerial post. Rothermere encountered strenuous departmental resistance to the sweeping reforms he had hoped to carry out. The strain on him was severe and he had to resign his ministerial post before his dream of forming the Royal Air Force as a third military arm could be realised. 'Your work,' Lloyd George wrote to him, 'has been of inestimable service to the nation, and time will bring with it a full recognition of your achievement.'[1]

Rothermere's interest in air power and his unshakeable belief in the future of aircraft in war marked him out, alongside Churchill, as a leading advocate of building a strong, well-trained air force, and this remained true long after his spell as Secretary of State. In the latter part of the 1930s, when Germany was manufacturing warplanes at a remarkable pace, Rothermere's view of the bomber as the 1930s' equivalent of the weapon of mass destruction, and his conviction that there was no adequate defence against it, dominated the campaigns he ran in his newspapers to persuade Britain to rearm, build up her air power and address her defences against aerial bombardment. He had held strong views on the potential of flying for many years. In 1906 the *Daily*

Mail had offered a prize of £1,000 for the first cross-Channel flight, and a prize ten times that amount for the first flight from London to Manchester. Rothermere's energetic promotion of these challenges in his newspapers drew ridicule in some quarters. *Punch* magazine thought the idea preposterous, and lampooned it by offering its own prize for the first flight to Mars. But Rothermere had the last laugh. By 1920 both his prizes had been won.

Much of Rothermere's extensive correspondence with his friend Winston Churchill is in the Churchill archives at Churchill College, Cambridge. One letter, written shortly after the start of the First World War, indicates that he lobbied Churchill as First Sea Lord, asking him to pull strings on behalf of Jack Kruse to gain him promotion to the rank of captain.[2] Rothermere was granted this favour by Churchill and Kruse secured his promotion. But Rothermere's intervention in no way guaranteed Jack Kruse an easy war. He was sent to Turkey to fight in the trenches in Churchill's ill-inspired and costly Gallipoli Campaign. Kruse was among the last to be evacuated from that disastrous adventure in which so many British and Anzac troops lost their lives. On his way home he faced further danger when his ship was torpedoed. But his luck held. He was one of those pulled exhausted from the water and he survived. Eventually, he returned to England to be transferred into the Royal Marines. When the Armistice came he resumed civilian life, rejoining Rothermere at the newspapers, now known as Amalgamated Press.

Rothermere himself was devastated by the war, having lost his two favourite sons, Vere and Vyvyan. Lieutenant Vere Sidney Harmsworth RNVR, like Jack Kruse, endured the horrors of Gallipoli only to die on the Western Front, gallantly leading a charge of his troops from the Royal Naval Division at the Battle of Ancre on 16 November 1916. Captain Harold Alfred Vyvyan Harmsworth died two years later of wounds suffered in action at the second Battle of Cambrai. Rothermere never fully recovered from the loss of his two eldest sons, and he had a fraught relationship with his only surviving son, Esmond. His married life had been just as tragic. He had married Lilian when she was 18. She went on to have a fairly open love affair with his younger brother St John, who was then paralysed in a car accident. Unsurprisingly, it had left Rothermere lonely and depressed, searching for a purpose other than his business, and to an extent living life at the mercy of events rather than entirely in control of them. The sadness of his personal loss in the First World War never left him and was certainly a factor in his later support of Chamberlain and his policy of appeasement.

Rothermere's brother, Northcliffe, fell out with Churchill over the disaster of the Gallipoli landings. In his newspapers Northcliffe directed much of the blame for what had happened at Churchill, who under severe criticism went on to lose his seat in the Cabinet, and, temporarily breaking from politics, took himself off to the Western Front. Despite his brother's newspaper campaign, Rothermere remained friendly with Churchill. But the war had taken its toll on him. Later in life, Churchill would recall an emotional moment while dining with Rothermere, when a weary Vyvyan was home on leave from the front line. Rothermere invited Churchill to tiptoe into the boy's bedroom where he proudly showed Winston the young officer fast asleep. As Churchill noted fondly, Rothermere was 'eaten up with love of this boy'.[3]

Possibly the tragic loss of his two sons explains Rothermere's kindness towards Jack Kruse. On his return home from war, Kruse was immediately welcomed back to employment with Amalgamated Press on a handsome salary, and it was not long before Kruse was one of Rothermere's closest, most trusted associates. Shortly before Jack's marriage to Annabel Wilson, Lord Northcliffe died, leaving a generous legacy in his will of a bonus equal to three months' pay to all 6,000 of his employees. Rothermere inherited the Amalgamated Press empire, becoming not only one of the most influential men in Britain, the Rupert Murdoch of his day, but also one of the wealthiest. He was owner not only of the *Daily Mail* and the *Daily Mirror*, two of the highest circulation newspapers in the country, but also the *Sunday Pictorial*, *Sunday Dispatch* and the *London Evening News*, together with a number of magazines. In conjunction with Lord Beaverbrook he also bought the Hulton Press, becoming, at the time, the largest newspaper owner in the world.[4]

3

THE GOLDEN COUPLE

When she met and married Jack Kruse, Annabel was not alone in being a divorcee. In July 1918, almost as soon as Jack had returned from war service, he had first married Lilian Kathleen Gilbert. Their marriage certificate describes Jack as an officer in the Royal Marines.[1] Just out of military service, he wanted for little. He was living in London at an expensive address, 41 Pall Mall, and he gave his occupation as 'of independent means'. Lilian was only 21 and came from Hastings on the south coast. A son, John, was born the following January while the couple were living at Tunbridge Wells. Jack had by then rejoined Rothermere at Amalgamated Press, and while he was described as private secretary to the newspaper owner, his responsibilities were increasingly demanding. They entailed constant travel, both in Britain and on the Continent. A second son, Anthony, was born in July 1920, but it seems Lilian rebelled at the demands Jack's job was making on their marriage and she began to see another man, George Ernest Took from Folkestone. Jack petitioned for divorce in 1921, citing Took as the co-respondent and claiming custody of the two children. By the following year, when he met Annabel in New York, Jack, father of two sons, was free to pursue her favours. Both were released from unsatisfactory marriages, seeking happiness in their new relationship.

Lilian soon remarried. Not to George Took, but to an army officer named Jennings with whom she moved away from the mainland to live on the Channel island of Jersey. Although Jack had won custody of the children, it would have been difficult for a single man, engrossed in a responsible and demanding job, to provide a suitable home for two young children. An amicable agreement was made that Lilian and her new husband would take the two boys with them to Jersey. Sadly, Annabel was unable to have children herself, so Kruse and his new wife later struck a deal with Lilian, whereby John, then aged 4, left his mother to live permanently with his father. As it turned out, the little boy would have no further contact with his natural mother for the next sixty years. Not surprisingly, he came to regard Annabel as his true mother.

Jack seems to have been spurred on to greater business activity following his marriage to Annabel, both on behalf of Amalgamated Press and on his own account. With the help of Rothermere's celebrated financial and business advice he set up a number of businesses in Amsterdam, London and later in Hartlepool. They all seem to have prospered. When business allowed, Jack and Annabel were enjoying a high-society life in London. They took up residence at 25 Park Street, Mayfair, one of the capital's most exclusive addresses. The two made an attractive and glamorous couple, and it was not long before they were being welcomed into some of London's most glittering society circles. The London scene in the climate of the 1920s was lively and carefree. The war had emancipated many women, irrevocably changing their place in society. Those who could afford to go to the best restaurants, to theatre premieres and be seen at society events enjoyed the freedom and the gaiety of the new era that peace had brought. There was a feeling, following the misery of war and its horrific human toll, that life was for living; a spirit reflected in the music, the dances, the fashion and the generally lighthearted attitude of the time. Jack and Annabel revelled in the newfound freedoms in the dance clubs and the revue bars. Smart venues, like the Embassy Club in Bond Street, were favourite haunts of glamorous 'couples around town'. In the overcrowded cellar room that was the Embassy, members of London's high society, all in evening dress, clustered at packed tables around the tiny dance area, the genial host Luigi in attendance, and Ambrose's band playing the latest quicksteps and foxtrots for the couples who squeezed onto the club's crowded dance floor. It was here in the early 1930s that the Prince of Wales and the still married Wallis Simpson would engage in raucous and lively conversation, while the long-suffering Ernest Simpson sat patiently in a thick fog of cigarette smoke on the periphery of the royal group. It was a place to be seen, and the Kruses were among the patrons who frequently danced the night away there.

In 1925 Jack and Annabel moved further upmarket to Upper Brook Street in Mayfair, where their next-door neighbours could hardly be higher up the social scale. Lord and Lady Mountbatten were not only cousins of royalty, they were influential in many areas of national life. Lord Louis was destined to become the last Viceroy of India, and later Chief of the Defence Staff. He and his new wife lived and entertained lavishly. It was said Edwina Mountbatten never understood the idea of living within one's means, the cash simply flowed.[2] A friendship with the Mountbattens was an entry to the top rung of society. Edwina and Dickie Mountbatten had married in the same year as Jack and Annabel. She was the granddaughter of the hugely wealthy Sir Ernest Cassel; he the son of the former Prince Louis of Battenberg. At Brook House the Mountbattens employed twenty-seven indoor staff and two outdoor staff when they were in residence, and fourteen indoor and three outdoor when they were away. This was the neighbourhood, and the aristocratic surroundings, in which the Kruses lived. And they kept up appearances themselves. In the summer they moved temporarily out of the city, renting houses in Sunningdale or Sunninghill near Windsor where they could escape from the bustle of central London and enjoy the 'season' of society events that inevitably included racing at Epsom and Ascot, polo, Wimbledon and the Henley regatta. It also meant that they were close to Fort Belvedere where the Prince of Wales had his residence, a magnet for all who aspired to the peak of society, and where Prince Edward entertained and pursued the favours of his mistresses.

In 1927 Annabel and Jack bought Sunning House at Sunningdale, a huge mansion standing at the heart of Sunningdale golf course. Together they virtually rebuilt the house, employing Spanish and Italian craftsmen to give it a distinctive 'Mission style' look. Inside, Annabel furnished the rooms with expensive antiques, collecting many of the pieces through her visits to the major London sales houses. The couple lived at Sunning House in conspicuous luxury and they employed servants on a scale more appropriate to times before the First World War than after, rivalling the aristocratic Mountbattens. Fifteen servants ran the domestic side of their lives, while a further seven were employed to tend the gardens and look after Jack's growing stable of sporting and touring cars. Of the seven outside staff, four were gardeners and no fewer than three were chauffeurs. In the grounds of their mansion they built a tennis court and a luxurious swimming pool. An extensive garage wing was added to the main mansion to accommodate Jack's cars – his fleet generally consisted of seven vehicles at any one time and most were iconic models of that most elegant era of motoring. During the years 1924 to 1937, records now in the National Motor Museum at Beaulieu show that Jack purchased no fewer than forty-seven cars.[3] Twenty of them were Rolls-Royce in a range of different models and styles – broughams, cabriolets, drop-head coupes, saloons, and sports tourers. The rest were mainly Bentley, and latterly Alfa Romeo, Bugatti, Lancia and Mercedes-Benz, with a Buick, a Lincoln Zephyr, an Invicta and a Ford as 'also rans'. Side by side with Jack's cars in the garage at Sunning

House were Annabel's vehicles, most of which displayed her personal crest and monogram emblazoned on their polished coachwork.

Jack had a voracious appetite for the fastest and most elegant models, and from the early 1920s he developed a well-recognised love for the finest hand-built cars the Rolls-Royce factory could produce. He was widely recognised as one of that famous manufacturer's leading and most discriminating customers, always in search of the optimum model for competitive events, sometimes changing cars so rapidly that he would keep a car for only a few weeks before swapping it for a new model. In the eyes of many experts, he represents the ultimate motoring sportsman of the 'Roaring Twenties'. In the correspondence columns of the motoring press he sparred with the Bentley Boys, that famous group of sporting characters led by Tim Birkin, who so captured the imagination of the public at the time. Several of Jack's cars still survive in different parts of the world, now hugely valuable because of their provenance and carefully tended by discerning collectors. Some have remained in England and are listed in the register of famous classic vehicles; others have passed to collectors abroad. The cachet of owning a vehicle that had once been in Kruse's ownership is enough to add thousands of pounds to its value today.

Although having chosen Sunning House as their main home, the Kruses had not entirely abandoned life in the city. Annabel maintained an apartment at the Grosvenor House Hotel, and a permanent suite at Claridge's. She was a major supporter of charities, as is clear from some of the entries in the court circular published in pages of *The Times*. For instance, in 1930 Annabel is mentioned as one of a handful of people sponsoring boxes, at a cost of 250 guineas a time, at a Midnight Revue organised by the impresario Charles Cochran at the London Pavilion, in aid of the Prince of Wales' personal fund in support of the British Legion. It reflects her friendship with Edwina Lady Mountbatten, who was chair of the organising committee.[4] Annabel and Edwina were both free spirits.

Kruse has been described by some commentators writing of that era as a cross between a character from *Jeeves & Wooster* and James Bond.[5] Whether he himself would have recognised that caricature is debatable, but what was probably his most famous car does in an indirect way link him to Ian Fleming, Bond's creator. In 1925 Kruse bought one of the first ever Rolls-Royce Phantoms, registration number 31HC, and in his quest to acquire the ultimate grand tourer he commissioned a talented engineer, Charles Amherst Villiers, to extensively modify it and fit it with a supercharger. Such modification of a Rolls-Royce was unheard of then and since. The purpose of the supercharger was to force more air/fuel mixture into the engine and increase the car's potential speed. The result was described in the motoring press at the time as 'The Stately Super-car'. It was an elegant car, a one-off and a classic example of the early days of supercharging. Jack himself referred to it as 'the first and last supercharged Rolls-Royce'.

Villiers was an engineering genius. He had built up a considerable reputation tuning cars for the celebrated racing driver Raymond Mays, increasing the power of his Brescia Bugatti, and successfully modifying his 1.5 litre AC sports car. Villiers later supercharged a 1922 Tourist Trophy Vauxhall. His most famous accomplishment was designing Malcolm Campbell's land speed record-breaking Bluebird. These achievements had been noted by Kruse, and he gave Villiers virtual carte blanche to rework his Phantom. Villiers was in fact a close friend of Ian Fleming. Indeed, when he wrote his Bond books, Fleming cast his master spy as a fast-car enthusiast who owned a supercharged 4.5 litre Bentley, which was his passion. As Bond enthusiasts will recall, he drove it with almost sensual pleasure. Fleming would have known that in 1929 Amherst Villiers, with the agreement of the Bentley company, had modified a number of 4.5 litre production Bentleys, fitting them with superchargers so that a team of these special 'Blower Bentleys' could be raced in 1930 at Le Mans. He would also have known that the forerunner of the supercharged Bentley was Kruse's 'Stately Super-car', fondly christened 'Sheila'.

As well as being an engineer, Villiers, who was a cousin of Winston Churchill, was also an accomplished portrait painter. His portrait of Fleming hangs today in the National Portrait Gallery. As a young journalist Fleming, as his Bond novels confirm, was devoted to cars, and in 1930 he reported the Le Mans 24-hour race for the press agency Reuters. The following year he participated in the Alpine Rally with Donald Healey as his co-driver. They won their class in a 4.5 litre Invicta. Kruse and Fleming were certainly known to each other, since Alpine rallying and touring was Kruse's first love and both he and Fleming participated in the same rally in 1931. As the two were acquainted, it is not entirely fanciful that Kruse's flamboyance, love of powerful, elegant motor cars, and his considerable wealth and charm may well have made him, at least in part, a role model for the famous character Fleming later invented.

It took Villiers two years to supercharge Kruse's Phantom, working on it at premises he acquired at a disused mill at Staines in Berkshire. To ensure he was not deprived of his favourite Rolls while work progressed, Kruse obtained a second Phantom. Villiers decided that the supercharger should not be driven by the Phantom's engine, because to do so would rob the car of its main unit of power, reducing the output the modification was aimed at achieving.

Instead, he designed a separate unit to drive the blower. This extra engine, which had its own ignition and starter, produced an additional 10hp. It was mounted beside the nearside front wing, where the spare wheel would normally have been housed. Two spare wheels were mounted on the other side of the car to provide the necessary balance for the 200lb engine/blower unit. The Phantom's dashboard was equipped with some fourteen instruments, which included an altimeter for use during Kruse's Alpine trips. There were also additional controls to prime and start the blower engine. The interior seats of the Rolls were pneumatic. However, the considerable additional weight, the whining of the blower, and the roar of the exhaust must have all made for an exhilarating, memorable, if queasy and ear-splitting, ride for those on board.

Villiers began testing the 'souped-up' Rolls at the Brooklands racing circuit, home of the British Grand Prix, in September 1927, running the modified chassis with a rig of testing equipment precariously balanced alongside him to assess the supercharger's effectiveness. Kruse was getting impatient to take delivery of his new 'baby'. He wanted to prove that it was the top British performance car in existence at that time. While he waited for delivery of the supercharged Rolls, possibly prompted by the exploits of the famous Bentley Boys, Kruse succumbed to the other prominent all-British marque, and in July 1927 he took delivery of one 6.5 litre Bentley with another, a Plas Tourer, as back-up for good measure. Yet despite having spent a great deal of money on his two Bentleys, Kruse was not won over by them.

The modified Phantom was at last ready for delivery in early 1928. Villiers himself delivered the car to Sunning House, only to find Kruse away on one of his frequent business trips to Europe. Villiers invited Annabel and young John Kruse to join him on a test run. He took them on a hair-raising trip to Bagshot and back in a heavy rainstorm. It must have been a hectic and far from comfortable first ride. John Kruse recalled glancing at the speedometer on the dashboard and seeing it indicate 110mph; there were no speed cameras or speed checks in those days, and no motorways either! The cost of the Phantom's conversion amounted to a small fortune, the equivalent of five standard Rolls-Royce cars, but Kruse was happy to pay the price. Indeed, on top of the bill, as a thank-you gift, he gave Villiers an almost new straight-eight, 2 litre Bugatti!

The supercharged Phantom proved an extraordinary and thrilling experience to drive, but because of the additional weight and noise, it was fairly impractical. The supercharger did not kick in automatically simply by accelerating. The driver had to lean far over to his left to prime the additional engine and then warm it up on the choke before engaging the supercharger. At speed, this manoeuvre would have been decidedly risky without the assistance of a chauffeur. This was not the only downside to the car in its reconstructed form. One of Kruse's chauffeurs, Reginald Powell, recalls that when the supercharger was engaged, fuel consumption plunged from 12–14mpg to something between 7–8mpg.[6] But fuel prices in the 1920s were not a significant concern to someone with Kruse's financial resources. Despite the time and money Kruse had lavished on his supercharged Rolls-Royce, he rapidly became disillusioned with it. He decided it was not the ultimate sports tourer he had hoped it would be. Nor was it the perfect sports tourer for which he had been searching. If a car did not match up to his high expectations, Kruse had a reputation for changing models with undue rapidity, undoubtedly to the satisfaction of the companies with whom he dealt. By April 1929 he had sold the supercharged Rolls to the famous Dorothy Paget, known as 'The Queen of the Turf' for her almost obsessive involvement in horse breeding and racing. In 1930 the Hon. Dorothy Paget temporarily switched her allegiance from the horse-racing track to motor racing, spending what today would be regarded as a fortune backing Birkin's Bentley team.

As a replacement for the supercharged Phantom, Kruse bought, in September 1928, another exotic 'Roller' – a special short chassis 'Sports Phantom' tourer, one of only four ever built by Rolls-Royce. This car, with its fabulous looks, complimented by a special paint finish of Curzon blue and enhanced by highly polished aluminium wings, was capable of 90mph. Maybe it is fanciful to think that this car inspired Fleming's Chitty Chitty Bang Bang, but with its stunning appearance it was certainly a car to dream about. However, Kruse was still not satisfied. Four months later he acquired another Phantom I, and later the same year, in an incredible display of the financial resources he was prepared to outlay, he took delivery of a couple of Phantom IIs. At the end of 1930 he laid out further cash on another Rolls-Royce, this time a magnificent Phantom II Continental, perhaps at last the ultimate touring car.

Touring was really his passion. He had little interest in the Monte Carlo Rally, although he had on occasions competed or entered vehicles. His real love was Alpine driving. He was beginning to become disillusioned in his search for a purely British-built, high-performance grand tourer which would fulfil all his demands, and he started to look more and more favourably on Continental manufacturers. The more he experienced driving on the Continent and in the Alps, the more he appreciated the touring performance of some of the finely engineered models being created by Continental builders like Lancia, Alfa Romeo and Mercedes-Benz.

For Jack and Annabel Kruse, life in London and at Sunning House was very comfortable. Their wealth, contacts and outgoing personalities made them welcome in the top echelons of society. But Jack's business increasingly took him into Europe. As a leading director on the board of Rothermere's Continental version of the *Daily Mail*, he was travelling extensively, often in company with his wife, and Annabel particularly relished their trips to the south of France. The French Riviera was a playground for the fashionable, sophisticated, moneyed classes from England, as indeed it was for the rich and influential from all over Europe. From the mid-1920s Jack and Annabel were regular visitors to the Côte d'Azur, as was Lord Rothermere. Both the press proprietor and his employee had luxurious villas there.

Rothermere, although estranged from his wife and still devastated by the loss of his two eldest sons in the war, was not averse to the attentions of attractive young women. Indeed, throughout his life he had many lady friends, some of whom were his mistresses. Despite his brusqueness he could be a vivacious companion and a 'good mixer', overcoming his inherent shyness. Without doubt Annabel was among those upon whom he lavished attention, and it almost certainly went beyond mere flirting and showering her with expensive gifts. The press baron was a complex character who liked to have familiar faces around him. One of his biographers described him as having a generous nature, although he never believed his own value extended beyond what he could give to another person. More and more the measure of his love became how much he could spend or lavish in presents and hospitality.[7] He was famous for his lavish tips and it was said he employed a member of staff for the sole purpose of giving away money! He had more than enough of it to worry about how to spend it all. By 1926 his fortune was estimated at between £15 and £26 million.[8] Rothermere's villa in the south of France, La Dragonnière situated at Cap Martin, was relatively small considering his huge fortune. The Kruses were frequent visitors there. The villa had gained its name from a legend which claimed that in the mists of time a terrifying dragon had been slain there. The myth added to the fairytale quality of the place. It stood in 2 acres of orange groves, 200yds from the sea, overlooking Monte Carlo. With the profusion of flowers clustered round its walls, their scents strong in the sunshine, and the sea close by, the place had a romantic atmosphere. It was this spirit that captured Churchill whenever he visited Rothermere there, and inspired him to get out his easel and paint. The press baron was a passionate gambler, and one of his favourite haunts was the Monte Carlo Sporting Club, where the amounts he waged on the tables were legendary.

With Rothermere putting his financial expertise to work, advising his colleague on the investment of his capital, Jack and Annabel were financially secure, comfortably rich enough to make their mark and keep up with the super wealthy. They enjoyed escaping to the playgrounds of the south of France and made many friends in the distinguished company they kept there. Indeed, it was part of Jack Kruse's job with the European *Daily Mail* to ensure that he had good contacts across Europe. In her book about the Harmsworth brothers, *The Great Outsiders*, S.J. Taylor describes the Kruses as 'a dazzlingly rich couple that would have been at home amongst the pages of a novel by F. Scott Fitzgerald'.⁹ And only a work of fiction could have dreamed up the consequences of Annabel's friendship with a remarkable, manipulative woman who was well known among the influential circles who frequented the luxury hotels, villas and casinos of Monaco. Annabel and Jack had a close friendship with Princess Stephanie Julianne von Hohenlohe-Waldenburg-Schillingsfürst. They saw her frequently in London, Paris and the French Riviera – it was a friendship that would fatally capture Rothermere in a web of intrigue, and eventually take him all the way to Hitler's inner circle and into the Führer's confidence.

4

THROW OF THE DICE

For large parts of the year, whenever Jack's commitments in Europe allowed, the Kruses immersed themselves in the high life of the top resorts on the Mediterranean coast. They frequented the casinos, hotels and fashionable bars, and inevitably they attracted to their circle others from all parts of Europe who were drawn to this arena of the rich and famous. Among those exotic personalities was their close friend, a princess of the Austro-Hungarian Empire, Princess Stephanie von Hohenlohe, who had her holiday villa in Biarritz. Only 5ft 5in tall, she possessed a magnetic personality, and her classic Grecian profile, striking Titian hair and beguiling charm engaged and fascinated all who met her. The princess had an intriguing reputation as a femme fatale, a temptress used to being showered with flowers, jewellery, furs and flattery from wealthy suitors who courted her as much for her title as her charismatic personality. She avidly accepted all the gifts that came her way, though some of those who lavished presents on her soon found that while their gifts were welcome, they were not! She was bold, adventurous, manipulative, persuasive, and, though few realised it then, she was potentially dangerous. The princess was a woman who would use her sophisticated charm and her seductive wiles to gain access to those she felt might repay her attention, and if she set her sights on meeting someone and winning them over to her wishes, her strength of character usually ensured she succeeded. She had the reputation of having exploited and rejected a catalogue of suitors, tapping the financial resources of many of them in the process.

In Monaco the princess welcomed warm relations with Annabel, because while they had common interests and enjoyed one another's company, the princess could see it gave her the ideal opportunity to get close to, and eventually to become acquainted with, the influential and extremely wealthy Lord Rothermere. The princess was skilled in positioning herself to meet and be introduced to those she chose to target. Her contacts book was filled with a cosmopolitan list of people of influence and wealth – entrepreneurs, financiers, politicians, diplomats, statesmen and European aristocracy and royalty. This was a world in which she moved with ease, using her charm, her social skills and inevitably her title to impress and to persuade.

However, Princess Stephanie Julianne von Hohenlohe-Waldenburg-Schillingsfürst, to give her the full title bestowed on her when she married into the family of the Austro-Hungarian Emperor, was not all she seemed. She had been born in Vienna in September 1891, when that city was the highly civilised and cultured centre of a great empire. But Stephanie was far from being born into the aristocracy. There was no silver spoon in her mouth, no high-level family tree in her background. In fact, she was the illegitimate daughter of Ludmilla Kuranda, a Jewish woman from Prague, who had had an illicit affair with a Jewish money lender by the name of Max Wiener while her real husband was serving a prison sentence for embezzlement.

Stephanie's Jewish parentage is beyond doubt, although later she contrived to convince the Nazi hierarchy, even Hitler himself, that she was of pure Aryan stock. The princess herself would never admit to Jewish blood. It was her half-sister, the writer Gina Kaus, who provided the evidence. Shortly after his illicit affair with Stephanie's mother Ludmilla, Wiener married another woman and a second daughter was born; this was Gina. Many years later, Gina confessed that Princess Stephanie was indeed her half-sister, though she added 'maybe she never knew it'. Gina went on to say that her Jewish father was an unsophisticated man. He had occasionally mentioned his affair with Ludmilla to Gina, and her understanding was that a sum of money probably changed hands when Ludmilla's husband, released from prison, undertook to accept Stephanie as his own daughter. Gina Kaus was born in Vienna in 1893. She became a successful novelist in the 1930s but the Nazis publicly burned her books together with those of many leading Jewish and anti-Nazi writers. She immigrated to California in 1938. Two of her novels, *The Devil Next Door* and *The Devil in Silk*, became bestsellers in post-war Germany, and in 1956 *The Devil in Silk* was turned into a successful film starring Curt Jurgens and Lilli Palmer.[1]

Her mother's actual husband was a lawyer, Hans Richter, a Catholic whose family came from Moravia. Shortly before her marriage to Richter, Stephanie's mother rejected her own Jewish faith and also became a Catholic. On his release from prison, Richter generously accepted the child as his own. Despite his term in jail, Richter was able to resume his rather lucrative legal practice and continued to earn a good income, certainly sufficient to give his family a comfortable standard of living. Stephanie had a fairly sheltered upbringing in Vienna, growing up as an only and somewhat spoilt child. 'School,' she wrote later, 'was something of a trial because I was a very erratic pupil. Abysmally poor at mathematics, for some reason I excelled at physics. My other strong points were history and P.E.'[2] After completing her schooling in Vienna, her parents sent her for several months to a college in Eastbourne in the south of England, where she became fluent in English and familiar with English customs and manners. In fact, Stephanie had a talent for languages, and by the time she was 21 she spoke several fluently; an asset she exploited fully in the life she embarked upon later. For a time she studied the piano at the Vienna Conservatoire. Her mother had ambitions for her as a concert pianist, but her hands were too small and narrow to allow her to span an octave with ease and it became clear this would prevent her from ever being able to aspire to a professional career in the concert halls of Europe.

Stephanie took little interest in handicrafts or household skills. But she was keen on sports and she excelled at tennis, swimming, riding and especially ice skating. Her prowess at performing graceful waltzes on the ice at the Vienna Skating Club drew many admirers, chiefly from the opposite sex. It seems to have been an early lesson for her that she possessed the ability to capture the interest of men, a talent she repeatedly used to good effect, and frequently to her financial benefit, in the years ahead. While on a summer holiday at the lakeside resort of Gmunden in the Salzkammergut, Stephanie, who was then only aged 14, entered a beauty contest and won. It was the first public recognition of her beauty and poise, and it made a deep impression on her. From then on her confidence and self-belief grew, fostered partly by studying ballet at the dance school attached to the Vienna Court Opera. Years later, in unpublished notes on her life, she claimed that at the age of 15 she set herself a goal – to marry a prince. 'By the age of sixteen,' she wrote, 'I had something of a reputation as a beauty.'[3]

So how did this friend of my Great-Aunt Annabel, from fairly lowly, inauspicious beginnings in Vienna, transform herself into a princess of the Austro-Hungarian Empire; admired, known and courted across the capitals of Europe? Stephanie first came into contact with members of the exclusive, aristocratic and at that time highly structured society in Vienna through her stepfather's law practice. One of his clients was the widowed Princess Franziska von Metternich, a lady Stephanie referred to as 'The Grande Dame'.

The princess took Stephanie under her wing. She made the young girl her protégée and tutored her in etiquette and manners. Stephanie, under the princess' patronage, learned how to behave in aristocratic circles. 'I remember her as a grande dame who used to invite me to treats as a little girl and later on to parties and balls where I flirted outrageously with all the eligible young men.'[4] People were enchanted by her smile, her personality and, what counted just as highly in Vienna society, her ability as a horsewoman. The first noble-man to show interest in the teenage Stephanie was the Polish Count Gizycki. As he was old enough to be her grandfather, she unsurprisingly rejected his proposal of marriage.

The death of her stepfather, Hans Richter, left the family in a poor finan-cial state, but, as at other times in her remarkable life, fate dealt her and her mother an ace. Her mother's brother, Robert Kuranda, whom the family had not heard from for years, arrived back in Austria from South Africa a rich man, having established a lucrative business on the African continent. Finding his family in reduced circumstances in his old home, he made generous pro-vision for his sister and his niece. Stephanie invested her share well. She also astutely made it her business to get close to her mother's sister, Clothilde. Her aunt had been married briefly to the Vienna correspondent of the London *Times*, and she owned a house in Kensington, London, an apartment in Berlin and a villa on the shores of Lake Wannsee, near Berlin. Clothilde had style and the means to maintain it. She was well known for throwing wonderful parties to which she invited the most famous dancers of the day – prominent ballerinas like the celebrated Anna Pavlova. She also broadened Stephanie's education by taking her on her travels in Europe to places like Venice, Berlin, Paris, Kiel, Corsica and Prague; widening Stephanie's knowledge, her fluency in languages and her appreciation of what it meant to move easily in aristo-cratic society.

Stephanie finally met her prince at a hunt dinner given by her grande dame Princess Metternich. She was asked to play the piano and a young nobleman joined her at the keyboard. He was Prince Friedrich Franz von Hohenlohe-Waldenburg-Schillingsfürst, who was military attaché at the Austro-Hungarian Embassy in St Petersburg, then the Russian capi-tal. According to Princess Stephanie's MI5 file, during the First World War Prince Friedrich became involved in the murky business of spying as chief of German propaganda and director of German espionage in Switzerland.[5] The courtship was swift and harmonious, but the betrothal was far from straight-forward because Stephanie, then 23 although she passed herself off as only 17, was pregnant, and not by her prince! The royal family could not risk a scandal, but because of the impending birth the marriage could not be long delayed. So instead of a prominent show wedding in Vienna, which would normally have been the case, it was decided to arrange a quiet, almost covert marriage ceremony far away in London. Why was Prince Friedrich willing to go through with this arrangement? The answer was that by now Stephanie was reasonably well off. She had sufficient money to settle his not inconsiderable gambling debts, with more to spare to maintain a realistic lifestyle. And there was strong pressure in the royal family for the wedding to take place to avoid causing a public scandal. Naturally, the fatherhood of the baby was a close-kept secret.

The wedding was held with a minimum of publicity and fuss on 12 May 1914 in Westminster Cathedral, London's Catholic cathedral. The required residence was fulfilled by a brief stay at the Ritz. As a marriage of convenience, it was not the kind of royal wedding one might have expected. Stephanie's mother was the sole guest, and the necessary witnesses were pressed into service at short notice. They left the same day for honeymoon in Berlin. It was to have been followed by a visit to India where they were to be hosted by maharajas and go on tiger shoots, but they never reached the subcontinent because within weeks Europe was at war.[6]

Who was the father of the child the bride was carrying when she married her prince? He was also of high rank – Archduke Franz Salvator, Prince of Tuscany and son-in-law of the Emperor Franz Joseph I of Austria and Empress Elisabeth. Stephanie had had a romantic liaison with the archduke from when they had first met in 1911, despite the fact that he already had ten children by his wife Archduchess Marie Valerie, youngest daughter of the emperor and empress. Stephanie's wedding may have been kept low profile, away from the press, the public eye and gossiping tongues in the capitals of Austria and Hungary, but it gave her the title and the connections to enable her to scale the highest reaches of European society. She was now either related to, or acquainted with, the majority of the royal families in Europe.

Her ambition to become a princess had been achieved as Europe was about to embark on the First World War. Soon after the birth of her illegitimate son, Prince Franz Joseph Rudolf Hans Weriand Max Stefan Anton von Hohenlohe-Waldenburg-Schillingsfürst, Stephanie volunteered to undertake war service as a nurse and went back to Vienna for training. Meanwhile, her husband had joined his regiment. Using her contacts, she arranged to be posted to the Russian front where she worked in a field hospital at Lemberg, which had just been recaptured from the Russians. But she was no ordinary nurse; she was conspicuously accompanied wherever she went in the theatre of war by her butler and her chambermaid. This retinue ensured she did not last long nursing close to the front line. But in 1917, minus her servants, she accompanied the Austrian Army as a Red Cross nurse as they advanced to confront the Italians at the battle of Isonzo River. There she served in field hospitals and witnessed Austria's defeat in June 1918 on the River Piave. When the Armistice came, it meant the break-up of the Austro-Hungarian Empire into which she had married. When the empire and its dual monarchy collapsed, Stephanie and her husband were both forced to choose whether to take up Austrian or Hungarian nationality, and both opted for Hungarian citizenship. Indeed, Stephanie held a Hungarian passport for the rest of her life.

Two years after the end of the First World War, the shot-gun marriage ended. On 20 July 1920 Stephanie's divorce was formalised in Budapest. She was now free to do whatever she wanted, and she enthusiastically pursued a life of pleasure. She spent a great deal of time in Vienna, cultivating friendships among the rich and powerful, and making contacts amongst diplomats, ministers, aristocrats and the wealthy; international contacts which would prove of incalculable worth to her in future.

The 1920s were good to her. She spent time in Paris, in the south of France and in the fashionable cities of Europe, developing friendships and intimate relationships with a number of powerful and influential men, some of whom she seduced and manipulated shamelessly to fund her lifestyle. Among them were the Greek Consul General in Vienna, a rich American called John Murton Gundy and a married millionaire. In 1922 she moved to Nice accompanied by a group of friends, including the Count and Countess of Nyari. In Nice she was a frequent visitor to the casino. The Duke of Westminster was among those who fell for her charms and she had a lucrative relationship with John Warden, an immensely rich American businessman from the family who owned Standard Oil. Indeed, an FBI memorandum written in 1941, recording her background, refers to her reputation as a 'gold digger' and suggests she endeavoured to marry Warden.[7]

In 1925 she moved to Paris, taking an exclusive apartment at 45 Avenue George V, where she employed a household staff of nine servants. A near neighbour was the British insurance tycoon Sir William Garthwaite, another wealthy man who fell for her and kept her in the style she now demanded. As a change from life in Paris she would follow the sun to the playgrounds of the rich and famous – Monte Carlo, Nice and Cannes – where she was again a frequent visitor to the gaming tables. Part of the summer season was spent in Deauville on the Normandy coast, where a flirtation blossomed with Solomon 'Solly' Joel, principal shareholder of De Beers, the South African diamond company. No one could fault Stephanie in her choice of lovers! It was when she was in Monte Carlo, however, that Annabel Kruse introduced her, over the roulette tables, to Lord Rothermere. Stephanie was 36 and the newspaper tycoon 59. It was destined to be an introduction that would significantly shape both their lives over the next fifteen years, and, although neither could have known it at the time, have a crucial impact on international events as Europe moved inexorably towards bitter conflict, and as Hitler sought influential friends in Britain and propaganda for his fascist aims.

5

WHOSE GO-BETWEEN?

Princess Stephanie knew exactly what she was doing when, in 1927, she targeted Lord Rothermere using her friend Annabel as the go-between. The subsequent record of her life shows she was always ruthless in getting what she wanted. The Federal Bureau of Investigation (FBI) in the United States noted as much in an extraordinary memorandum sent to President Roosevelt after the start of the Second World War. It said that 'she was reputedly immoral, and capable of resorting to any means, even bribery, to get her ends'.[1] The FBI knew there was plenty of evidence from Europe and indeed America to support their conclusion. A 1938 British intelligence report had spelt out the potency and the danger of her manipulative skills in stark terms. 'She is frequently summoned by the Führer who appreciates her intelligence and good advice. She is perhaps the only woman who can exercise any influence over him.'[2]

She was well aware it would take time before a relationship with the press baron paid the dividends she sought, but she seems to have instinctively known that here was a man whose friendship was worth cultivating and eventually exploiting, and she used her charm and intelligence to cement the friendship. Stephanie and Annabel had known each other for some years. They were close friends and in many ways shared some of the same characteristics. Much of the Kruses' wealth, which financed their extravagant lifestyle, had been built from inherited money originating from Jack's family's banking business. But Kruse had multiplied his riches through the stock market; benefiting from tips which Rothermere generously passed on to him. Together the Kruses were, as one contemporary described them, the ultimate 'golden couple'. With Jack

Kruse and Annabel so obviously in Rothermere's circle, it would have been clear to Stephanie that the route to the press baron's attentions was through Annabel, who was a prominent member of his group of close friends. In his understandably defensive biography of his mother, Prince Franz Hohenlohe notes that Annabel had, a few years earlier, been Rothermere's mistress and as such was adept at seeking his favours.[3]

Recalling that era many years later, Stephanie told her son that Jack Kruse, or 'Jimmy' as she knew him, was an extremely likeable man; blonde and handsome. She described Annabel as full of fun, tiny, slim and petite, even by the 'boyish' fashions of the 1920s. Annabel, she remembered, sparkled with life and laughed like a child. She was a captivating and exciting companion. The evident luxury of Annabel's life, Stephanie said, was plain to see. Not content with having the finest silk sheets, pillow cases, nightgowns and underwear all handmade and embroidered with her initials, Annabel also had her stockings specially woven and with her name worked into the top. She remembered Annabel as possessing a kind of frenetic compulsion always to be active; a characteristic Stephanie sometimes found hard to understand. Later, it became clear where that supercharged energy came from – for years Annabel had been taking drugs.

Cunning and opportunistic, but radiating personality and charm, the princess cut a fascinating figure. It was not just her title and her confidence that impressed, it was the daring way she behaved. Few aristocratic, titled ladies in society had the nerve to openly smoke Havana cigars as Stephanie did. It was a habit she had picked up to avoid the stench of festering wounds when she was nursing on the front line in the First World War. But she added to the outrageous image by striking her matches on the soles of her shoes. Guided by Annabel, Rothermere fell for Stephanie despite the age difference of twenty-three years. Stephanie later noted that she thought she had made a conquest – but the meeting was to have a far greater impact on both of their lives than a passing flirtation.[4] It was inevitable that they would continue to see each other since both enjoyed playing the tables at the casinos, and it was at the Monte Carlo Sporting Club that Stephanie again saw Rothermere for the meeting that changed both of their lives.

She found him on this occasion moody and depressed. Recalling the meeting later in conversation with her son, she said Rothermere appeared to be concerned at the lack of an interesting and significant news story which would give his newspapers a headline.[5] Her response was to say she could give him a story guaranteed to sell his papers. Having aroused the press owner's interest, he promised to invite her to his villa at Cap Martin so she could give him the details. He must have been suitably impressed and eager to hear what she had to say, because the following day she received a telephone call inviting her to lunch.

That 1927 meeting led to a close, ongoing relationship whenever the two were in Monte Carlo. Rothermere habitually spent up to four months a year on the Riviera and travelled frequently in Italy and Spain. He and Stephanie realised they shared a common interest in ballet. Rothermere was patron of the famous Diaghilev ballet company, and he was entranced by the beauty of some of its leading ballerinas. He fell for the charms of the famous Komarova, and in particular he admired the petite figure of Lydia Sokolova, the first English dancer in Diaghilev's company. He was won over by the childlike nature of Alice Nikitina, another of Diaghilev's prima ballerinas, and his fascination with her led to a long-lasting and largely platonic affair that persisted, on and off, almost until his death.

As well as a shared passion for ballet, Rothermere and the princess were both inveterate gamblers. In fact, in a colourful phrase she described Rothermere as 'a fabulous plunger at the casino tables' – in other words, someone who played for high stakes on a whim.[6] Stephanie was a keen player of chemin de fer and baccarat, and she enjoyed some spectacular successes. In Cannes in 1928 she had a handsome winning streak that continued for days on end, which, according to her son, enabled her to pay every single bill over a period of sixty days solely with cash she won at the tables.[7] Whenever she played she insisted on occupying a certain chair which she was convinced brought her luck. If that chair was occupied, she refused to play until it became available.

At lunch, following their meeting at the Sporting Club, the princess persuaded Rothermere that the *Daily Mail* should publish an article outlining the dire situation in Hungary, following the crude readjustment of the country's boundaries after the peace settlement after the First World War. The Treaty of Trianon, signed in 1920, had been hastily concluded to resolve outstanding issues following the lengthy and tedious international arguments that had produced the Treaty of Versailles. It had imposed particularly unjust and damaging terms on Hungary, brutally partitioning the country. There were strong feelings over the unfairness of the treaty towards Hungary, and the resulting hardships being suffered by many hundreds of thousands of Hungarian nationals who, as a result of its terms, were excluded from their own country. Hungary had lost two-thirds of its territory under the treaty; the area ceded to Romania alone was larger than that left to Hungary. Countless families had suddenly found themselves citizens of a foreign nation whose language they did not speak and whose customs they did not share. They were divorced from their homeland and from their birthright. Before the First World War, Hungary had a population of 21 million; after 1920 its population was reduced to less than 8 million. The country was isolated, surrounded by hostile neighbours and defended by an army that was restricted by the treaty to no more than 35,000 men.

Stephanie argued passionately for a campaign to right these injustices imposed on her adopted country. It was her first venture into international politics. She had targeted the press baron carefully to voice her views and to persuade him to give them widespread publicity in his newspapers, where she knew they were bound to achieve international impact. Rothermere was impressed by her arguments and her understanding of the problem. He was aware of the cynicism in Germany over the Treaty of Versailles and the country's determination to evade the terms that had been inflicted upon it. He now became absorbed in the parallel problems in Eastern Europe. He believed, or maybe he was persuaded to believe, that the situation there constituted a potential 'powder keg', which could well threaten the hard-won peace. Inspired by the princess' arguments, Rothermere subsequently wrote and published two editorials for the *Daily Mail* in June and August 1927. In them he pointed out in no uncertain terms the dangers of Hungary having been forced to cede land, where so many millions of native Hungarians lived, to Czechoslovakia, Romania and Yugoslavia. His editorials argued that the so-called land deals amounted to some of the worst frauds that had ever taken place in Europe. The articles called for these wrongs to be recognised and addressed before they could cause further conflict in Europe.

In the first article, headlined at the princess' suggestion 'Hungary's Place in the Sun?', Rothermere wrote:

> Eastern Europe is strewn with Alsace-Lorraines. By severing from France the twin provinces of that name the Treaty of Frankfurt in 1871 made another European war inevitable. The same blunder has been committed on a larger scale in the peace treaties which divided up the old Austro-Hungarian Empire. They have created dissatisfied minorities in half a dozen parts of Central Europe, any one of which may be the starting point of another conflagration.[8]

His campaign had an immediate effect in Hungary and it was greeted with ecstatic gratitude. No one else with such authority and clout had raised the matter so effectively or with so much international impact. The *Daily Mail* was bombarded with letters and messages of support. At home, the Hungarian press lauded Rothermere, and people went crazy with appreciation that at last the injustices they had suffered were being recognised. The consequences were almost certainly more dramatic than Rothermere could have imagined. There were calls for the restoration of the Hungarian monarchy. A group of monarchists even offered the throne to Rothermere himself. Briefly, he took that offer seriously. But he quickly realised it was totally unrealistic.

What were Stephanie's motives in persuading Rothermere to embark on the campaign in the first place? It is possible, given her place in the former Austro-Hungarian aristocracy, that she entertained ideas that her own son could have a claim to the throne? After all, both she and he held Hungarian nationality. In 1928 the Hungarian Parliament adopted a resolution expressing the thanks of the Hungarian people to Rothermere. The University of Szeged offered him an honorary doctorate in recognition of his selfless efforts for the Hungarian cause. Rothermere declined to attend himself; instead he sent his son Esmond to receive the doctorate on his behalf. Esmond Harmsworth was generously and widely feted throughout Hungary, and he brought back with him, as a gift to his father from the Hungarian people, a unique hand-built car. Its chassis incorporated reinforced silver and its radiator was lavishly enhanced with gold plate. The press baron was amazed that what had at first appeared to be an issue merely of current news interest had resulted in such an outburst of support and respect. In April 1928 he wrote to the princess:

> I had no conception that a recital of Hungary's sufferings and wrongs would arouse such world-wide sympathy. Now from all parts of the world I am in receipt of such a flood of telegrams, letters and postcards that the work entailed in connection with the propaganda is rapidly absorbing all my energies.[9]

The impact of her intervention with Rothermere made a deep impression on the princess. It would spur her on to a future role of influence in international intrigue.

Stephanie's ambitions for her relationship with the powerful British newspaper proprietor, and what she might achieve by encouraging the partnership to grow, took second place for the next few years to travel in Europe and the incessant building of contacts with powerful people whose influence she could turn to her own advantage. Some of these contacts were members of the Nazi Party in Germany, then plotting to seize power. Others were wealthy admirers who were in a position to help her maintain her finances and to pay for the lifestyle she relished. In 1932 her position as a French resident was becoming increasingly difficult. She was getting deeper into international political intrigue. Among her contacts was Otto Abetz, a German who was claiming to work for better relations between his country and France. But there was more to the conspiratorial manoeuvring in which Abetz was involved than met the eye, as became clear when he later joined the Nazi Party, and in the fullness of time he appeared in the role of Hitler's ambassador in occupied Paris. For his crimes against the French he was sentenced, in 1949, to twenty years' imprisonment, dying before his term was completed.

In Paris Stephanie was increasingly becoming involved in problems which upset the French government. One issue that French ministers were particularly concerned about was her persistent campaigning for a revision of the Treaty of Trianon, with a view to Hungary being restored to its former size and power. It flew in the face of the French government's alliance with Czechoslovakia, Yugoslavia and Romania – known as 'The Little Entente' – a policy which as far as the French government was concerned was designed to contain a resurgent Hungary, the very opposite of what the princess and Rothermere were working to achieve.

The former Berlin journalist Bella Fromm, who in the 1930s wrote for the prominent German newspaper the *Berliner Zeitung* and had high-level contacts which made her well placed to know the truth, insisted in an unpublished memoir years later that Princess Stephanie had been expelled from France because of her espionage activities. British intelligence files, only declassified and deposited in the Public Record Office in Kew in 2005, disclose the truth. In 1933, the year after she left Paris to take up residence in London, and the year Hitler gained power in Germany, the British secret service circulated a government report stating that files had been found in the princess' flat in Paris showing she had been commissioned by the German authorities to persuade Rothermere to campaign in his newspapers for the return to Germany of territory and colonies ceded at the end of the First World War.[10] She was to receive the then massive sum of £300,000 (equivalent to some £13 million today) if her mission succeeded. Meanwhile, the princess was on the verge of concluding a separate deal with Rothermere to become his representative or 'fixer' in Europe on a retainer of £5,000 a year (£200,000 at today's values), plus additional payments for each assignment she carried out.

She had finally secured the role she had aimed for back in 1927. Via the mouthpiece of Rothermere's newspapers, she would be in a prime position to influence British politics and British government policy. The arrangement also gave her the opportunity to influence Rothermere's personal views, which since 1930 had been strongly in support of the rise of Hitler's National

Socialists, and steer him closer to Hitler's inner circle. Regardless of her loyalties, playing both sides in a 'game' of international politics could potentially be very lucrative for her. And this was convenient, because in 1932 the Great Depression following the Wall Street Crash caught up with her. She was heavily in debt. At one time, according to her son, she had been worth some $4 million, a colossal sum at that time. Now she seriously needed to economise and to find a new and regular source of income.[11]

As was so often the case in Stephanie's life, she was dealt another ace. The luxurious Dorchester Hotel in London's Park Lane was newly opened. Its first manager had also been manager of the Hotel du Palais in Biarritz, where she had frequently stayed. Recognising that having a princess as a guest would help to attract the right sort of clientele to his new hotel, the manager offered the princess cut-price terms if she would stay there instead of Claridge's, her usual base when she was in London and where she frequently met Annabel Kruse. Stephanie settled into a magnificent apartment on the Dorchester's sixth floor. It had a private entrance to Park Lane, a massive sitting room overlooking Hyde Park and four bedrooms. Her latest beau, an American banker by the name of Donald Malcolm who had studied at Harvard and Oxford, also moved from Paris to London with her, joining her at the Dorchester. Malcolm was a genius in the field of finance and he took over managing and boosting her finances. It was Malcolm who advised her to negotiate a contract with Rothermere.

Clinching the contract was not difficult to achieve. She reminded Rothermere of the success of her intervention over Hungary, and persuaded the press baron to appoint her as his emissary in Europe. She argued – and this was undoubtedly true – that she had the contacts to gain admittance to many of Europe's most powerful people, and that she could open doors to almost every exclusive social circle on the Continent. Hoping to build on his initial success in raising Hungary's profile, and desirous to restore the Hapsburg monarchy, Rothermere now instructed Stephanie to make contact with the ex-empress Zita, widow of the last Austro-Hungarian emperor, and also with Admiral Horthy, Regent of Hungary. Rothermere was an ardent monarchist; his argument was that a monarchic constitution was the best bulwark against Bolshevism and his hopelessly optimistic ambition was to restore both the Hapsburg and Hohenzollern thrones. In reality, following war in Europe, the cause of both monarchies was beyond revival. When neither of Stephanie's missions showed any chance of success, he next instructed her to seek a meeting with the exiled ex-Emperor of Germany, Kaiser Wilhelm II.

This was a simple assignment for her. She was a close friend of the kaiser's eldest son, Crown Prince Wilhelm; indeed, they had been flirting for years. Crown Prince Wilhelm, who unlike his father had not been condemned to exile, lived at Potsdam outside Berlin and had been a member of the Nazi Party since 1930. In 1933 he had joined the party's paramilitary wing. As a result of the princess' visits to him on Rothermere's behalf, and probably influenced by her arguments, the Crown Prince sent Rothermere a crucial letter, dated June 1934, from his office in the Unter den Linden in Berlin. It praised the actions of Hitler's new government: 'The rearmament of the nation was recognised as a necessity,' he wrote. 'The withdrawal from the League of Nations and from the Disarmament Conference announced to the world at large the determination of the new German government, behind which for the first time the whole nation was concentrated, not to tolerate any longer being treated as a second-class people.'[12]

The Crown Prince said his respect for, and confidence in, the personality of the Führer had gown month by month. His personal relations with Hitler were moreover friendly and enjoyable. He made it clear that he thought Hitler had come to power at the right psychological moment. The people had faith in the National Socialist movement following all the humiliations of the peace treaty of Versailles, the senseless destruction of Germany's entire war material, the degrading war reparations which had burdened the people with insane debts, and the subsequent inflation which had ruined the most valuable parts of the nation. While the letter expressed some concern for the views and influence of Goebbels, the Reich Minister for Propaganda, in all other respects its support for Hitler and his policies must have been music to Princess Stephanie's ears. It would prove crucial in her efforts to persuade Rothermere to put the powerful influence of the *Daily Mail* behind Hitler and the Nazi Party.

6

A FRIEND IN BERLIN

A growing number of people in England in the early 1930s agreed with Lord Rothermere that the Treaty of Versailles had been excessively harsh on Germany. Many who shared the press baron's views on Bolshevism were also obsessed by a fear of the spread of Communism. They argued that Germany, if released from some of the more humiliating terms of Versailles, could be an important bulwark against Bolshevism and the growing power of Russia. Meanwhile, Rothermere's own political views were becoming increasingly nationalistic and right wing. In 1929, disillusioned with the mainstream Conservative policies, he joined with fellow press baron Lord Beaverbrook to form the United Empire Party. Rothermere urged the Tory Party to dispense with its leader Stanley Baldwin and replace him with Beaverbrook. He also argued for the reform of the House of Lords to make it possible for peers to be elected to the Commons. But the row he stirred up backfired. It divided Conservative voters to such an extent that the Labour Party won the 1929 election.

As early as September 1930, when the National Socialists had just emerged in Germany as a major party from the Reichstag election, Rothermere published in the *Daily Mail* an article extremely supportive of Adolf Hitler. It was headlined 'A Nation Reborn' and Rothermere, someone who always preferred to seek evidence first hand and see for himself before committing his views to print, had travelled to Munich to gain information about what he described in the article as 'the beginning of a new epoch in the relations between the German nation and the rest of the world'.[1] He could not have imagined how correct he would be in terms of Germany's impact on the outside world. But the impact would be far more devastating and destructive than Rothermere could possibly have imagined at that time. He wrote:

> What are the sources of strength of a party which at the general election two years ago could win only 12 seats, but now, with 107, has become the second strongest in the Reichstag, and whose national poll has increased in the same time from 809,000 to 6,400,000? Striking as these figures are, they stand for something far greater than political success. They represent the rebirth of Germany as a nation.

Rothermere pointed out that the great majority of those who had voted for the National Socialists were between the ages of 20 and 30. He welcomed the fact that the new trend represented the values and the resurgence of youth. Whatever his views on Hitler and his Nazi Party, as a press proprietor and journalist he was uncannily prophetic. When the majority in Britain, including those in government, were indifferent to or ignorant of it, he realised the crucial significance of what was happening in Germany.

In September 1930 the *New York Times* was reporting on Rothermere's pro-German views, saying that the newspaper proprietor was urging the British government to 'examine diligently the potential sources of conflagration which are smouldering beneath the present peaceful surface of Europe'; it warned that to make enemies of the younger generation in Germany would mean that sooner or later there would be another terrible awakening facing the European nations.[2] So when Hitler swept to power in 1933, Rothermere wanted to meet and get the measure of the man who was now Germany's chancellor. He gave the task of engineering that meeting to Princess Stephanie. Surprisingly, he was aware that she had been publicly accused of being a spy, as he certainly had not been when he commissioned her to undertake assignments for him. But Rothermere refused to believe the slurs about her activities in the Continental press; indeed, he thought he had sound reasons not to believe them.

In December 1932 a number of European newspapers had carried allegations of espionage against her. One published the sensational headline: 'Princess Stephanie Hohenlohe arrested as a spy in Biarritz.' It transpired that the story had originated in the French newspaper *La Liberté*. The following day, Christmas Day, the same newspaper carried a further report: 'Le Mystère de Biarritz.'[3] Other European newspapers followed with reports referring to her as a 'political adventuress', even 'the vamp of European politics'.[4] *La Liberté* asked, 'Is a sensational affair about to unfold?', alleging that she had been arrested by agents of the Sûreté Nationale because of political activities harmful to France.[5] But as Stephanie had not spent a single day in Biarritz during 1932, had given up her villa there and had sailed for New York at the time she was alleged to have been arrested in the French resort, it was reasonable for Rothermere to believe there was not a shred of truth in it. It is now clear from declassified British intelligence papers that both the French and British secret services had evidence which pointed to the accuracy of at least some of those allegations, although the facts as presented in the newspapers at the time were wrong. Indeed, British intelligence had had serious suspicions about the princess' motives and her true allegiance since 1928, and they had been routinely intercepting the princess' correspondence and tracking her movements in and out of the country from 1928 onwards.[6]

The declassified files show clearly that she was a target of British intelligence during the decade from 1928 until war broke out in 1939. Copies of her intercepted letters have been removed from the heavily weeded files, and a number of pages continue to be withheld under a section of the Public Records Act of 1958, invoked as recently as May 2004. But there is enough in the records of the British secret service to show that the monitoring of her communications and movements was extensive. As early as April 1931 the Foreign Office was questioning the condition of the princess' residence in Britain, as she was suspected of having connections with highly placed Germans, including the Crown Prince, eldest son of the kaiser, who was known to be an ardent Nazi sympathiser. The FBI also suspected her of being a Nazi agent. Those suspicions were summarised in great detail in a lengthy memorandum dated October 1941.[7] French intelligence, the Deuxième Bureau, informed the British secret service in August 1938 that, in their opinion, the princess was in all probability an important German agent. They further commented that they found this curious, since according to their information she was of Jewish origin.[8] Stephanie, against all the evidence, for years robustly contested her Jewish parentage and the claims that she was involved in espionage. On many occasions before and after the Second World War she said she would publish her memoirs and prove these allegations to be entirely false, but she never did.

An indication of how seriously MI5 treated her during the latter half of the 1930s can be gauged from the fact that while MI5 were certainly alert to the potential dangers of Oswald Mosley and his Blackshirts, and indeed had infiltrated the British Union of Fascists, at no time were any Home Office warrants issued to monitor Mosley's correspondence and his movements. In contrast, warrants were repeatedly issued throughout those years, covertly, against Princess Stephanie. What is surprising is that the British government never seem to have warned Rothermere of their suspicions. As a prominent newspaper owner he clearly had contacts in the highest levels of government. Why so influential a person in public life, with powerful organs of the media in his power, was not tipped off by MI5 is a mystery. Presumably they had sound reasons.

Stephanie turned to Rothermere for advice on how she could clear her name over the damaging newspaper reports. Rothermere's response was it was better for her to do nothing about it. Anything she did would only make matters worse and would lead to people believing there was indeed substance in the stories. He had been in the newspaper business long enough, he said, to realise that a denial usually resulted in merely refreshing the story, and was likely to stir up new rumours. His advice was to let the matter lie. Her friends would know it was untrue after all. Rothermere also appreciated that further publicity could be extremely damaging to him as well. But Stephanie would not let the issue drop. As long after the original publication as July 1936, Rothermere was writing to her to say 'the libels were of such a preposterous character that my lawyers advised me that you and myself should treat them with the contempt they deserved'.[9] Stephanie remained dissatisfied, although it appears she never considered suing in the French courts to clear her name. Her belief that Rothermere should have done more to squash the 1932 allegations formed part of the notorious court case she pursued in the High Court some weeks after the Second World War had begun.

The story of the princess' secret life refused to die, however. In January 1933 an article headlined 'Fairy Tales around Princess Hohenlohe, Franco-Polish Intrigues' appeared in a major German newspaper. The report stated that the princess, whom some French newspapers had reported had been arrested in Biarritz, had now arrived in Southampton aboard the liner *Europa* and had immediately travelled to London. She had spent the month of December in New York, the paper explained, and was exceedingly put out by the reports that had appeared in the 'chauvinist' French press. 'It would appear that the whole story is an intrigue,' the article went on, 'instigated by Poland against the Princess.' The report added that the princess was being held responsible for the editorial policy of Lord Rothermere who, in a series of articles in the *Daily Mail*, had argued for the return of the Polish corridor to Germany. It went on to allege that during Rothermere's stay in Berlin, the princess was repeatedly seen in the company of his lordship, with whom she was on 'close' terms, and she had also been in the company of leading German politicians. But again, the reports were basically untrue. Rothermere, at that point, had not been in Berlin, nor indeed had Stephanie. But as is so often the case, there was no smoke without fire, even though some of the details of the press reports were inaccurate.

Writing forty years later, her son, Prince Franz Hohenlohe, said that the ugly label 'spy' turned out to be a persistent one.[10] The mud stuck, and his mother's subsequent work for Rothermere did little to help remove it. His account says that the evil wrought by the 'irresponsible news stories' pursued his mother for the remaining decades of her life; though the majority of her friends remained steadfastly loyal to her throughout. 'People remembered the accusation, not the denial,' he wrote. Had he, or her friends, had access to her British intelligence files, they may not have been quite so unquestioning. Rothermere now realised it was totally unrealistic to believe, as he previously had, that the restoration of any of the old and now defunct monarchies of central Europe could be seen as a way of assuring the integrity of post-war countries and guaranteeing their stability. Instead of placing his faith in a restoration of the old Hapsburg and Hohenzollern thrones, he now turned his attention to the new dictators. They were becoming, he believed, the guarantors of future peace in Europe: Mussolini in Italy, and now with his appointment as chancellor, Hitler and his National Socialists in Germany.

In July 1933 Rothermere wrote probably the most famous of his pro-fascist *Daily Mail* editorials, hailing Hitler's rise to power in an article headlined 'Youth Triumphant', and captioned 'from somewhere in Naziland'.[11] Rothermere wrote of the Germans: 'There has been a sudden expansion of their national spirit like that which took place in England under Queen Elizabeth. Youth has taken command.' His editorial praised the regime for what it had achieved both in 'spiritual' and 'material' terms. Germany, he wrote in a subsequent article, had been 'liberated' by Nazism from 'the rule of the frowsty, down-at-heel German republic … where fraud and corruption had begun to spread on a large scale'. He continued:

> I urge all British young men and women to study closely the progress of the Nazi regime in Germany. They must not be misled by the misrepresentations of its opponents. The most spiteful detractors of the Nazis are to be found in precisely the same sections of the British public and press as are the most vehement in their praises of the Soviet regime in Russia … They have started a clamorous campaign of denunciation against what they call 'Nazi atrocities' which, as anyone who visits Germany quickly discovers for himself, consists of a few isolated acts of violence such as are inevitable among a nation half as big as ours, but which have been generalised, multiplied and exaggerated to give the impression that Nazi rule is a bloodthirsty tyranny.

Collin Brooks, at the time one of Rothermere's editors, later to become his close confidant, wrote in his journal that Rothermere's mood was one of deep depression over what he saw as Britain's decline.[12] The country had lost its former militant virtues and was adopting policies that were beginning to sap the traditional self-reliance the British had demonstrated so successfully in the past in its role of empire builder. Rothermere had long been attracted to Germany, its national character and its historic cities. He had travelled widely in the country, had studied its culture and its history, and he owned a superb collection of photographs and postcards of Germany's towns and cities.

Once Hitler had achieved power Rothermere said there were three possible policies Britain could pursue: negotiate with Hitler and disarm in order to reassure him; give not an inch to Hitler's demands and rearm at full speed (the line Churchill advocated); or open a dialogue with Germany while steadily rearming. The latter was the view Rothermere took, and there were plenty of others in public life and among the Establishment in Britain who echoed it. One who espoused very similar views was Rothermere's neighbour and fellow Norfolk landowner Lord Lothian, whose country seat was at Blickling Hall. Lothian later went on to become British ambassador to Washington from 1939–40.

In November 1933 the press baron gave Princess Stephanie the task of establishing personal contact with Hitler. It did not take her long. She was soon reporting that she was making progress through contact with someone who she conspiratorially called 'my friend in Berlin'. That friend turned out to be none other than Hitler's personal adjutant, Captain Fritz Wiedemann. The princess, using the female wiles she had so often employed to her advantage, set out to form an intimate relationship with the already married Wiedemann. It was to be a long-lasting liaison that would prove both passionate and productive for many years, continuing well after the start of the Second World War across the Atlantic in the then neutral United States.

Fritz Wiedemann was a handsome, 6ft tall, dark-haired professional soldier who had known Hitler since the First World War. They had served together in the 16th Reserve Infantry Regiment. At that time Wiedemann had been Hitler's superior officer, a staff adjutant, while Hitler was a mere messenger; a humble soldier in the lower ranks. The future Führer never rose above the rank of lance corporal and was based behind the lines at regimental headquarters. When he was not required to deliver a message, he passed his time painting and talking politics. There was no obvious demonstration to his fellow 'squaddies' of the mesmerist qualities that were later to bring him to power. Indeed, it is a mystery how someone so relatively undistinguished managed to gain for himself the award of the Iron Cross. Aside from a brief scribbled entry, Hitler's army pay book contains no evidence of the incident that led to the award, and Hitler later saw to it that his military records and correspondence were destroyed or falsified. Nazi propagandists in the early 1930s found it difficult to present to the public, in any convincing way, the historical facts about the award. The chances are Wiedemann knew the real background of how Hitler had contrived to gain such a distinction when he was rarely, if ever, close to any front-line action. If so, Hitler must have realised that he needed to ensure his former senior officer remained a close confidant.

Following the Armistice, Wiedemann left the army in the rank of captain and became a farmer in south-west Bavaria. In 1933, suffering financial difficulties, he asked two former army friends to approach Hitler, remind him of their former active service together, and ask whether Hitler would pull strings to get him into the regular army. Hitler went further. He offered him the post of his personal adjutant. So, in a remarkable role reversal, Wiedemann, who once in wartime France had ordered Hitler to paint the unit canteen, was now personal adjutant to the Führer at the Reich Chancellery in Berlin and was one of the most influential men in the new Germany. There was undoubtedly a close bond of friendship between the two men. Hitler trusted Wiedemann implicitly and they enjoyed one another's company. Wiedemann was at Hitler's side daily; he attended to the Führer's private correspondence, acted as his gatekeeper, ensured the smooth running of his office and even accompanied him on important visits abroad to confer, for instance, with Mussolini. Hitler frequently gave his old commander expensive presents, on one occasion a six-seat Mercedes-Benz saloon. For the princess, Wiedemann was to turn out to be an important and influential conquest.

Hitler initially approved of the princess' friendship with his adjutant, though later he was to change his mind. As the friendship blossomed he authorised Wiedemann to spend lavishly in order to encourage the relationship to become even closer. It was Hitler's personal instruction that Wiedemann should use a fund of 20,000 Reichsmarks as a maintenance allowance to ensure the princess had her hotel, restaurant bills, telephone bills and taxi and travel fares paid. Sometimes the generosity even extended to purchasing expensive clothes and gifts for her. In early December 1933 she used her friendship with the Crown Prince, the kaiser's son, and her closeness to Wiedemann to gain her first meeting with Hitler in Berlin. The Führer appears to have been highly impressed by her sophistication, her intelligence and her charms. At that first meeting she wore one of her most elegant outfits, calculating it would impress him. It seems to have done so, because Hitler greeted her with uncharacteristic warmth, kissing her on the hand. It was far from usual for Hitler to be so attentive to women, particularly women introduced to him for the first time. The princess was invited to take tea with him, and once seated beside him, according to her unpublished memoirs, Hitler scarcely took his piercing eyes off her.[13] The princess handed the Führer a personal letter from Rothermere, and passed on a verbal message to the effect that on the day the outcome of the Reichstag election had been announced, Rothermere had told some of his staff: 'Remember this day. Hitler is going to rule Germany. The man will make history and I predict that he will change the face of Europe.'[14] As she took her leave, Hitler, in an ostentatious show of affection that did not go unnoticed by members of his staff, kissed her and presented her with a personally addressed reply, asking her to convey it direct to Lord Rothermere in London.

After he came to power, Hitler had the reputation of often being downright rude to his women, even to those he knew intimately. But if he thought that it was in his interests he could also be charming in a rather over-sentimental way: kissing their hands, presenting them with huge bunches of flowers and addressing them in endearing terms by pet names. He had mastered the technique of disciplining his behaviour. One minute he could be charming and sentimental, the next he could become a demanding demagogue. But, by the accounts she left in notes for her memoirs, the only side of Hitler's behaviour Princess Stephanie saw whenever they were together was of generosity, warmth and affection. He began referring to her as his 'dear Princess', or '*Hochverehrte Prinzessin*' – 'revered princess'. Writing some years later, and with an eye to distancing herself from the many allegations and suspicions that surrounded her, Stephanie commented:

> Seldom in history has a former enemy demonstrated as much goodwill to
> a dangerous dictator than the British in the Thirties. There I stood near the
> centre of events. Rothermere came from a family that had experienced the
> novel possibility of influencing international politics through newspapers
> and was determined to sound out Hitler. He chose me for a 'consultant'
> and several times between 1934 and 1938 I witnessed history from a very
> close perspective.[15]

Hitler's first letter to Rothermere, like the majority he exchanged with the *Daily Mail* proprietor, was long and rambling. Hitler wrote as he spoke, using lengthy, ponderous sentences. His letter made clear that Germany was determined to defend herself against attack, but he assured the British newspaper owner he had not the slightest intention of provoking a war:

As old soldiers of the World War – I was myself in the frontline for four and a half years, facing British and French soldiers – we have all of us a very personal experience of the terrors of a European war. Refusing any sympathy with cowards and deserters, we freely accept the idea of duty before God and our own nation to prevent with all possible means the recurrence of such a disaster.

In a reference to the hated humiliations of the Treaty of Versailles, he wrote:

This cannot definitely be achieved for Europe unless the treatment of the critical problem, whose existence cannot be denied, is transferred from the climate of hatred in which victors and vanquished confront each other, to a basis where nations and states can negotiate with each other on an equal footing.

Adopting a more personal tone about Rothermere's *Daily Mail* article, Hitler wrote:

I should like to express the appreciation of countless Germans, who regard me as their spokesman, for the wise and beneficial support which you have given to a policy that we all hope will contribute to the final liberation of Europe. Just as we are fanatically determined to defend ourselves against attack, so do we reject the idea of taking the initiative in bringing about a war … I am convinced that no one who fought in the front line trenches during the world war, no matter in what European country, desires another conflict.[16]

Hitler thanked Rothermere profusely for his 'shrewd and well directed journalistic support' of his policies. He wrote that he saw no reason for war either in the west or the east, but he emphasised his demand for Germany to establish an army of 300,000 men which he said would constitute a menace to no one, given that Germany faced over 600,000 men across her frontier with France, 370,000 in Poland and 250,000 in Czechoslovakia.

Encouraged by the success of her first mission, Rothermere arranged for the princess to travel again to Berlin. This time she was bearing a gift for Hitler, a portrait photograph of Rothermere, mounted in a solid gold frame, made by Cartier of Paris and worth more than £50,000 at today's prices. On the reverse of the frame was a reprint of the page from the *Daily Mail* of September 1930, which reproduced Rothermere's initial editorial, hailing the 'New Germany'. In Berlin it fell to Stephanie to translate the article for

Hitler, and the Führer was duly impressed, as well he might be. Rothermere was delivering the propaganda he sought, and putting it in front of the largest newspaper audience in the whole of the British Isles. As he said goodbye to the princess, Hitler insisted Stephanie convey his warmest thanks to the press baron. He urged Rothermere to continue to use his publications to convince the British people that a strong and contented Germany was the best guarantee of lasting European peace. Hitler's hopes were more than fulfilled. In all his newspapers Rothermere proclaimed loudly that the Reich Chancellor had only peaceful intentions; that a defeated Germany had at last found its saviour.

There is no doubt after that first meeting with the new chancellor that Hitler was deeply impressed by Princess Stephanie. She certainly believed she had won his confidence and his respect. But there were people in Hitler's immediate circle who resented the favours the Führer was showing her. His press spokesman, Dr Ernst von Hanfstaengl, warned the Führer against getting too involved with Stephanie, describing her as a 'professional blackmailer and a full-blooded Jewess'. (Ironically, Hanfstaengl, Nazi Party press chief from 1933–37, defected and fled to America before the war began, later serving as a White House expert on Nazi policy.) Hitler promised Hanfstaengl he would have the princess' family history researched. And in answer to a later warning to exercise caution, Hitler said the Gestapo had investigated her background thoroughly and had found the allegations that she was Jewish totally unfounded. The Nazi leader probably calculated that Stephanie's value to him at that time greatly outweighed any vague allegations of Jewish heritage.

Princess Stephanie's son, in his book about his mother, puts a rather different complexion on the episode. He claims his mother was acting only as a 'high-ranking postmistress' and as a result she acquired two camps of enemies. The anti-Nazis in Britain and elsewhere in Europe and the United States called her 'Hitler's mistress', 'Hitler's spy', 'Germany's paid agent'. Whilst those in Germany, jealous of the attention she was receiving from Hitler and others in the Nazi hierarchy, cast aspersions on her 'non-Aryan' origins.[17]

In March 1934 the invitation Rothermere had been angling for – a face-to-face meeting with Hitler – finally arrived. Making another visit to the Reich Chancellery at Hitler's express request, Stephanie was handed a letter by the Führer which invited his 'kindred spirit' – Rothermere – to visit him in Germany. Princess Stephanie had at last delivered on the task Rothermere had set her. But who, now, was she working for – the British press baron, or the German Führer?

7

THREAT FROM THE SKY

An objective commentator might have concluded that Hitler had far more to gain from any association with Princess Stephanie than Rothermere. But the press proprietor believed that the opportunity to give wide-scale publicity to Hitler's policies was in fact a patriotic duty. In British political circles Rothermere was not universally liked. Some regarded him as a maverick, unreliable in certain of his judgements and apt to be dominated by impulse. He was passionately anti-communist and it was his firm belief that by offering friendship to Hitler, and allowing him the freedom to confront and destroy Bolshevism, was in Britain's national interest. He regarded it as the only policy that would avoid another disastrous war in Europe. Rothermere was also a passionate proponent of British rearmament, particularly the strengthening of the country's air force.

He may not have had the general support of most mainstream politicians in Britain, but he was a good deal more far-sighted than many who held office in Parliament and public life at the time. His apprehension about Europe's lack of stability, threats from Communism and fear of the possibility of war devastating Europe once more were genuine, and they contrasted with a lack of concern being expressed about these issues in government. To someone with Rothermere's insight, who frequently visited the countries of central Europe and was well-acquainted with their history, it was clear Hitler and those around him in 1933 represented a significant new force. He regarded them as resolute men who felt deeply the degradation of their race, who believed they had much to avenge and who had attained power by the exercise of determination and self-sacrifice. Rothermere pointed out that:

The new German Chancellor was a man of obscure origins. The Austrian house-painter who had been battalion runner and a corporal in the German army had raised a standard of revolt in Munich, only to be cast into prison for his pains. It seemed to the unimaginative eyes in London and Paris that his appointment as Reich Chancellor was rather in the nature of a bad joke than an event in the serious history of Europe.[1]

But Rothermere concluded that, 'a man of known resolute and daring character pledged to the wiping out of the Peace Treaties who had made himself in a very few years the master of the German Parliamentary machine was a man neither to be derided nor ignored'.

There was no secret about Hitler's aims for those willing to look for them. His three most significant objectives were his pledge to wipe out the humiliating clauses imposed by the peace treaties, to win the return of Germany's ex-colonies and to recognise the Jew as an alien. Rothermere wrote:

Germany, a decade and a half after the end of the World War was in odium surrounded by armed neighbours and herself unarmed ... It was surely a simple deduction that such men as now controlled the German nation would turn from requests to demands, and would strive to back those demands with adequate military force, whatever the rejected treaties might say.[2]

He argued that demands for redress from a revitalised Germany could only be addressed to two nations – France and Britain. Of these Britain had, in pursuit of her treaty pledges, spent fifteen years reducing her armaments, and now the British government was showing no signs of waking up to the menace which the new National Socialist government in Germany posed.

In November 1933, a month before the princess had her first meeting with the German chancellor, Rothermere published a peculiarly prophetic article in the *Daily Mail* headlined 'We Need 5,000 War-Planes'.[3] In it he predicted that the next war in Europe would begin with mass air attacks upon the cities of the weaker powers. Britain, he argued, was powerless to resist these perils. Successful defence in the air demanded a lead in aircraft numbers of at least 2:1, and of all the great European powers Britain was weakest, with a home defence force of a mere 490 aircraft. The French in contrast had 3,000, the Italians 1,500. Rothermere wrote:

No other country on earth is so exposed to devastating air attack. Our capital city offers an almost ideal target for enemy bombers. It lies in the corner

of the kingdom which is most accessible to air-raiders with a broad estuary
to guide them to its heart ... Though we were to double the size of our
Navy and our Army we could at present be decisively defeated in any new
European war by aerial action alone.

Rothermere's fear was that in a war, an armada of enemy planes laden with
bombs, some filled with poison gas, would rain destruction on Britain and
particularly on its capital city.

He was not alone in warning of the bomber threat. Stanley Baldwin in a
well-publicised speech said: 'I think it is as well for the man in the street to
realise there is no power on earth that can protect him from being bombed.
Whatever people may tell him, the bomber will always get through.'[4]
Alexander Korda produced an alarming film, *Things to Come*, written by H.G.
Wells, which depicted the dire effects of an aerial bombardment on an aver-
age town. Public fears were stoked by the experience of attacks from the air
in the Far East, Africa and during the civil war in Spain. It was estimated in
the late 1930s that in the first week of a war against Britain, 83,000 people
would be killed by bombing; that every ton of bombs dropped would result
in fifty casualties; and in a concentrated campaign of aerial bombing on the
UK, more than half a million people would die.[5] It was widely believed that
sustained bombardment from the air could produce a revolution in the country. All of this, of course, would prove to be a huge exaggeration, although
no one at the time could have realised that. In fact, in the whole of the Blitz
– and London was bombed on fifty-seven consecutive nights with 20,000
tons of bombs being dropped – British civilian deaths from bombing totalled
43,000, with 71,000 seriously injured. The authorities had prepared for nearer
600,000 deaths.

Rothermere argued that Britain needed 5,000 warplanes if she were not
to remain at the mercy of her European neighbours. Based on her already
substantial civilian flying industry, he forecast that when Germany started
to equip herself with a strong Luftwaffe, she would surpass Britain almost
overnight. He called the British government's failure to embark upon a realistic policy to create a properly equipped air force a policy of suicide. It
appalled him that since 1925 Britain had cut the annual budget for its air
force by almost 10 per cent. As Rothermere wrote in his book, *Warnings and
Predictions*, published in the year the Second World War broke out, 'by one
section of the British population my policy was called "war-mongering",
by the other it was called "pro-Nazi"'. In reality, he said, it was a policy to
achieve peace.

In 1935 Rothermere had translated his views into action, funding and founding an association called the National League of Airmen. This was his personal effort to give wider expression to the need to start building a strong and effective air force. He invested £50,000 (equivalent to £1.7 million at today's values) in his campaign, and he attracted to the league experienced pilots and supporters, aiming to convince the population, and in particular the government, of the dire need for a modern air force. Full membership of the league was awarded to pilots who had a minimum of 100 hours' flying time. Associate membership was offered to others who had the ambition to learn to fly. He set up a system to help those who wanted to qualify as a pilot. They could achieve their aim for only £14, and he funded a series of public meetings which swiftly led to the recruitment of several thousand members and potential flyers.

Hermann Goering, Commander-in-Chief of the Luftwaffe, had told an acquaintance of Rothermere's in 1936 that Germany was adding one new aircraft to her fleet every half an hour, and the German munitions and aircraft factories were working seven days a week. It was an exaggeration, but appalled by what this meant if Britain had to face a future war, Rothermere published a further broadside in the *Daily Mail* in April 1936.[6] The words from Goering, he wrote, had been translated into deeds. Under his programme, Germany was to have had 87,000 aeroplanes by the end of 1935, all of the newest type: 'There is every reason to believe that this programme, at least has been fulfilled, and that since that date the total number of aeroplanes has rapidly increased. It has been estimated that some fifty new aeroplanes, all of the most modern design, are added to Germany's air fleet daily.' Rothermere declared that Britain should not waste a moment more and should proceed swiftly to deal with the inadequacy of her own air force.

Not satisfied with conducting his campaign through words alone, he took practical steps and invested a considerable amount of his own money to commission a high-performance aircraft from the Bristol Aircraft Company, which he christened 'Britain First', after the slogan of the British Union of Fascists. It was initially designed as a civil transport aircraft and was delivered within a year. It flew for the first time on 12 April 1935. Fitted with two American variable pitch propellers, it was capable of 307mph; 80mph faster than any fighter being flown by the RAF at that time. Under pressure from Rothermere, the Air Ministry asked the RAF to test it at Martlesham Heath airfield in Suffolk. Some of the RAF's top pilots who had the chance to fly it formed the opinion that its handling qualities made it a potentially excellent aircraft for military purposes. The RAF enquired if they could use it as a

prototype, suggesting a similar model could be adapted for large-scale manufacture. In the name of the *Daily Mail* Rothermere presented the aircraft to
the RAF. He wrote: 'The building of "Britain First" conclusively showed that
Britain's lack of efficient modern bombers was not because we couldn't make
them, but because we wouldn't make them.'[7] 'Britain First', suitably adapted,
eventually became the RAF's Blenheim Bomber, one of the most successful medium bombers Britain possessed at the outset of the Second World
War. When the king toured RAF airfields in July 1936, the Spitfire and the
Blenheim were the two aircraft the RAF chose to display in front of him. By
1937 the Air Ministry had placed an order for 150 Blenheims.

Meanwhile, Jack Kruse, undoubtedly influenced by his colleague and
employer, had thrown his support behind the campaign for rearmament. He,
too, was lobbying for the strengthening of the RAF. In letters to *The Times* he
expressed his views on the urgent need for a stronger air force to defend the
country in a possible forthcoming war. He also wrote in support of enlistment into the British armed forces from far-flung outposts of the empire.
Kruse was always extremely well informed, but his views supported a rather
less extreme middle way between, on the one hand, Churchill's hawkish anti-
appeasement stance, and on the other, as he saw it, his employer's rather too
well-disposed attitude towards Hitler. He still kept in touch with Princess
Stephanie, but perhaps Jack Kruse was beginning to realise that the introduction his wife Annabel had engineered nearly a decade earlier was leading
to a rather too close relationship with Hitler and his henchmen for either
Rothermere's or his country's good.

8

ENTER THE BLACKSHIRTS

The invitation for Rothermere to visit Hitler was handed to Princess Stephanie in March 1934, but because of Rothermere's business commitments and his constant travelling, it was not until December that year that he was able to accept. When he arrived in Berlin, Rothermere received an overwhelmingly friendly reception. Hitler appeared to genuinely hold him in esteem. The significance of the visit to the National Socialists was not hard to see; there were potentially huge benefits if the Reich Chancellor was able to exploit the power a proprietor of such mass-circulation newspapers wielded in the UK. From Hitler's point of view there was no more effective way of achieving a propaganda coup for National Socialism and for his policy to reclaim territory ceded in the settlement that followed the First World War and boost German influence in Britain.

At that first meeting, Hitler made the comment, 'Lloyd George and your brother won the war for Britain'.[1] Hitler admired strong men and had a high regard for the late Lord Northcliffe, who had placed his considerable journalistic skills to great effect behind Lloyd George's conduct of the First World War. Northcliffe had aimed fierce criticism at the Asquith government during the early part of the First World War. He had swung the power of his newspapers behind a campaign to ensure that more and better munitions reached the front line, and he had galvanised the government into action; persisting even when his criticisms, notably of Lord Kitchener, were reflected in substantial falls in the circulation of the *Daily Mail*. When Lloyd George replaced Asquith as premier he asked Northcliffe to join him in his Cabinet. However, Northcliffe refused, saying he was a journalist and that was where his talent and his influence could be exercised. To enter politics as a minister would undermine his ability to criticise government. Hitler admired Northcliffe's stance and his patriotism. Now he was dealing, face to face, with the great propagandist's brother, and on his own terms. The dividends, if he played his cards cunningly, could be significant.

It was just before Christmas 1934 and Rothermere and his son Esmond, together with Princess Stephanie, were accorded the honour of being entertained by Hitler at the first major dinner party he had given for foreign visitors at his official residence in Berlin since he had taken office. The Nazi leader was accompanied at the dinner by twenty-three high-level guests, among them Goebbels, Goering and Joachim von Ribbentrop. In Rothermere's party was George Ward Price, the *Daily Mail's* European correspondent who was to become one of the few British reporters to get close to the Führer; one of the very few reporters that Hitler greatly admired. On 20 December Rothermere returned the hospitality, hosting a dinner at Berlin's famous Hotel Adlon. Twenty-five guests attended, including Germany's Foreign Minister Baron von Neurath and his wife; Dr Joseph Goebbels and his wife Magda; Joachim von Ribbentrop, Hitler's foreign policy adviser, and his wife Annelies; and Hermann Goering, accompanied by the actress Emmy Sonnemann, later to be his wife. Rothermere had also invited the British banker E.W.C. Tennant, one of the principal founders of the Anglo-German Fellowship and a friend of Ribbentrop's who had been instrumental in introducing Ribbentrop to a number of influential people in English society.

Princess Stephanie had taken great care over the seating plan. Rothermere, as host, sat at the centre of the table, with Hitler on his right and Stephanie, as hostess, opposite. Hitler began to talk at length about his imprisonment in Landsberg Castle. By sheer coincidence, it was ten years to the day that he had been released from internment and he relished talking about the impact of the experience on his politics and policies. No official interpreter was present, so the princess struggled to keep up with the Führer's torrent of words. When the main course was served, Hitler again dominated the conversation, speaking at length on the topic of Anglo-German friendship and his view that the future of the two nations, Britain and Germany, lay in a strong partnership. With Hitler in full flow, very few of the other guests were able to get a word in edgeways. Though he wanted to, Rothermere was unable even to propose a toast, because Hitler went on talking. Finally, when his guest paused for a few moments, Rothermere grabbed the opportunity to rise and make his speech, but at that moment someone accidentally knocked over a large vase of flowers which fell to the floor with a thunderous crash. Immediately, armed men from Hitler's SS bodyguard rushed into the room, pistols drawn, convinced the noise signalled an attempted assassination. Although the whole incident was a pure accident, the Reich Chancellor left the hotel without waiting for the final course to be served. He was followed out by the other senior Nazis. To Rothermere's consternation the evening, which up to that time had been convivial, ended in some confusion.

The year 1934 was a significant one for Rothermere. In Berlin he shook hands with the Führer. In London he voiced powerful support for Britain's would-be Führer. It was the year of his notorious acclamation, in an article he published in the *Daily Mail*, of the Blackshirt movement in Britain; the popular name for Sir Oswald Mosley's British Union of Fascists, the British version of the National Socialism movement which Mosley had formed in 1932.² Mosley had been a darling of the British Establishment. He had served in the Royal Flying Corps in the First World War, where he had performed with distinction. But he had never really got over the sense of betrayal that he felt his generation had suffered in the terrible slaughter of trench warfare. He had first been elected to Parliament at the age of 22, in 1918 as a Conservative, and soon established a reputation as a powerful orator. He was a 'man in a hurry', impatient with his party's 'old guard', among whom were many who, as he saw it, had allowed the tragedy of war to decimate the young men of the nation and had not done enough to keep them from poverty once the war was over. Mosley was a figure in high society as well as in politics. Those with whom he was identified were in the main rich, young and glamorous. Stanley Baldwin was perceptive in remarking of Mosley as a Tory: 'He's a cad and a wrong'un and they will find it out.'

Mosley had emerged from the war a dashing figure, much in demand by political hostesses, with a barely disguised contempt for what he regarded as middle-class morality; blandly describing his well-known pursuit of married women as 'flushing the covers'. Disappointed and disillusioned by the Tories, in 1924 Mosley changed sides and joined Labour, believing them to be the party more capable of delivering the change he wanted. Some, including Aneurin Bevan, saw him as a potential Labour leader, and Mosley was promoted by Ramsay MacDonald to the Labour Cabinet. But when the economic programmes he passionately advocated to tackle unemployment and his brilliant analysis of the economic problems facing the country were rejected, he resigned from the Labour Party to become an Independent, only to rejoin Labour and then to rebel again.

In 1931 he launched his own party, the New Party. When that failed he departed to Italy, attracted by Mussolini and the politics that had brought the

Italian dictator success. Returning to Britain in 1932 he founded the British Union of Fascists (BUF). Many found him an intriguing character – vain, arrogant and ambitious. He certainly possessed charisma and was socially acceptable, a protégé of some of the leading politicians of the day; not only of Bevan and Ramsay MacDonald, but also Winston Churchill. The views Mosley was advocating also appealed to Rothermere: they embraced youth, action and rearmament. The violence and anti-Semitism the BUF eventually espoused emerged later. Mosley convinced himself, and many others, that fascism would appeal where weak and spineless conservatism was putting off those who would be considered natural supporters of the right.

In some people's minds, Mosley and his Blackshirts represented not much more than an extreme, energetic and youthful wing of the then Conservative Party, inspired by patriotism and loyalty. Plenty of middle- and upper-class people were attracted to his movement, many of them natural Tories driven to a new radical dynamism against the perceived socialist threat. Quite a number of peers and aristocrats were drawn to his ideas, although they found the way the Blackshirts were organised and the violence displayed at some of Mosley's rallies and marches vulgar. It was to attract such people of influence that on New Year's Day 1934, Mosley formed the January Club as a front to engage members of the political Establishment and people influential in British society with his ideas of the corporate state. It was in effect a 'half-way house' for those who sympathised with BUF aims but felt unable to come out and publicly join the Fascists. Certain Conservative MPs, senior military officers, businessmen and members of the aristocracy (many of them friends and acquaintances of Princess Stephanie) were January Club members. In contrast to those sympathising with the BUF, there were plenty of people who supported socialism and who genuinely feared the prospect of a fascist revolution in Britain. Rothermere's nightmare was the absolute reverse. He, as one of the country's richest men, worried about a communist takeover and all that might imply for those who had considerable wealth. He even planned to purchase an estate in Hungary as a 'bolt hole' against this eventuality.

Having met and in some respects tried to emulate Mussolini, Mosley now went to see Hitler in Berlin. To Mosley, Hitler was another example of how the politics of the extreme right could reinvigorate a country and inspire its youth. Initially Hitler was not wholly convinced by Mosley and he doubted the depth of his commitment to National Socialism. However, Hitler was impressed by Mosley's fiancée Diana, one of the famous Mitford sisters who were considered the epitome of high society in England. Mosley later married Diana, after the death of his first wife Cimmie, in a private ceremony in the drawing room of Goebbels' house to which Hitler went as a guest. Hitler clearly had a soft spot for Diana; as a wedding present he gave her a personally signed photograph of himself in a silver frame, decorated with the German eagle. Diana kept it at her bedside. But Hitler was even more smitten by Diana's sister Unity, and both girls were regular and welcome visitors to Hitler's homes. In fact, British secret service files show that intelligence officers were more interested in the Mitford sisters and their close relationship with Hitler than they ever were in Mosley himself.[3] The growing attraction between the Mitford girls and Hitler, which was mutual, proved useful to Mosley who was receiving financial support from Europe to help fund his growing Blackshirt movement in Britain. Mussolini is thought to have funded him to the tune of over £2.5 million a year in today's money. There were rumours of a £1.7 million gift from Germany, although MI5 were of the opinion that Hitler was unwilling to provide secret funding.[4]

In January 1934 Rothermere published his notorious article in the *Daily Mail* headlined 'Hurrah for the Blackshirts', which praised Mosley for his 'sound commonsense and Conservative doctrine'.[5] But privately, Rothermere went further. He took steps to win Hitler over to the British fascist movement by sending a personally written note via Princess Stephanie in which he expressed his view that the Blackshirts would 'rule Britain within three years'. In America the FBI noted that Princess Hohenlohe had in her possession a 'long-hand notation in Rothermere's own hand writing declaring his belief that the Blackshirts would indeed take over as the leading political force in the United Kingdom'. Further evidence that Rothermere instructed Stephanie to convey his conviction that in Britain the Fascists would eventually emerge as the leading party, is recorded in the legal documents prepared for the princess' notorious court case against Rothermere which reached the High Court in November 1939.[6]

The BUF was initially anti-communist and protectionist. It supported strong state intervention in the economy. Rothermere described the BUF in his article as 'A well organised party of the right ready to take over responsibility for national affairs with the same directness of purpose and energy of method Hitler and Mussolini have displayed'. The *Daily Mail*'s supportive articles boosted Blackshirt recruitment. The Home Office expressed concern that the BUF was growing in numbers and influence, and attracting 'a better class of recruits'. In 1934 MI5 estimated it had between 35,000 and 40,000 active members, although this figure might have been somewhat higher than was factually correct.[7] The influx included a smattering of senior service officers, prominent businessmen, and even debutantes; all of them hooked by the patriotic side of Mosley's appeal. But the drive for members extended across the class divide. It reached out to the middle classes, to working-class Tories and even to some Labour voters. One Conservative MP, Col. Thomas Moore, writing in the *Daily Mail* in April 1934, declared: 'Surely there cannot be any fundamental difference of outlook between the Blackshirts and their parents, the Conservatives?'[8] A number of prominent people contributed anonymously to BUF funds, believing it was a movement that had the ability to secure a national renaissance. It was even rumoured that the Prince of Wales made a donation. However, despite Mosley's strong appeal to certain elements in British society, the BUF did not contest a single seat in the 1935 election, which was strange given Mosley's belief that the Conservatives were the representatives of a failed past and needed to be swept away. His objective, not helped by the violence his Blackshirts demonstrated in London's East End and in some other big towns and cities in the Midlands and the North, was to challenge the existing political Establishment in Britain. In fact, despite Mosley's ambition to take extreme right-wing politics from the streets into the House of Commons, the only fascist candidate to stand for Parliament in the late 1930s was at a by-election in Hythe, Kent, in 1939. That candidate was Harry St John Philby, ironically the father of Kim Philby, the most prominent, and from the Soviet view most successful, of the notorious Cambridge spy-ring recruited by the Russians to work within the British Establishment.

Another of Rothermere's newspapers, the *London Evening News*, found a more popular and subtle way of supporting the Blackshirts. It procured 500 seats for a Blackshirt rally at the Royal Albert Hall and offered them as prizes to readers who sent in the most convincing reasons why they liked the Blackshirts. A further Rothermere title, the *Sunday Dispatch*, even sponsored a Blackshirt beauty competition to find the most attractive BUF supporter. Embarrassingly, there were no entries! Mosley himself was forced to explain this away by saying that these were serious young women, dedicated to the cause of their country rather than 'aspirants to the Gaiety Theatre chorus line'.[9] The *Daily Mirror* weighed in with its support even though Rothermere had disposed of his shares in the newspaper in 1931. It declared:

> Timid alarmists all this week have been whimpering that the rapid growth in numbers of the British Blackshirts is preparing the way for a system of rulership by means of steel whips and concentration camps.
>
>   Very few of these panic-mongers have any personal knowledge of the countries that are already under Blackshirt government. The notion that a permanent reign of terror exists there has been evolved entirely from their

own morbid imaginations, fed by sensational propaganda from opponents of the party in power.

As a purely British organisation, the Blackshirts will respect the principles of tolerance which are traditional in British politics. They have no prejudice either of class or race. Their recruits are drawn from all social grades and every political party.[10]

Meanwhile, George Ward Price, the *Daily Mail*'s European correspondent who by 1934 had built up a unique rapport with Hitler, was a close friend of Mosley's and a leading figure in the January Club, conceived the idea for Mosley and Rothermere to go into business together by forming a company, in May 1934, called New Epoch Products Ltd. The plan was for the company to manufacture a range of goods, including cigarettes, which would be distributed via the 500 or so Blackshirt chapters that had been formed throughout the country.

It was New Epoch Products of which my father, as a young chartered accountant of 25, became company secretary. Jack Kruse knew my father, James 'Jimmy' Wilson, well through his marriage to Annabel Wilson, my father's aunt. They were 'family', and got on well together socially. On occasions my father accompanied Kruse on Alpine and Monte Carlo rallies. He shared Kruse's interest in fast sports and touring cars, and had even driven some of Kruse's iconic cars when Kruse toured on the Continent. My father had frequently visited Jack and Annabel in London and at their North Yorkshire, home, Moor Top near Castleton. It was natural that Jack Kruse should introduce my father to Rothermere, Kruse's employer and close colleague. Rothermere perhaps saw in my father a substitute for one of the two sons he had lost during the war. It was through the circle around the newspaper baron, and in particular the Kruses, that my father also met and became on friendly terms with Princess Stephanie. My father had worked for an agency, based in London's Leicester Square, dealing with writers' and publishers' contracts, and in that role he came into contact with the princess. Rothermere was particularly generous to my father and he appointed him to a key role in his new company. Rothermere invested £70,000 (equivalent today to around £2.4 million) in a factory and all the necessary plant. With an eye on business as well as politics, he saw the project as an opportunity to use spare capacity from his Canadian paper mills, normally used in producing his newspapers, in cigarette production. For a time the factory prospered, but the commercial relationship with Mosley did not last for long. It faltered after the notorious Olympia riot that marked out the Blackshirts as an unsavoury, un-British intervention into the politics of the time and all but sealed the prospects of National Socialism taking root in any serious way in the UK.

Almost certainly the catalyst for Rothermere's disillusion with the BUF came as a result of the massive rally Mosley held at Olympia in June 1934. It was planned along the lines of Hitler's Nuremberg rallies and Mosley set out to make it the largest, most spectacular public gathering in the history of British politics. Fifteen thousand gathered to hear the leader of the Blackshirts, and as with the huge rallies Hitler and the Nazis organised in Germany, the proceedings were carefully stage-managed on an impressively theatrical level. Instead of swastikas there was a profusion of Blackshirt banners bearing the 'bolt of lightning' symbol Mosley had chosen to emulate the Nazi swastika. Opponents sarcastically dubbed it 'the flash in the pan'. Union Jacks fluttered everywhere, amid the black uniforms of Mosley's followers. But the strutting and bogus ceremonial were provocative to those opposed to Mosley's brand of fascism. The communists, who were there in numbers, were determined to express their opposition. The proceedings were delayed by at least half an hour by violent protests outside the building. When Mosley arrived, he paraded the 200yds down the central aisle of Olympia towards a raised platform at the end of the hall. The Blackshirt leader was flanked by his bodyguards and preceded by a procession of uniformed BUF members bearing fascist banners. This attempt to whip the crowd into a frenzy, in much the same way as at Hitler's rallies, failed to work. The communists had infiltrated around 2,500 agitators into the hall, and as Mosley began to speak, a well-organised campaign of disruption began. Agitators shouted slogans like 'Fascism means murder' and 'Down with the Blackshirts'. There was chaos in the hall, and savage fighting broke out. The Blackshirt stewards were brutal in their efforts to suppress the uproar and expel the agitators. Outside the auditorium, 200 Blackshirts patrolled the corridors, beating up those already ejected from the main hall. Many ejected from their seats were handled quite brutally and suffered injuries. Fifty needed hospital treatment and five were detained as a result of the beatings they received.

The potent combination of pageantry and violence at a political rally was totally foreign to Britain and the British middle classes viewed it with distaste and alarm. Among the crowd that night was Collin Brooks, former editor of Rothermere's *Sunday Dispatch*, and, at the time of the Mosley rally, a confidant and assistant to the press baron. He wrote in his diary:

The advertised time of the great oration was eight o'clock. At 8.45 the searchlights were directed to the far end, the Blackshirts lined the centre corridor – and trumpets brayed as a great mass of Union Jacks surmounted by Roman plates passed towards the platform. Everybody thought this was Mosley and stood and cheered and saluted. Only it wasn't Mosley. He came some few minutes later at the head of his chiefs of staff. In consequence the second greeting was an anti-climax. He mounted to the high platform and gave the salute – a figure so high and so remote in that huge place that he looked like a doll from Marks and Spencer's penny bazaar. He then began – and alas the speakers hadn't properly tuned in and every word was mangled. Not that it mattered – for then began the Roman circus. The first interrupter raised his voice to shout some interjection. The mob of storm troopers hurled itself at him. He was battered and biffed and bashed and dragged out – while the tentative sympathisers all about him, many of whom were rolled down and trodden on, grew sick and began to think of escape. From that moment it was a shambles. Free fights all over the show. The Fascist technique is really the most brutal thing I have ever seen, which is saying something. There is no pause to hear what the interrupter is saying: there is no tap on the shoulder and a request to leave quietly: there is only the mass assault. Once a man's arms are pinioned his face is common property to all adjacent punchers.[11]

Brooks observed that one protestor had climbed into the high beams in the roof of the hall after being chased by six Fascist bouncers, risking a fatal fall onto the frightened audience below. His diary continued:

[The] breaking of glass off-stage added to the trepidation of old ladies and parsons in the audience who had come to support the 'patriots'. More free fights – more bashing and lashing and kickings – and a steady withdrawal of the ordinary audience. We left with Mosley still speaking and the loud speakers still preventing our hearing a word he said, and by that time the place was half empty. Outside, of course, were the one thousand police expecting more trouble, but I didn't wait to see the aftermath. One of our party had gone there very sympathetic to the fascists and very anti-Red. As we parted he said 'My God, if it's to be a choice between the Reds and these toughs, I'm all for the Reds'.[12]

In his diary Brooks commented that the whole thing was a fiasco and had probably done more to rally opinion to the National Government than anything else since 1931. His view was that the personal appeal of fascism had been drowned out by the display of un-British behaviour. To answer communist brutality with fascist brutality in the middle of an orderly audience of peaceful citizens was to undermine the whole theory of the modern state, and the government seemed to have realised that.

They had indeed. It was the bloody rally at Olympia that was the catalyst for the 1936 Public Order Act which banned the wearing of uniforms during political rallies and marches, and required police consent to be obtained for any political marches to take place. Nevertheless, the *Daily Mail*'s Ward Price, who regarded Mosley as a more eloquent and persuasive speaker than Hitler, Mussolini or Goebbels, chose to put a different gloss on the rally in the next day's paper.

> If the Blackshirt movement had any need of justification, the Red Hooligans who savagely and systematically tried to wreck Sir Oswald Mosley's huge and magnificently successful meeting at Olympia last night would have supplied it. They got what they deserved. Olympia has been the scene of many assemblies and many great fights (the sporting version) but never had it offered the spectacle of so many fights mixed up with a meeting.[13]

That was one view, but it was not the conclusion most shared, and it led to the BUF largely being publicly discredited.

The anti-fascist disruption of the Olympia rally was debated in the House of Commons and there was surprising support for the BUF among some Conservative MPs.[14] Michael Beaumont, Conservative member for Aylesbury, said of the British Fascists: 'a lot were respectable, reasonable and intelligent people'. Another Conservative, H.K. Hayles, member for Hanley, said the BUF contained 'some of the most cultured members of our society'. But MI5 took a more proportionate view. Their report to the Home Office in October 1934 said:

> It is becoming increasingly clear that at Olympia Mosley suffered a check which is likely to prove decisive. He suffered it, not at the hands of the Communists who staged the provocations and now claim the victory, but at the hands of Conservative MPs, the Conservative press and all those organs of public opinion which made him abandon the policy of using his 'Defence Force' to overwhelm interrupters.[15]

The riot at Olympia finished Rothermere's brief support for the Blackshirts, but opposition to the fascists became even stronger following an event in Germany two weeks later. On 30 June 1934 the brutal violence that came to be known as The Night of the Long Knives marked out the true terror of National Socialism. Hitler's colleague and long-time supporter Ernst Röhm, together with some seventy-seven of his SA followers, were butchered in the most chilling circumstances. It became clear that Hitler was personally implicated. When the full horror of what had happened at Hotel Hanslbauer at Wiessee dawned, it was clear that fascism was not just a political campaign for economic reform and national re-dedication; it was an organisation capable of orchestrating terror on a horrific scale. In Britain, Mosley and the BUF never really recovered from the backlash.

Rothermere began to face pressure from his Jewish advertisers over the *Daily Mail's* pro-Blackshirt campaign. Important businesses were threatening to withdraw their support from his papers which would have represented a serious commercial blow to him. He wrote to Mosley listing his reasons for cutting off his relationship with the BUF: he deplored the term fascist; he feared the growing anti-Semitism of the movement; he disliked the policy of a corporate state run by officials and industrialists in place of Parliament; and he now believed a dictatorship would not work in Britain.[16] But his disillusion with Mosley and the Blackshirts did not curtail his pursuit of closer relations with Hitler.

In August 1934 he received an intriguing letter from Princess Stephanie, designed to draw him deeper into an ever-closer relationship with Hitler:

> I have seen both your friends and have much of interest to tell you ... Please let me impress upon you that you ought to see H now. I know he already has some doubts as to your sincerity. I hope you have not forgotten that you assured him in your last letter you would see him in the latter part of August ... He intends to discuss his present and future plans with you, and I think it is, for the first time, more in your interests than his, for you to see him.[17]

In the way she phrased the letter, and baited the hook, it seems Stephanie was well aware of Rothermere's thinking following the Olympia riot and the horrifying events in Germany. The message she conveyed seemed more concerned with fulfilling Hitler's interests than serving Rothermere's. It disclosed an intoxicating mix of double-dealing, and in her increasingly intimate relationship with Hitler's right-hand man, Fritz Wiedemann, sexual attraction was now added to the excitement of political intrigue. In London the British secret service, at the request of the Foreign Office, asked the Home Office to renew the warrant which allowed them to intercept and read the princess' correspondence. In January 1935 the Foreign Office expressed further concerns over her activities, asking the Home Secretary to restrict her visits to the UK. Documents in her MI5 file indicate that the Home Office foresaw 'considerable difficulties with taking such a move because of the milieu in which the princess moved in this country'.[18] In other words, the intelligence services knew that she had powerful friends in the Establishment who could exercise influence in her favour.

A document in her MI5 file, prominently marked 'most secret', states that she first came to the notice of British intelligence as a visitor to the country in 1928, 'exercising considerable influence on Lord Rothermere'.[19] One of those instrumental in introducing her to Rothermere, the files note, was an individual named Andre Rostin, 'not of good repute and strongly suspected of being a German secret agent'. It may well have been Rostin who first advised Princess Stephanie to find a way of getting close to Rothermere, suggesting that the perfect conduit would be her friendship with my Great-Aunt Annabel. In her son's biography of her, he makes it clear that it was through Annabel Kruse that she met the press baron. But neither Prince Franz Hohenlohe nor Stephanie herself would have wanted to credit a known German agent as having any hand, however minor, in her subsequent alliance with the newspaper proprietor. Her MI5 files go on to record that British agents were conscious of her wooing wealthy and influential members of the British aristocracy. In 1933/34, the file states, she became acquainted with Lady Oxford, Lady Cunard and Lady Snowden, with whom she had formed 'a most intimate friendship'. Through introductions by these individuals, the file records, she had 'wormed her way into society circles in London'.

9

NAZI PARTY GOLD

A personal invitation to the princess from the Führer to attend the Nuremberg Nazi Party Rally arrived in London in 1935. It was the occasion on which Hitler announced the notorious Nuremberg Laws, which launched legislation restricting the basic human rights of German Jews; laws that led inevitably to the concentration camps and the gas chambers. Others who received personal invitations to the huge Nazi jamboree included Lady Ethel Snowden, wife of Philip Snowden, Chancellor of the Exchequer in the Labour governments of 1924 and 1929, and an intimate friend of Stephanie. Lady Snowden was also a writer and journalist who had frequently contributed articles for the *Daily Mail* at Rothermere's request.

Among other British supporters at the rally worshipping the ceremony, the passion with which the crowd was being whipped into a frenzy and hanging upon every word the Führer uttered, was Unity Mitford. Unity was jealous of Hitler's fondness for Princess Stephanie, and of the compliments he paid her. She had complained loudly to him about his relationship with the princess and she was said to have told Hitler: 'Here you are, an anti-Semite, and yet you have a Jewish woman, Princess Hohenlohe, around you all the time.' Hitler apparently made no response. It was an indication of what was now widely suspected across Europe: that the princess was working for German intelligence and supplying the Nazis with important information and influential contacts in Britain. The link the princess provided to Rothermere, his newspapers and to right-wing elements in British society was a propaganda tool Hitler greatly valued. Unity hated Stephanie. She referred to her as a '*rusée*', a wily manipulator; she feared the influence Stephanie was exerting on Hitler, and was furious when she learnt that the Reich Chancellor had presented the princess with a large, signed photograph of himself. It was a memento Stephanie treasured and she kept it in pride of place on her desk at her London flat, as British intelligence noted in her MI5 file. The portrait was personally signed by Hitler and was dedicated 'To my dear Princess'.

Albert Speer, Hitler's architect and close friend, believed Unity was in love with Hitler. She was often included in the Führer's party when he travelled, and she referred to him in correspondence as 'the greatest man of all time'. Unity herself, though, was not trusted by the head of the SS, Heinrich Himmler; in fact, he could not stand her. But he had no such distrust of Stephanie, despite those rumours of her Jewish background. By 1937 Unity was under active surveillance by the SS. She was also being closely watched by British intelligence who described her as 'more Nazi than the Nazis'. Significantly, Stephanie was never placed under similar surveillance by the SS. Wilhelm Brückner, one of Hitler's adjutants, so disliked the close relationship between Hitler and Unity that on one occasion he broached the subject directly with his boss: 'What if she's an agent of the British secret service, cleverly placed right under our noses?' he asked. 'We should be more cautious.' The suggestion was rejected in Hitler's close circle, but no such suspicions seem ever to have been voiced about Hitler's other admirer, Stephanie, until later. Indeed, she received VIP invitations on the Führer's instructions to the huge annual rallies of the Nazi Party in 1936, 1937 and 1938.

Stephanie was deeply impressed by the hypnotic and quasi-religious character of these spectacular events. Later in life she described the 'tribal excitement of Nuremberg … a shrine of Nazidom … an orgy of dedication' to the Nazi creed.[1] Lady Snowden accompanied her again in 1937, and that year Goebbels noted in his diary: 'Lady Snowden writes an enthusiastic article on Nuremberg. A woman with guts. In London they don't understand that.' In 1938 Stephanie was on the dais for the Reich Party Congress of Greater Germany. She was distinctly unhappy at having to share the privileged seating area set aside for Hitler's personal guests with Unity Mitford and Unity's parents Lord and Lady Redesdale. There was an intense jealousy growing between them, each of them angling for the Führer's favours. Much to Stephanie's annoyance, it was she who had been instrumental in enabling Unity to meet Hitler in the first place. Back in 1935 she had told Unity that Hitler frequently patronised the Osteria Bavaria, his favourite Munich restaurant. It was there that Unity first met him. Determined to get herself noticed and introduced to him, Unity did so by the simple expedient of sitting quietly at a table by the door, day after day, wearing her British Blackshirt uniform and waiting for Hitler to spot her when he walked in. After that first meeting she rapidly became part of the Osteria Bavaria circle, and later of Hitler's close court. Hitler was well aware of the propaganda value of having a faithful follower drawn from the ranks of the British aristocracy. Stephanie blamed herself for initiating the relationship, and it made the jealousy she felt for Unity all the more bitter. Two of the Mitford girls, Unity and Diana, in private called Hitler 'Sweet Uncle Wolf'. For his part, the Führer was totally fascinated by them.

The exchange of letters between Rothermere and Hitler continued throughout 1935. The press baron made sure that when it was appropriate, Hitler's views were communicated to government ministers and even, on some occasions, to the king. In a long letter in May 1935, Hitler wrote:

An Anglo-German understanding would form in Europe a force for peace and reason of 120 million people of the highest type. The historically unique colonial ability and sea-power of England would be united to one of the greatest soldier-races of the world. Were this understanding extended by the joining up of the American nation, then it would indeed be hard to see who in the world could disturb peace without wilfully and consciously neglecting the interests of the white race. There is in Germany a fine saying: that the Gods love and bless him who seems to demand the impossible.[2]

Hitler set his sights high, but while he was writing in this reasonable and apparently peaceful vein to the owner of the *Daily Mail*, and signing his letter 'with sincere friendship', he was simultaneously launching his first steps towards the Final Solution – the Holocaust, the greatest crime of the twentieth century. He was enacting the Nuremberg Laws that would take away the citizenship of Jews, prohibit marriage between Jews and Aryans, and exclude Jews from leading professions, depriving them of their livelihoods. From burning thousands of books by Jewish authors, he was in the process of making the chilling leap to incinerating human beings in their millions.

The invasion of Abyssinia by Italian troops in October 1935 caused a storm of protest in England. The Italian dictator, Mussolini, was intent on seizing the whole of that vast country and turning it into an Italian colony. Rothermere was anxious to exert pressure to stop the conflict, or at the very least to prevent it spreading. He wanted to find out Hitler's views so he could write with authority about Germany's stance in his newspapers and pass on first-hand information to the British government. He asked Stephanie, once again, to be his go-between. Initially Hitler sent word, via the princess, that he had no time to answer detailed questions on the matter. He was possibly stalling for time because he was playing a devious hand in the conflict. On the one hand, Hitler was seeking closer relations with Mussolini and supplying him with coal and steel. On the other, he was secretly prolonging the war by supplying war materials to the Abyssinians, as a means of further increasing Mussolini's dependence on him. When Hitler did respond to Rothermere, in December, it was to emphasise his belief that a time would come when England and Germany would be the solid pillars in a worried and unstable world:

> There is nobody in Germany with any political insight who welcomes this conflict, except perhaps some enemies of the state who may cherish the hope that it might constitute an international example which could one day be applied to Germany. But these elements must not be confused with the German people.[3]

Rothermere met Hitler again in September 1936, and signalled his continuing friendship with the Nazi leader that Christmas by asking the princess to take the German chancellor a personal gift of a valuable Gobelin tapestry which would attract a value of more than £85,000 in today's money. Stephanie was happy to oblige. In a letter accompanying his gift, Rothermere wrote that he had selected the tapestry guided by the thought of Hitler the artist, rather than Hitler the 'great leader'. He added it was a pleasure to hear from Princess Stephanie that in spite of the Führer's tremendous workload, and the burden of responsibilities he shouldered, he was in high spirits and excellent health. Rothermere signed off his Christmas letter 'in sincere admiration and respect'.[4]

A letter of thanks arrived from the Reich Chancellery at Rothermere's villa on the French Riviera, where he escaped from the English winter whenever he could. Hitler's letter said the 'magnificent tapestry' had given him great pleasure and his letter included an invitation for Rothermere to be his guest in January 1937 at the Führer's mountain retreat, amid the spectacular mountain scenery on the Obersalzberg. It was the first occasion Rothermere had been asked to meet Hitler at his mountain retreat and it was to be an especially memorable occasion.[5] In a gesture Hitler rarely offered to his guests, he sent his personal railway saloon carriage to meet Rothermere and the princess at the Austrian border. The Berghof was isolated and difficult to reach. It was poorly served by road and rail, but the railway line to Bad Reichenhall, some 20km from the Berghof, had been improved and the station enlarged to accommodate Hitler's and Goering's private trains. Hitler had had his home there since 1927. Goering and Martin Bormann, Hitler's deputy chief of staff, also had residences on the Obersalzberg. In 1939 the Nazi Party, as a 50th birthday present, gave Hitler what became known as 'The Eagle's Nest', a building constructed on the very summit of the Kehlstein Mountain, high above the Berghof. Because of the exposed and rugged site on which it was built, it was one of the most costly and complicated building projects of its time; a showpiece of German engineering. However, Hitler rarely visited 'The Eagle's Nest' or the Teehaus with its breathtaking views and spectacular sun terrace. He disliked the rarefied air high on top of the mountain and he had a fear of heights. Nevertheless, suppressing his own fears Hitler was proud to show off the building whenever he had prominent political guests visiting him at the Berghof.

Rothermere's party arrived late in the evening and spent the night at the Berghof, a distinct privilege seldom granted to foreign visitors. Fellow guests at Hitler's lair while Rothermere and his party were there were Magda and Joseph Goebbels. Hitler was immensely proud of the Berghof. Its great hall was dominated at one end by a glass wall that provided a magnificent view of the spectacular scenery. The hall's walls were hung with Gobelin tapestries, all of them every bit as valuable as the one his guest had presented to him. There were numerous paintings by Italian masters, including nudes by Titian and Bordone which were displayed either side of the entrance to the dining room. As well as expensive paintings, the rooms were adorned with beautiful pieces of sculpture and exotic porcelain. The dining room was almost as big as the great hall, and leading from it was an enclosed winter garden, one of the few places in the Berghof where smoking was allowed. Hitler was a fanatical anti-smoker. Upstairs, bedrooms and offices were arranged either side of a long corridor. Hitler's private suite consisted of sitting room, study, bedroom and bathroom. The bathroom was clad in Italian marble and embellished with gold-plated fittings.

After experiencing a night in the splendour of the Berghof, the group breakfasted together late as Hitler rarely rose early. In the afternoon Hitler took Rothermere for a walk – downhill, because the Reich Chancellor disliked too much physical exertion. At the end of their stroll, during which the two men discussed the possibility of a German alliance with Britain, a car met them and returned them to the comfort of the Berghof. There the discussions continued on the threat of international communism and the Nazis' attitude to the Jews. Hitler claimed that the anti-Nazi campaign in Britain was being backed by Winston Churchill on behalf of his Jewish paymasters, and asserted that it was the Jews who controlled much of the press in Britain, too – an indication perhaps of the value he placed on the mouthpiece for National Socialism Rothermere was providing for him.[6]

Goebbels' diary for 7 January 1937 records the visit by Rothermere and Princess Stephanie:

> Rothermere pays me great compliments ... Enquires in detail about German press policy. Strongly anti-Jewish. The princess is very pushy. After lunch we retire for a chat. Question of Spain comes up. Führer won't tolerate a hot-bed of communism in Europe any longer. Is ready to prevent any more pro-Republican volunteers from going there. His proposal on controls seems to astonish Rothermere. German prestige is thus restored. Franco will win anyway ... Rothermere believes British government also pro-Franco.[7]

In the evening Hitler treated his guests to a showing of the film *Stosstrupp 1917* (*Shock-troops 1917*). Rothermere, who had lost two of his sons in the Great War, was deeply moved by it. Stephanie apparently wept. Hitler seemed fascinated by her, stroking her hair and giving her intimate pinches on her cheek.

As a result of the meeting at the Berghof and the discussions that took place there, Hitler and Goebbels agreed that Rothermere's continued supporting voice in Britain on behalf of the Nazis via his newspapers was of valuable service to the German Reich. The relationship should be encouraged as actively as possible, and the British peer should be treated well to ensure he continued to write favourably of an Anglo-German alliance and remained a strong supporter of the Führer. However, on the orders of the Reich propaganda chief, little was published in the German press about Rothermere's visit.[8]

Stephanie left the Berghof delighted with what had been achieved and honoured that she had been personally presented with another signed photograph of Hitler in a silver frame, in this case inscribed 'In memory of your visit to Berchtesgaden'. Rothermere returned to his villa by the Mediterranean, while Stephanie remained for a few days in Munich. Again Hitler showered her with favours. A massive bunch of roses arrived at her hotel, along with a personal message that as a further token of his friendship and admiration, he wanted to present her with a sheepdog puppy. She christened the puppy Wolf, after Hitler's own favourite Alsatian dog.

Later, from her apartment at Bryanston Court, London, Stephanie wrote a personal letter of thanks. 'You are a charming host,' she told Hitler. 'Your beautiful and excellently run home in that magnificent setting all leave me with a wonderful and lasting impression. It is no empty phrase when I say,

Herr Reich Chancellor, that I enjoyed every minute of my stay with you.' Thanking Hitler for the gift of the dog, she wrote: 'It has given me great pleasure, not only because I love dogs – but also because, to me, dogs symbolise loyalty and friendship – which in this instance pleases me all the more.'[9]

By January 1937, when the visit to the Berghof took place, Stephanie was deeply in love with Fritz Wiedemann. The previous year, when she was staying at the Hotel Adlon in Berlin, Wiedemann had visited her there. Both of them were aged 45. Although married for eighteen years and the father of three children, Fritz Wiedemann missed no opportunity to lavish his charms on her. He was 6ft tall, dark and muscular, with beetling eyebrows and friendly eyes. Some said he exuded eroticism. He was extremely charming and well educated. But, according to the daughter of the American ambassador to Berlin, Martha Dodd, who attended many parties given by leading Nazis, he had the shrewdness and cunning of an animal and could behave completely without delicacy or subtlety. 'Certainly, Wiedemann was a dangerous man to cross,' she wrote, 'for despite his social naiveté and clumsiness he was as ruthless a fighter and schemer as some of his compatriots.'[10]

Stephanie was extremely keen to cement her relationship with Wiedemann. She knew how close he was to Hitler and the influence he was able to exert on his leader. Devious as ever, she advised Rothermere to send Wiedemann a gift and Rothermere duly instructed her to go to Cartier, select a gold cigarette case, have it engraved with Wiedemann's name, charge it to his account and take it to Berlin. In response, Rothermere received a handwritten letter of thanks from Wiedemann.[11] Rothermere's keenness to maintain good relations with Hitler extended to another expensive gift. In May 1937 he sent a precious jade bowl to the Nazi leader. Again, it was Princess Stephanie who delivered it personally. In his letter expressing 'heartfelt thanks', Hitler said he would display the bowl in his rooms at the Obersalzberg as a lasting token of Rothermere's 'friendship and esteem'. He added that he was following closely Rothermere's efforts to establish a true Anglo-German friendship. 'Your leading articles published within the last few weeks, which I have read with great interest, contain everything that corresponds to my own thoughts as well.'[12]

Later in 1937, Princess Stephanie received a personal honour from a grateful Reich Chancellor – proof of the value the Führer placed on her work for the Nazi regime. On Hitler's orders she was awarded the Honorary Cross of the German Red Cross as a token of her 'tireless activities on behalf of the German Reich'. Wiedemann travelled to Paris, where Stephanie was staying at the Ritz Hotel, and personally decorated her with the medal, which was accompanied by a document confirming Hitler's personal authorisation of the award. But this honour was totally eclipsed the following year, 1938, when she was cabled in Paris by Wiedemann summoning her urgently to Berlin 'as the Chief wants to speak to you'. On 10 June 1938 she had an audience lasting several hours in the Reich Chancellery. It was an extraordinary event; at a solemn ceremony Hitler pinned on her, a Jewess, the Nazi Party's Gold Medal of Honour. In the Third Reich it was a badge that elevated the recipient to the level of 'Nazi royalty'. It was rarely awarded and reserved for a small group of people, mainly long-standing Nazi Party members who had given outstanding service to the National Socialist movement. It was regarded as the mark of a so-called true patriot. The princess, born a Jew, was now a de facto member of the Nazi Party – 'an honorary Aryan', as Heinrich Himmler declared her. The honour meant she had been acknowledged personally by Hitler as a significant contributor to the Third Reich. Three years later, in 1941, when she was in internment in America, FBI agents searched her house in Alexandria, Virginia, and found and photographed the medal with its gold swastika symbol. It was in a jewel case in her bedroom, close to her signed photographs of the Führer. It is unlikely that Rothermere ever knew of this extraordinary meeting in Berlin, or the honour bestowed by Hitler on Princess Stephanie. Had he known about it, the implications to him must surely have been obvious. Her loyalty as his ambassador had been fatally compromised. But her loyalty to Hitler was plain to see.

Many surrounding Hitler and in his inner circle were far from pleased that the princess had been favoured in this very prominent way by their leader. Hitler had devoted four hours in a one-to-one meeting with her, an almost unheard-of audience in the circumstances. Even Goering expressed his surprise to her. As Stephanie sarcastically recorded, using Hitler's first name:

> Everyone of their clique [the leading Nazis] yearned to have the Führer, or at least his ear exclusively to himself. Every visit of mine to the Reich Chancellery seemed to them an impudent encroachment upon their sacred privileges, and every hour that Adolf wasted upon me was an hour which he might have spent to so much greater advantage in their devoted company.[13]

Long after the war had ended and years after Hitler's grim suicide in the claustrophobic madness of the Berlin bunker, Stephanie set down her impressions of Hitler in what seems like an effort to distance herself from her Nazi relationships in the 1930s. 'When I saw Adolf Hitler for the first time,' she wrote in a lengthy memorandum now in the Hoover Institution Archives at Stanford University in California, 'I remember distinctly how astonished

I was at the insignificance of his appearance. A suburban schoolteacher, or better, some small employee, that is exactly what he looked like.'[14] No one could have seen anything extraordinary or outstanding about him:

> His manners are exceedingly courteous, especially to women. At least that is how he has always been towards me. Whenever I arrived or left he always kissed my hand, often taking one of mine into both of his and shaking it for a time to emphasise the sincerity of the pleasure it gave him to see one, at the same time looking deep into my eyes.

Stephanie's notes comment on Hitler's 'truly Chaplin-like moustache' emphasising his small mouth, but she describes his very light blue eyes as 'beautiful, with a slightly far-away expression'. She says his best feature were his hands, 'truly the sensitive hands of an artist'. She wrote:

> He hardly ever smiles, except when making a sarcastic remark. He can be, he often is, very bitter. I think I can truthfully say that with the exception of his very intimate circle I am one of the few persons with whom he held normal conversations. By that I mean one where both parties speak in turn; a conversation of two human beings. Usually this is not the case. He either makes a speech and one has to listen, or else he sits there with a dead serious face, never opening his mouth … He once told me when I expressed my astonishment at his never learning English that the reason he would not be able to learn any other language outside of German was his complete mastery of the latter, which was an all time job. But I have never found that Hitler speaks or writes German as well as he claims or thinks. I have had many occasions to read letters of his, where all he did was revel in heavily involved Teutonic sentences. A single sentence often attains as much as eight or ten lines. The same is true of all his speeches … In 1938 during the September crisis Hitler sent for Unity Mitford. When she arrived he told her that in view of the gravity of the situation he wanted her to leave Germany. Though it would seem that such a gesture was prompted only by friendly concern towards one of his most ardent admirers, his intention was of a different nature. His real purpose in sending for Unity Mitford was to make her return to England and impress her people and all those she would naturally talk to with the gravity of the situation. This is an example of his cunning and supreme ability to make use of even the slightest incident. He is a master at the understanding of, and playing upon, the psychology of people, which I consider his greatest gift and asset. In January 1939 I was

staying at the Adlon Hotel in Berlin when Hitler gave his opening speech at the Reichstag in which, denouncing all political pessimists and the war prophets, he shouted to his audience the words: 'I prophesy a long peace.' Naturally such a statement made by Hitler was taken up by every newspaper the world over and spread in headlines around the globe. Hitler, reading the result and the favourable echo his pronouncement had created, declared in private: 'This was the best piece of bluff I have pulled in a long time!'

10

THE LANGUAGE OF BUTTER

Rothermere's motives in cultivating close relations with Hitler, by wholeheart-edly supporting Hitler's policies and using his newspapers as a mouthpiece for the Nazi leader's views, are not easy to fathom. In Rothermere's opinion he was using his influence in a sincere attempt to avoid future bloodshed. But the supportive terms of some of his private correspondence with Hitler might well have been regarded, certainly by 1938, as beyond negotiating for an understanding between Britain and Germany, and verging on downright disloyalty. The press baron believed a firm alliance between a strengthened Germany and an adequately rearmed Britain was a guarantee of peace in Europe, and a bulwark against the spread of communism. While appeasing Hitler he was also profoundly convinced it was in Britain's interests to rearm, particularly by building up Britain's air power and extending the Royal Navy's submarine fleet. To this extent he was a patriot. But wooing Hitler, long past the point at which it should have been obvious Hitler's policies were moving against Britain's interests, was tantamount to flirting with treachery, particularly in view of the huge influence he wielded through his mass-media newspapers.

In many respects Rothermere was a visionary. He could show remark-able foresight in predicting events to come. But he was spectacularly wrong in October 1929 when he wrote a leader in the *Daily Mail* entitled 'Does Germany mean Peace?' His prediction was that Germany quite definitely did mean peace: 'She means it for the simple reason war has failed. In 1914 the Germans tried to dominate Europe by military conquest. Now they are work-ing for the same end by industrial conquest. Germany will not again stake its fortune on a chance that proved so costly and complete a failure. If Germany could not win in 1914 with resources intact and preparations complete, her prospects of victory now with a military system so disorganised and disarmed, are hopeless and must long remain so.'[1] It was his conviction that the Weimar Republic had learned a bitter lesson – that military aggression never solved anything – that made Rothermere accept Hitler's peaceful intentions. As it turned out, the Second World War was declared a decade later.

Rothermere was right, however, in 1930. In September that year he was sending a dispatch to the *Daily Mail* from Munich, stating that 'the gains made by Adolf Hitler's young supporters have so thrilled the German nation that if new elections were held the National Socialists would emerge as definitely the strongest party in the state'.[2] A report in the *New York Times* noted Rothermere's prediction that within the next few years, the forces at work in Germany will have altered not a few features of the map of Europe; features which politicians assembled in Paris in 1919 complacently believed had been fixed forever. 'They should set themselves to examine diligently the potential sources of conflagration which are smouldering beneath the present peaceful surface of Europe. Sooner or later a terrible awakening is in store for Europe.'[3] Rothermere was not naive. Despite espousing Hitler's policies far too enthusiastically for both his own and his country's good, as war looked more and more inevitable he saw it his duty to pass on to the British government any information he learnt through his German connections. Too often British ministers and their senior civil servants preferred to ignore his warnings. They saw him as a maverick, someone outside the Establishment. When it came to rearmament, for which Rothermere was an early advocate, the politicians should have listened more intently.

There is no question that Rothermere positively admired the German chancellor. He believed that Hitler was driven by ideology; that Hitler was strong, talented, and had intense conviction in his policies. In comparison, he thought the majority of British politicians, with the exception of Churchill, were weak and lacked the unshakeable belief the Nazi leader showed. He believed if Hitler was offered friendship and allowed the freedom to carry out his expansionist policies in Eastern Europe, he could confront and destroy Bolshevism. It would be in Britain's interests and the best chance of avoiding a second major war. Earlier, Rothermere had hailed Mussolini when he came to power, and he was not alone in doing that. In the late 1920s Churchill had praised Mussolini too. 'Fascism has rendered a service to the entire world,' he is reported to have written to the Italian dictator. 'If I were Italian I am sure I would have been with you entirely.' Two years after Hitler's rise to power,

Churchill seemed uncertain what Germany with Hitler as chancellor would mean to the world. Would he 'be the man who will once again let loose upon the world another war', or would he 'go down in history as the man who restored honour and peace of mind to the great Germanic nation and brought it back serene, helpful and strong, to the forefront of the European family circle'?[4]

Rothermere was far from alone in dreading the possibility of another war in Europe and wanting to do all he could to ensure it could never happen. The widespread notion in Britain was that any future war would be even worse than the war that had decimated a generation just a few years earlier. To the horrendous slaughter on the battlefield would be added the unspeakable destruction that a further conflict would wreak from the air. Based on the experience of the Spanish Civil War, it was widely estimated that the first few weeks of a German air assault would result in incalculable casualties among the civilian population. Those who feared German air attack in the 1930s, in much the same way that fear of nuclear attack dominated the Cold War years, had not fully appreciated that until the German Air Force had access to forward airfields in France, their aircraft did not have the range to mount sustained aerial attacks on major cities in Britain. The assumptions of devastating bombardment from the air were exaggerated, but fear of a new and horrific means of warfare against the civilian population fuelled a policy of appeasement which had considerable support amongst the public and politicians.

Critics today might say the appeasement policy of the British government between the wars constituted a huge foreign policy betrayal. But without the advantage of foresight, and viewed from the perspective of the times, it was a policy many in Britain felt more than justified in pursuing. The truth was British politicians underestimated their adversary. They were slow to detect his cunning, and only realised his untrustworthiness when it was too late. Although the extent of Nazi intentions was not fully apparent before 1939, every one of Hitler's foreign policy initiatives up until then, with perhaps the sole exception of the Prague coup, could be explained away by the appeasers as a legitimate policy of righting the wrongs of the Versailles treaty. For his part, Hitler, once war had broken out, considered the British leaders as criminals. 'They could have had peace on the most agreeable terms,' he said. 'But there are some people whom you can talk sense into only after you've knocked out their front teeth.' Nevertheless, the British government cannot say it was not warned.

The Cambridge historian Christopher Andrew records in his book, *The Defence of the Realm: The Authorised History of MI5*, that from 1935 onwards

MI5 had an informant inside the German Embassy in London, a diplomat by the name of Wolfgang zu Putlitz.[5] He consistently provided clear warning, as first Leopold von Hoesch and then Ribbentrop were German ambassadors in London, that negotiations with Hitler were likely to be fruitless and the only way to deal with the Nazi dictator was to stand firm. By 1938 he was flagging to his contacts that Britain, through her policy of appeasement, was 'letting the trump cards fall out of her hands. If she had adopted, or even now adopted, a firm attitude and threatened war, Hitler would not succeed in this kind of bluff.' MI5's frustration over the government's failure to take heed of the intelligence it was receiving from Putlitz and other agents resulted in an unusually frank and hard-hitting report to government. MI5 never usually commented in explicit and forthright terms. But this time the agency did not hide its concerns. The MI5 report stressed how exasperated their agent was. It appeared to him, they said, useless trying to help the British withstand Nazi ploys. MI5 said information received from Putlitz had always proved to be accurate and free of bias. Intelligence from another agent, who had risked his life to communicate it, had also called for a 'stiff attitude on the part of Britain to resist Hitler's demands'. In essence, British policy during the Munich crisis had convinced Hitler of England's weakness; that the English were decadent and lacked the will to defend themselves and their empire.

MI5 were desperate to harden Chamberlain's will and make clear that appeasement, far from achieving 'peace for our time', was bolstering Hitler's aggressive policies. There was every reason to believe the Nazi dictator was only in the first stages of his planned programme of territorial expansion. Their extraordinary note quoted Hitler as saying: 'If I were Chamberlain I would not delay for a minute to prepare my country in the most drastic way for a total war ... It is astounding how easy the democracies make it for us to reach our goal.' MI5's note went on: 'If the information which has proved generally reliable and accurate in the past is to be believed, Germany is at the beginning of a Napoleonic era and her rulers contemplate a great expansion of German power.' When even these stark warnings apparently failed to shake Chamberlain out of his policy of appeasement, MI5 officers decided to emphasise to Halifax, the Foreign Secretary, how insultingly Hitler was referring to Chamberlain behind his back. The Nazi leader, MI5 said, habitually described the British Prime Minister as an 'arsehole', a word Halifax had probably never seen written down in his life before, and certainly never in an official internal government communication! Halifax was so shocked, as MI5 intended he should be, that he underlined the word three times in red pencil. He then showed it to the Prime Minister, who was infuriated by Hitler's crude

name-calling and his mockery of the British Prime Minister's 'umbrella paci-
fism'. Nevertheless, MI5 were convinced that Chamberlain's policy during
the Munich crisis gave Hitler the confirmation he wanted of the weakness of
Great Britain and her lack of will to defend the British Empire.

Like Chamberlain, Rothermere was duped into thinking that Hitler was a
man of reason and able to compromise; a man who could be trusted to keep
his word. While he was unguarded in his dealings with the Nazi leadership,
he was foolish in his trust of Princess Stephanie. Had he known how keenly
MI5 had been watching his titled go-between ever since she had first become
involved with him and the *Daily Mail*, he would perhaps have been a great deal
more circumspect in his dealings with her. He was allowing himself to be the
'fall guy' in Nazi hands. Why, since MI5 clearly had legitimate misgivings about
her, was Rothermere not taken on one side and warned? Was it because he had
plenty of friends in high places? Rothermere sometimes gave the impression
of a man with a split mind. He adopted one approach when dealing with the
Nazi Führer and his fellow National Socialists, and another, far more realistic one, for domestic appearance. In October 1934, several months after The
Night of the Long Knives, Rothermere was writing with remarkable foresight
to Neville Chamberlain, who at the time was Chancellor of the Exchequer:

> The oligarchs of Germany are the most dangerous, ruthless men who have
> ever been in charge of the fortunes of a people 67,000,000 in number. They
> will stop at nothing. Violent as they were on 30th of June in internal politics,
> they will be equally or more violent in external politics.[6]

Yet at the very same time, Rothermere was still corresponding with Nazi
leaders in friendly, supportive and encouraging terms.

The government chose to regard some of Rothermere's warnings as alarmist. In 1933 he had predicted that: 'Hitlerism means war. Unlike the last war,
the next war will be fought with the entire concurrence and endeavour of
every German man, woman and child.'[7] But such stark predictions did not
appear in the editorial columns of the *Daily Mail*. His reason for maintaining
close relations with Herr Hitler, he said in a letter to Lady Vansittart, wife of
the Permanent Under-Secretary of State for Foreign Affairs, was in the hope
that he would be in a position to exert influence on the German leader if the
need arose. 'When the emergency comes,' he wrote, 'this relationship might
be of great value to this country. My policy is quite clear. It is to endeavour
to keep on friendly terms with Germany, but to say all the time that circumstances and not personalities rule events.'[8] For his part, Hitler praised

what Rothermere was doing. Naturally, it was hugely valuable in assisting the Nazi leader's expansionist ambitions. The Reich Chancellor once remarked to Ribbentrop (who passed it on to Ward Price, one of Rothermere's most trusted journalists and Hitler's favourite British reporter) that he had the greatest admiration for the newspaper owner. 'He is the only Englishman who sees clearly the magnitude of this Bolshevist danger,' Hitler said. 'His paper is doing an immense amount of good.' Hitler generally detested journalists, but at an event in the Deutsch Hofhe he was seen to embrace Price, affectionately holding him by the shoulders with both hands and loudly proclaiming his friendship.

Rothermere's patience was sorely tried by Britain's refusal to rearm realistically, even in the face of conclusive evidence that the Nazis were dangerously set on breaking the fragile peace that had existed since the end of the First World War. His policy, he said, was to speak to the Nazis using 'the language of butter because these dictators live in such an atmosphere of adulation and awe-struck reverence that the language of guns may not go nearly as far'.[9] Rothermere's 'soft soap' policy was certainly fawning. 'I esteem it a great honour and privilege to be in correspondence with Your Excellency,' he wrote to 'My Dear Führer' on 20 April 1935. 'It is not often that anyone has an opportunity of learning the views of one who may occupy the first place in all European history.'[10] In December the same year he made very clear to Hitler the terms of their correspondence. 'Any information you might give me, my dear Reichskanzler, will be dealt with, as you know, only in the way you may desire.' What an opportunity for the Nazi dictator – access to mass-circulation newspapers in Britain, and on his own terms![11]

The flattery was still there in February 1938 at the time of the notorious Blomberg crisis, when Hitler began systematically getting rid of the 'old guard' of the military and aristocracy – on the whole the less fanatical leaders – and replacing them with his own appointees, in the process making himself Supreme Warlord. Rothermere's response was to congratulate him on the 'salutary' changes he had made. Adulation was in evidence two months later in April 1938 in a telegram to compliment Hitler on his 'triumph' in the Austrian plebiscite that led to the Anschluss. 'I beg to tender you my dear Führer my heartiest congratulations. Your star is rising higher and higher, but has not yet shone with its full effulgence.'[12] In October 1938, following the capitulation of the Czechoslovakian government after the so-called Munich Agreement, Rothermere was again ladling out excessive compliments. In a telegram to Berlin he enthused: 'Everyone in England is profoundly moved by the bloodless solution of the Czechoslovakian problem ... Frederick the

Great was a great popular figure in England, may not Adolf the Great become an equally popular figure.'

Churchill was not privy to the contents of the letters passing between Rothermere and Hitler; they may well have shocked him had he seen them. However, in a letter to his wife Clementine in August 1934, he echoed the sentiments Rothermere had expressed. He wrote that Rothermere wanted Britain to be strongly armed and frightfully obsequious at the same time, and that in such a way he hoped to avoid living through another war. Churchill conceded that it was a more practical attitude than that adopted by Britain's socialist politicians, who wished to remain disarmed and at the same time be exceedingly abusive to Hitler and his Nazi colleagues. The *News Chronicle* put it rather more brutally: 'There is nothing in modern politics to match the crude confusion of the Rothermere mentality. It blesses and encourages every swashbuckler who threatens the peace of Europe – not to mention direct British interests – and then clamours for more and more armaments with which to defend Britain presumably against his Lordship's pet foreign bully.' Among all leading British politicians it was really only Churchill who took note of Rothermere's warnings. The bulk of the Establishment regarded Rothermere as a 'wild card' and unpredictable. He was discredited as alarmist, a collaborator, inconsistent and disloyal. Yet, as Churchill admitted, he was right in predicting many of the significant events leading up to the Second World War, for instance by campaigning for rearmament, calling for a strong air force, forecasting how rapidly the French Army would capitulate at the first sign of German might and even prophesying that Hitler would be the eventual leader of Germany, years before he achieved that office. Yet in all this Rothermere seemed oblivious to the double role his protégée Princess Stephanie was playing; oblivious too to the possibility that via the princess and her lover, Fritz Wiedemann, Hitler was making use of him.

Few in the British Establishment were prepared to give Rothermere any credit. That was clear when, in September 1938, Hitler annexed the Sudetenland and Chamberlain flourished his piece of paper recording 'Peace for our time'. Rothermere, as perceptive as ever, cabled Churchill: 'If it hadn't been for you and me the country wouldn't be nearly as well prepared for the encounter as it is today.'[13] It was a truth that Churchill acknowledged in December 1939, when he wrote: 'I know how ungrudgingly you have spent time, energy and money in your endeavours to make the nation aware of its danger and its need to re-arm. I have appreciated to the full your patriotism and your sincere desire to see Britain virile and secure.'[14] At the time of Munich Rothermere's fears spilled out in a confidential letter to Churchill.

The accuracy of his prophecies now seemingly lost, he told Churchill that the Munich Agreement would last no more than nine or ten months and thereafter the British people would 'fold'. In a struggle, he wrote, between a parliamentary system and a dictatorship, the outcome was decided before the struggle even started. Britain was passing into the twilight, he gloomily forecast. 'A moribund people with a moribund government cannot stand up to the perils of these times.'[15] It was one prophesy he got wrong, but he never lived long enough to see the tide of war change.

There were others in high places who shared many, if not all, of Rothermere's views. One such figure was the 11th Marquess of Lothian, whose family estate was at Blickling in North Norfolk, close to Rothermere's country seat at Stody. During the Great War Lothian had served as private secretary to Prime Minister Lloyd George, and in the opening two years of the 1930s he had held the posts of Chancellor of the Duchy of Lancaster, and Under-Secretary for India in the National Government. Later, he was a prominent spokesman for the Liberal Party in the House of Lords. When Hitler came to power, Lothian argued that by winning German co-operation and allowing Germany to regain some of the territory it had lost as a result of the Treaty of Versailles, Britain would have the best chance of not only avoiding another bitter conflict, but also of preserving its empire. He persisted in his policy of friendship with Hitler and his fellow Nazis almost as long as Rothermere did.

In July 1938 Lord Lothian hosted a four-day gathering of German visitors, including a number of dedicated Nazis from the Deutsche Gruppe, at his stately home, the magnificent and picturesque Jacobean Blickling Hall. During a lavish weekend of hospitality, his guests, who included a representative of the Reich Propaganda Ministry, discussed ways of furthering Anglo-German relations with a British group who were mostly very sympathetic to the new Germany. Those present included several who Princess Stephanie had befriended. Among them were Lord Astor, owner of the *Observer* newspaper; Sir Thomas Inskip; and Arnold Toynbee, who had just returned from a meeting with Hitler in Berlin. Another was the influential editor of *The Times*, Geoffrey Dawson. The Blickling weekend resulted in a document entitled 'How to deal with Hitler', which painted the Nazi leader as a reasonable statesman. The outcomes from the weekend debate were transmitted next day to the government. Lothian, like others, was convinced the best hope for a peaceful Europe and a sound future for the British Empire was the removal of Germany's sense of grievance and injustice. In his pursuit of this cause he was prepared to turn a blind eye to the brutal excesses of the Nazi regime, even as late as a few months before war broke out. Hitler had been told by his London ambassador that Lothian was 'without doubt the most important non-official Englishman who has so far asked to be received by the Chancellor'.[16] When the two met face to face for a two-and-a-half-hour audience on 29 January 1935, Hitler emphatically ruled out using force against Poland, France, the Low Countries and Austria, and emphasised his determination not to provoke a war. Lothian, like so many others, took it all at face value and put forward his assessment of what the Führer had told him in a series of letters to *The Times*. Two years later, in 1937, Lothian made another trip to meet Hitler. This time the *Observer* printed an article lauding the success of Lothian's mission and crediting Hitler as being 'genuinely anxious for an understanding with the British Empire'.

Unlike Rothermere, Lothian's reputation hardly suffered from his overtures to the Nazis, despite the fact that the American ambassador to Berlin, William Dodd, had referred to Lothian as 'more Fascist than any other Englishman I have met'.[17] Ironically, Lothian was appointed British ambassador to Washington from 1939–40, a key position when Britain stood alone and Churchill was desperate to gain American support, if not as a participant, then as a generous supplier of war machinery. In September 1940, little more than two years after hosting that get-together of pro-Nazi guests at his Norfolk stately home, Lothian was responsible for the negotiations with President Roosevelt to conclude a crucial agreement for the still neutral United States to transfer fifty destroyers to Britain in exchange for naval and air bases in British territories in the Atlantic. Shortly after achieving that agreement, Lothian fell ill and died. Meanwhile, Blickling Hall, where the infamous 1938 pro-Nazi weekend was held, became the officers' mess of nearby RAF Oulton.

The Nazis had a misplaced belief that almost any Englishman with an impressive title and friends within the British Establishment could exercise influence on British foreign policy, hence their keenness to court members of the aristocracy sympathetic to their cause. It is clear from the MI5 documents that Princess Stephanie was actively recruiting these British aristocrats in order to promote Nazi sympathies.[18] Indeed, it appears one of her major tasks on behalf of the Nazi leadership was to canvass and infiltrate pro-Nazi views into British society. It was a mission in which she excelled – her title gained her access; her personality and flirtatious charm provided an effective means of persuasion. In the notes she later wrote for her unpublished memoirs, she lists many names of prominent Britons whom she considered either friends or close acquaintances. They go to the very top of British society. Her list is headed by the Prince of Wales and Wallis Simpson, and includes Lady Mendl, Lady Cunard, Lord and Lady Londonderry, Lady Oxford, Lord Brocket,

Lord Carisbrooke, Lord Rothschild, the Aga Khan and Dawson, editor of *The Times*.[19] It is reasonable to speculate she was at the notorious gathering at Blickling Hall herself, given the closeness of Blickling to Rothermere's country residence, Stody Lodge. The opportunity to promote further pro-German propaganda through the influential pages of *The Times*, which rightly or wrongly was considered by foreigners as the authentic voice of the British government, would have been too good an opportunity to miss.

Rothermere and Lothian were just two from the ranks of the Establishment who fell for these pro-Nazi overtures. The Duke of Westminster, who Princess Stephanie had befriended, having met him in France some years before, was another. The duke even took her on holiday to Scotland and it is clear that for a time romance blossomed between them. Two other prominent Nazi supporters were the Marquess and Marchioness of Londonderry, members of one of Britain's grandest and wealthiest aristocratic families, and owners of more than 50,000 acres. It is well documented, both in the notes kept by British intelligence and in her own personal notes, that the Londonderrys were close friends of the princess.[20] Indeed, her MI5 file describes Lady Londonderry as 'among her most intimate friends in England'. Londonderry, a cousin of Churchill, had, like Rothermere, been Secretary of State for Air. He was a flying enthusiast and believed passionately in the potential of aircraft in modern warfare. He held the ministerial post at the Air Ministry from 1931 until 1935. But in the second half of the 1930s, when to his bitter disappointment he lost high office, Londonderry and his wife became strong supporters of Nazi Germany. During his time in government, echoing Rothermere and Churchill, Londonderry pressed hard to increase the RAF's capacity to offer a strong and reliable defence. However, he was constrained by budgetary problems and fears of stimulating a new arms race when Britain was publicly pressing for a policy of disarmament in Europe. He was well aware that Britain was falling dangerously behind other countries, particularly Germany, in the numbers of squadrons at its disposal, but he faced difficulties in making headway because of strongly held policies against aggressive rearmament elsewhere in government.

When his term in office ended in June 1935 he was unfairly discredited and felt, with some justification, that he had been made a scapegoat for the ineffective policies of the National Government. His time as Secretary of State for Air produced some real and lasting achievements for which he was never really acknowledged, probably because of his later relationship with the Nazis. His strong support of the design of modern fighter aircraft gave the initial push that resulted in the two famous aircraft which were the saviours of the

Battle of Britain: the Spitfire and Hurricane. The beginnings of research into radar – the invention which together with the iconic fighters played such a massive part in the air defence of Britain – dated to his period in office, as did the prototypes of the early generation of the RAF's Second World War bombers – the Wellington, Hampden and Blenheim. The latter, of course, was developed from the prototype that Rothermere personally commissioned and paid for.

Within months of losing his post at the Air Ministry, Londonderry began to emerge as a strong champion of Germany. It was his fervent, if misguided, belief that a personal mission to meet Hitler and his fellow Nazis might lead to an arrangement with Germany. Londonderry was particularly keen to meet his erstwhile opposite number, Goering. In January and February 1936 Londonderry combined his first visit to meet the Nazi leadership with a trip to the Winter Olympics in Bavaria. Goering was more than happy to facilitate the trip, even sending a Junkers JU52 to Croydon to fly Londonderry and his wife to Berlin. The Nazi hierarchy did everything possible to impress their new admirers, showing them Luftwaffe installations and airfields, and introducing them to key players in the Third Reich. The day after their arrival they were invited to witness a huge procession of thousands of storm troopers gathered in the Wilhelmstrasse to mark the third anniversary of Hitler's rise to power. The following day they were guests of Goering at Carinhall, his vast hunting lodge and estate north of Berlin. Goering was an enthusiastic hunter and conservationist. He had introduced elk, bison and wild horses to his estate, and the sport there for any keen hunter was outstanding; far removed from the traditional shooting of game on the landed estates in Britain. In extensive talks, which followed a hunting expedition, Goering advocated a bilateral agreement between Germany and Britain, implying an Anglo–German air pact. On 4 February came the high point for the British aristocrat – a two-hour audience with Hitler in the Reich Chancellery followed by a reception and lunch hosted by German Foreign Minister Baron von Neurath. Two days later Lord and Lady Londonderry were flown in Goering's personal plane to Berchtesgaden to visit Goering's mountain retreat, before moving on to the Winter Olympics.

To say Londonderry was impressed is to understate the effect the three-week trip had on him. He returned home determined to work for the relationship with Britain Hitler and Goering so desired. He was reassured that by his friendship with Princess Stephanie he would be able to maintain direct contact with the Nazi power brokers in Berlin. In a speech delivered in Durham shortly after his return, Londonderry referred to Hitler as 'a kindly man with a receding chin and an impressive face'. He said Britain would be lacking in statesmanship if, in the event of war, it found itself engaged on a different side to Germany. Nazi organisational brilliance, he said, had enabled rapid expansion of its air force, and the German armed forces would be the strongest in the world. He expressed his conviction that 'The German nation as a whole, and the German government, are actuated by a desire for friendliness towards this country'.[21] The Londonderrys found, however, that not everyone was impressed by the enthusiastic praise they gave their Nazi hosts. The *Manchester Guardian* carried a report sarcastically headlined, 'An Innocent's Return', pouring scorn on the former British Air Minister.[22] He was met in influential political circles with derision. His trip, and the message he brought back, were treated with deep suspicion.

Their poor reception did not deter Lord and Lady Londonderry from writing with lavish praise to their German hosts. Lady Londonderry in a personal letter to Hitler said: 'To say I was deeply impressed is not adequate. I am amazed. You and Germany remind me of the book of Genesis in the Bible. Nothing else describes the position accurately.'[23] In May 1936 the Londonderrys hosted the Ribbentrops for a weekend at their mansion at Mount Stewart in Northern Ireland – a weekend which became christened and derided in the province as the weekend of the 'swastika over Ulster'. Ribbentrop was about to be appointed Hitler's ambassador to London. He was a well-known figure in London society, having been introduced by Rothermere to a number of prominent British businessmen. He was a frequent guest at some of the most fashionable society parties in London, many of them social events where Princess Stephanie also figured high on the guest list. Lady Londonderry was one of the hostesses who ensured Ribbentrop met important contacts in high society and the weekend house party in Ulster, which was given prominent exposure in the press, only served to heighten the reputation of the Londonderrys as notorious German sympathisers. Indeed, in England Lord Londonderry was considered so pro-German that behind his back he was referred to in jest as the 'Londonderry Herr'.

The Nazis regarded their assiduous courting of members of the British aristocracy as an important diplomatic coup. They truly believed such leading people in British society, certainly those with a voice in the Upper House, had far more influence than in fact they actually had – hence the importance of Princess Stephanie's mission to capture the sympathies of so many in the ranks of the British aristocracy. The Berlin Olympic Games of August 1936 nevertheless provided the Nazis with an unmatchable opportunity to strengthen links with those members of British society they believed important to their cause. The princess was feeding back to the Reich Chancellery information on who should receive such privileged treatment, who was most sympathetic to Nazi ambitions and who might be susceptible to persuasion. There were huge receptions in Berlin for selected foreign guests hosted by Ribbentrop and Goebbels. Most impressive of all was a massive garden party for 800 people staged by Goering. Hitler took the opportunity to welcome members of the Anglo-German Fellowship, together with the two leading British press barons Rothermere and Beaverbrook. From the Nazi point of view, the Olympics provided a world stage on which the growing strength of Germany could be paraded. More importantly, it was an event at which the fears of those deeply concerned about Nazi dictatorship and Nazi policy could be soothed. Privately, Hitler's ambition was that after 1940 the Olympics would be held permanently in Germany in a 400,000 capacity stadium in Nuremberg, that would also be used for the Nazi Party's mass rallies. He had asked his personal architect Speer to design such a stadium, believing that when the Third Reich dominated all of Europe, he would have the power to insist that the Olympics become a fixture in Nazi Germany.

The year 1936 was in many ways the pivotal one leading to the Second World War. It has been described as the 'hinge of the Devil's decade'. It began with the death of King George V, encompassed Mussolini's rape of Ethiopia, Hitler's occupation of the Rhineland, the outbreak of the Spanish Civil War, the battle of Cable Street in London in opposition to Mosley's Blackshirts and the Jarrow hunger march. It ended in the Abdication Crisis. For those alert enough to recognise the signs, it was the year the world changed from a post-war era to a pre-war one.

Although the Londonderrys were unable to attend the Summer Olympics, they were back in Germany in October 1936 at Goering's personal invitation. After a hunting trip to Carinhall, they again had an audience with Hitler, who as ever was keen to express his thanks for everything Londonderry and his wife were doing to encourage friendship between Germany and Britain. Privately, by the end of 1936 Londonderry was beginning to get increasingly gloomy about his chance of preventing war by pursuing an overtly pro-Nazi line. He blamed the disastrous attitude taken by the Foreign Office and wanted Britain to pin Hitler down on his policy options, and ensure he adhered to a peaceful policy whatever the circumstances.

In September 1937 Londonderry paid his third visit to the Nazis, again accepting an invitation to hunt with Goering at Carinhall. Goering told him that because Britain had shown repeated unwillingness to take the still-offered German hand in friendship, Germany had had to seek allies elsewhere, namely Italy and Japan. Britain appeared forever reluctant to help Germany attain her rightful place as a world power.[24] Londonderry, like others who had been the recipients of Nazi hospitality, detected growing impatience from his hosts. The leaders of the Third Reich were beginning to feel that all their wining and dining of British aristocrats was producing very small dividends. Londonderry was disappointed and frustrated. His report back to Chamberlain was treated by the British Prime Minister with only superficial interest. But Lord Londonderry was nothing if persistent. In November he was invited, again personally by Goering, to attend a banquet in Berlin to launch the International Hunting Exhibition. To his disappointment, when he was in the German capital he had only a fleeting discussion with Goering and no opportunity to meet Hitler. In June 1938 Londonderry made his last trip in a final effort to try to win a lasting peace through personal diplomacy. The British government was far from keen for him to go, concerned that someone so well known as a German sympathiser would send out the wrong messages. Londonderry had the opportunity on this occasion for talks with Himmler and Ribbentrop. He also made another visit to Carinhall for a further chance to indulge in the sport he loved. But when he reported back in London, the British government was dismissive of what he had been told by the Nazi leaders. They thought he had swallowed far too much propaganda, particularly from Goering.

Princess Stephanie commented on an embarrassing encounter between Goering and Lord Londonderry during one of these visits to Carinhall. She recalled Reichsmarschall Goering asking her: 'Tell me Princess, is it true that Lord Londonderry's daughter is married to a Jew?' Stephanie said there was no way she could deny that Londonderry's daughter, Helen Maglona, had indeed committed what the Nazis called *Rassenschande*, by marrying the Hon. Edward Jessel, a Jew. If she had been a German citizen, that very fact would have been enough to declare the marriage null and void, and her 'crime' would have been punished by a sentence of three to five years' hard labour. 'Goering seemed perturbed. He threw his arms up and shouted: That's dreadful. I made a terrible blunder. I was arguing with Lord Londonderry about race and religion and I asked him what he would do if his own daughter should want to marry a Jew.' Stephanie said she asked Goering what answer Londonderry had given. Goering said: 'He didn't. Imagine, he never said a word. It wasn't fair. He let me go on and never said a word. He should have stopped me. How tactless of him. Would you expect an aristocrat to behave like that? It just wasn't fair.'[25]

As the Czechoslovakian crisis began to boil up, Londonderry's passionate overtures to the Nazi hierarchy, after a period of three years, effectively came to an end. In the public's view, when war came Londonderry was the most notorious German sympathiser of all. Though Rothermere's track record of praising Hitler in his private correspondence with the Reich Chancellor, even as late as Hitler's march into Prague in 1939, was a good deal more outrageous, it had not been public knowledge. Indeed, the bulk of that highly damning evidence remained classified in MI5 files until 2005. Rothermere's close confidant Collin Brooks was well aware of what was contained in most of Rothermere's correspondence with the Nazi leaders. Nevertheless, when he heard of his master's death in December 1940, as Britain stood alone and in great danger of invasion and defeat, his verdict on Rothermere's wooing of Hitler and other leading Nazis was generous. He wrote in his diary: 'Everybody now seems to realise that the nation owes him a true debt both for the rearmament campaign and the attempts to keep Germany and Britain in some kind of accord.'[26]

11

THE PRINCESS, THE KING
AND WALLIS

MI5 noted in the late 1930s, with some obvious alarm, that Princess Stephanie had, in their words, 'wormed her way into British society' through her contacts with an expanding circle of aristocrats and political power brokers.[1] Her charm, her devious and disarming skills and her title took her to the very top of British public life, though she failed in her mission to deliver what Hitler most wanted: an ally, sympathetic to his policies, on the English throne.

The abdication of King Edward VIII in December 1936, to allow him to marry Wallis Simpson, his twice-divorced American mistress, caused a shockwave throughout Britain. In Germany, Hitler viewed it as little short of a disaster. For Princess Stephanie it was a rare failure for the brand of intrigue in which she excelled. She had worked hard behind the scenes, no doubt on instructions from Berlin, to steer the king and his mistress further towards the Nazi cause. Both Edward and Wallis were sympathetic to National Socialism. That much was becoming disturbingly clear to government ministers. But it was a key aim of the princess, and of Hitler's diplomats in the German Embassy in London, to keep Edward on the throne, preferably with Wallis at his side.

The princess had an apartment in Bryanston Court, close to London's Marble Arch. It was no coincidence that her apartment was in the very same building in which Mrs Simpson was living. Stephanie had known Edward when he was Prince of Wales. He was a keen golfer and she had met him at some of the well-known golf clubs he frequented in England and in the south of France. Before and after he became king there were social functions both of them attended in London.

The Prince of Wales was not the only member of the royal family the princess knew well. She was also close to Edward's youngest brother, Prince George, Duke of Kent, who, like the heir to the British throne, also showed a deep interest in the political philosophy of the Nazis. He regarded Hitler as a worker of economic and social miracles in Germany. He had met Hess and the influential Nazi ideologue Alfred Rosenberg, and dined frequently in London with Ribbentrop. From the early 1930s Prince George was involved in fostering closer relations between Britain and Germany, and as war loomed he was a participant in moves to avert hostilities. His involvement in the mysterious flight Hess made to Scotland in May 1941, and his subsequent death in an air crash in Scotland, has left many questions still unanswered.

Stephanie's closeness to Prince George is illustrated by the fact that letters between them were invariably handwritten and personally signed and addressed. One letter that has survived in the princess' personal papers is an effusive note to her from the prince dated 10 November 1934, expressing 'a million thanks' for the present of an expensive piece of furniture. There is no doubt the two saw a great deal of one another and shared political views. Indeed, both were at the lavish party given by Ribbentrop at the German Embassy in London to mark the coronation of King George VI in May 1937.

The Nazi hierarchy knew Stephanie had positioned herself adroitly to cultivate Edward and Wallis' fascist sympathies, in the same way she had influenced others in the upper reaches of the British aristocracy. What was almost certainly known to Stephanie – but definitely not common knowledge in London – was that while in Shanghai in 1925 with her first husband, an officer in the US Navy, Wallis had had an affair with the handsome fascist Count Galeazzo Ciano, son-in-law of Mussolini. Ciano was soon to become Italy's Foreign Minister in Mussolini's Fascist government and was a key figure in the alliance between the dictators of Italy and Germany. The affair had resulted in a pregnancy, and a carelessly carried out abortion had left Wallis unable to have any more children. But the friendship persisted, and it gave Wallis a direct link to the Italian dictator.[2]

Edward cherished his German ancestry. He felt a strong affinity with Germany and he spoke the language fluently. Until the First World War the name of the British royal family, indeed the name Edward was born with, was German – Saxe-Coburg-Gotha. Because of the need to distance the court from its German ancestry during the First World War, the royal family name was changed by George V to the very English title of the House of Windsor. Edward regretted the deep divisions the First World War had caused with his German relatives. In his teens he had been very friendly with the kaiser's family and he had spent many of his youthful holidays in Germany in the company of his favourite cousin, the Eton-educated Charles Edward, Duke of Saxe-Coburg-Gotha, who under the Third Reich became a member of the Schutzstaffel, the SS. When the Duke of Saxe-Coburg-Gotha was in London, representing Hitler at the funeral of George V, he told Edward there should be a high-level meeting between the British Prime Minister and the Führer. Edward welcomed the idea and the duke reported back to Hitler that as head of state in Britain and head of the British Empire, the new king fully supported bringing Britain and Germany closer together. Henry 'Chips' Channon, Conservative MP, leading socialite and commentator, noted in his diary that Edward 'was going the dictator way and is pro-German. I shouldn't be surprised if he aimed at making himself a mild dictator – a difficult enough task for an English King.'[3]

One of Stephanie's closest friends in London was Lady Emerald Cunard, an American who had married the heir to the Cunard Steamship line. She was well known in society circles as a lavish and generous host, and her parties in London were a major centre of Nazi influence. Wallis and Edward were frequent guests at her house in Grosvenor Square, and they regularly shared her box at the opera at Covent Garden. One commentator described Emerald's parties:

> Her drawing room, glowing with Marie Laurencin paintings, was alive night after night, with excited conversation about the merits and demerits of Mussolini, of the British prime minister, and of the new Führer. The conversation would eddy and flow as Emerald twittering and extravagant on her tiny feet and bedecked in gold lame, would lead Wallis, the prince, Ernest [Wallis' husband whom she divorced in favour of Prince Edward] and all her other guests into the dining room … [4]

Joachim von Ribbentrop, by then German ambassador, was frequently among the guests, and naturally Princess Stephanie was a regular part of the company too. As MI5 recorded: 'She has succeeded through introduction from Lady Oxford, Lady Cunard and others in worming her way into certain society circles where she speaks favourably of the present regime in Germany.' British intelligence also noted that the Nazi leadership had a scheme to invite people of influence in England to meet Hitler personally. 'The difficult job of selecting from British "neutrals" possible future friends of Hitler and Nazi Germany has been given to some of Hitler's most trusted friends in this country. Hitler is counting on the help of Princess Hohenlohe, his Vienna-born friend and talent spotter.'

1 Princess Stephanie von Hohenlohe photographed in 1932. The FBI called her 'dangerous and clever', others considered her a temptress and a femme fatale. To Hitler she was 'my dear Princess'. (Ullstein bild)

2 Above: Lord Rothermere conferring with Hermann Goering in Berlin, January 1934. (Ullstein bild: Heinrich Hoffman)

3 Left: Lord Rothermere, Princess Stephanie and Hitler at the Berghof, Obersalzberg, January 1936. With them are Ward Price, Fritz Wiedemann, and Joseph and Magda Goebbels. (Prince Franz von Hohenlohe Collection)

4 Hitler in 1935 with his friend and personal adjutant Fritz Wiedemann, who had been the Führer's senior officer during the First World War. (Ullstein bild: SV–Bilderdienst)

5 Princess Stephanie and her son, Prince Franz, photographed for a society magazine in London, June 1937. (*Illustrated London News*/Mary Evans)

6 *Daily Mail* correspondent George Ward Price with Hitler in 1938. Ward Price was one of the few journalists Hitler admired. (Ullstein bild)

7 Lord Rothermere, co-founder with his brother Lord Northcliffe of the *Daily Mail*. (*Illustrated London News*/Mary Evans)

ADOLF HITLER

BERLIN, DEN 20. Mai 1937.

Sehr geehrter Lord R o t h e r m e r e !

Für die mir durch meinen Adjutanten übermittelte Jadeschale sage ich Ihnen meinen herzlichsten Dank. Ihr wertvolles Geschenk wird eine Zierde meiner Räume auf dem Obersalzberg und für mich eine bleibende Erinnerung an Ihre Freundschaft und Wertschätzung sein.

Ihre Bemühungen zur Herstellung einer wirklichen deutsch-englischen Freundschaft verfolge ich , lieber Lord, auf das eingehendste. Ich bin wie Sie wissen, seit je der Ansicht, daß unsere beiden Völker am Ende doch auf einander angewiesen sind, und daß es keine bessere Sicherung für den Weltfrieden gibt als eine dauernde deutsch-englische Verständigung. Ihre in den letzten Wochen veröffentlichten Leitartikel, die ich mit großem Interesse gelesen habe, enthalten alles, was auch meinen Gedanken entspricht. Ich weiß, sehr verehrter Lord Rothermere, daß das Neue Deutschland in England keinen aufrichtigeren und warmherzigeren Freund hat als Sie.

Der Trauerfall, der Sie betroffen hat, ist mir erst durch Ihre Mitteilung zur Kenntnis gekommen. Ich darf Ihnen aus diesem Anlaß meine aufrichtige Teilnahme aussprechen.

8 Left: Dated May 1937, Hitler writes extolling Lord Rothermere's 'sincere and warm-hearted friendship'.

9 Below: Just seven months before the Second World War, Rothermere was writing to Hitler inferring a growing disillusion with Parliamentary democracy in England. (Hoover Institution Archives)

Ostern, 1938 Jan 1 — 1939

An den   Fuhrer und Reichskanzler Adolf Hitler, Berchtesgaden

May I tender You Fuhrer und Reichskanzler my heartiest good wishes for another successful year of Your wonderful regime. In England there is a steadily growing appreciation of Your Excellency and what You have accomplissed. Powerful influences are at work, to effect an enduring rapprochment between Your great country and mine. I am most hopeful, that in this new year a long stride will be taken to mett Germanys just demands. Every day in England there is developing the opinion that parliamentarism is unable to meet the needs, and solve thetproblems which confront modern democracies.

Rothermere

La Dragoniere Cap. Martin

10 Above: The Duke and Duchess of Windsor enjoy red-carpet treatment from the Nazis on arrival at Friedrichstrasse Station, Berlin, October 1937. (Ullstein bild)

11 Left: Nazi Foreign Minister Joachim von Ribbentrop with Italian Foreign Minister Galeazzo Ciano. Wallis Simpson was alleged to have had a romance with Ciano in China in 1925. (Ullstein bild: Heinrich Hoffman)

12 Left: Sir Oswald Mosley addressing a Blackshirt rally in Trafalgar Square, London, 1937. (Ullstein bild: Heinrich Hoffman)

13 Below: Schloss Leopoldskron, Salzburg. Hitler made Princess Stephanie chatelaine of the magnificent palace after the Gestapo had ejected its Jewish owner, the theatre director Max Reinhardt. (GNU Free Documentation Licence)

ADOLF HITLER

BERLIN, DEN 28.12.1937.
z.Zt. Obersalzberg.

Hochverehrte Prinzessin !

    Für die Bücher über amerikanische Hoch-
und Brückenbauten, die Sie mir als Weihnachts-
geschenk übermitteln liessen, sage ich Ihnen recht
herzlichen Dank. Sie wissen, wie sehr ich mich
für Architektur und die damit zusammenhängenden
Gebiete interessiere und können daraus ermessen,
welch' grosse Freude mir Ihr Geschenk bereitet.
    Ich habe mir ferner berichten lassen,
wie aufrecht und warmherzig Sie auch im vergan-
genen Jahre in Ihren Kreisen für das neue Deutschland und seine Lebensnotwendigkeiten eingetreten
sind. Ich weiss wohl, dass Ihnen manche Unannehm-
lichkeiten daraus erwachsen sind und möchte Ihnen
deshalb, hochverehrte Prinzessin, aufrichtigen
Dank sagen für das grosse Verständnis, das Sie un-
serem Volke im ganzen und meiner Arbeit im beson-
deren immer entgegengebracht haben.
    Ich verbinde mit diesem Dank meine herz-
lichsten Wünsche für das neue Jahr und verbleibe
mit ergebensten Grüssen

14 Letter from Hitler to Princess Stephanie, December 1937, thanking her for her Christmas
gift of books on American architecture, bought during her trip to the United States with
her lover, Hitler's personal adjutant, Fritz Wiedemann. (Hoover Institution Archives)

15 The Gold
Badge of the Nazi
Party (NSPD)
awarded to
Princess Stephanie
personally by
Hitler in 1938.

<u>Abschrift.</u>

Der
     Führer und Reichskanzler Adolf Hitler,
           B e r l i n .

The news of your excellencys marvellous

triumph in the plebiscite has just reached

me on the German ship Europa on which I am

travelling to New York stop I beg to tender

you my dear Führer my heartiest congratu -

lations stop your star is rising higher and

higher but has not yet shone with its ful

effulgence.

                       Rothermere.

16 Telegram from
Lord Rothermere
in April 1938
praising Hitler's
'triumph' in
the Austrian
plebiscite which
led to Germany's
annexation of
Austria. (Hoover
Institution
Archives)

Generalfeldmarschall Göring

Carinhall, den 19. Sept.1938.

Hochverehrte Fürstin!

Mit dem schönen Gartenruhebett haben
Sie mir eine grosse Freude bereitet. Ich habe es
nach meiner Rückkehr nach Carinhall bringen las-
sen und möchte Ihnen nunmehr für dieses wunder-
volle praktische Geschenk meinen herzlichsten
Dank aussprechen.

Mit den verbindlichsten Grüssen

Ihr

17 Letter from Hermann Goering, September 1938, thanking Princess Stephanie for the gift of a garden lounger for his home at Carinhall. (Hoover Institution Archives)

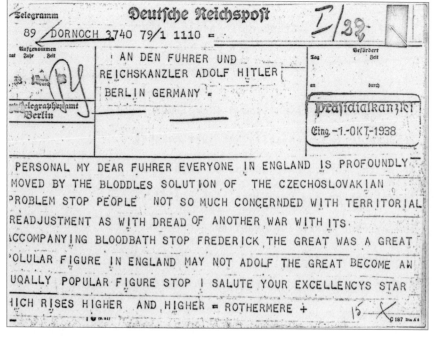

Telegramm **Deutsche Reichspost**

89 DORNOCH 3740 79/1 1110 =

AN DEN FUHRER UND
REICHSKANZLER ADOLF HITLER
BERLIN GERMANY =

Präsidialkanzlei
Eing. -1.-OKT-1938

PERSONAL MY DEAR FUHRER EVERYONE IN ENGLAND IS PROFOUNDLY
MOVED BY THE BLODDLES SOLUTION OF THE CZECHOSLOVAKIAN
PROBLEM STOP PEOPLE NOT SO MUCH CONCERNDED WITH TERRITORIAL
READJUSTMENT AS WITH DREAD OF ANOTHER WAR WITH ITS
ACCOMPANYING BLOODBATH STOP FREDERICK THE GREAT WAS A GREAT
POLULAR FIGURE IN ENGLAND MAY NOT ADOLF THE GREAT BECOME AN
UQALLY POPULAR FIGURE STOP I SALUTE YOUR EXCELLENCYS STAR
HICH RISES HIGHER AND HIGHER = ROTHERMERE +

18 Effusive telegram from Lord Rothermere to 'Adolf the Great' in October 1938, following the capitulation of the Czechoslovakian government after the so-called Munich Agreement. (Hoover Institution Archives)

Consul's Letter Is Bared

Wiedemann's Note to Princess Read in Rothermere Suit

LONDON, Nov. 10 (AP).—A letter which counsel said was from Captain Fritz Wiedemann Adolf Hitler's former adjutant and now consul general in San Francisco, was read today in the breach of contract suit of Princess Stefanie Hohenlohe-Waldenburg against Lord Rothermere, British publisher.

It credited the princess with laying "the groundwork which made the Munich agreement possible."

HITLER APPRECIATIVE

Asked "is that true?" the princess replied: "yes."

(The Munich agreement of September 29, 1938, began the break-up of Czecho-Slovakia through cession of the Sudetenland to Germany.)

The letter, described as being from Captain Wiedemann to Lord Rothermere, also said:

"You know the fuehrer greatly appreciates the work the princess did to straighten out the relations between our countries."

It added that Hitler, although it would be unpleasant, would allow her to use his correspondence with Rothermere in her suit.

(In San Francisco, Captain Wiedemann declined to comment on the London development, explaining that the records in the matter were not available to him.)

HITLER 'HATES PUBLICITY'

The princess explained it would be unpleasant for Hitler "because he hates publicity." Laughter interrupted the proceedings, which were adjourned until Monday.

In her suit the princess charges breach of a contract under which she asserted she was to receive 5,000 pounds (about $20,000) a year for acting as Lord Rothermere's political representative in Europe.

Sues Britisher
Letters From Hitler

Princess Stefanie Hohenlohe-Waldenburg, well known in local social circles, whose breach of contract suit in London against Lord Rothermere was featured today by a letter from Captain Fritz Wiedemann, German consul general in San Francisco.

19 How the American press reported the breach of contract case in the High Court in London in November 1939, in which Princess Stephanie attempted to sue Lord Rothermere after war had broken out between Britain and Germany. (Hoover Institution Archives)

In the High Court of Justice.

KING'S BENCH DIVISION.

Fos. 53.

Writ issued the 24th day of June 1938.

Between HER SERENE HIGHNESS THE
PRINCESS STEFANIE HOHEN-
LOHE-WALDENBURG   -   -   Plaintiff

and

THE RIGHT HONOURABLE HAROLD
SIDNEY VISCOUNT ROTHER-
MERE -   -   -   -   -   -   Defendant.

Statement of Claim.

1. In July 1932 it was orally agreed between the Plaintiff and the Defendant that the Defendant should employ the Plaintiff and that the Plaintiff should serve the Defendant as his foreign political representative it being the desire of the Defendant that she should carry communications to, and conduct negotiations with, statesmen and royal personages on the Continent with a view to securing the re-establishment of the Hohenzollern family on the throne of Germany and the placing of one of the Hapsburg princes or some other person on the throne of Hungary and that the Defendant should remunerate her for her said services at the rate of £5,000 a year and should pay her necessary expenses. It was an implied term of the said engagement that the Plaintiff's said employment should not be determined without reasonable notice.

2. The Plaintiff in pursuance of the said agreement herein-before referred to in paragraph 1 duly performed the services required of her by the Defendant as the Defendant's foreign political representative, and the Defendant in pursuance of the said agreement paid to the Plaintiff the said agreed remuneration from the time of her employment till the 19th January 1938 when in breach of the said agreement the Defendant wrongfully purported to determine the Plaintiff's said employment without giving her a reasonable or any notice.

3. While the Plaintiff was performing her said service it came to her knowledge that false and defamatory statements which

20 Princess Stephanie's 'Statement of Claim' in her notorious case against Lord Rothermere in the High Court in London, November 1939 – Her Serene Highness versus the Right Honourable Viscount. (Hoover Institution Archives)

21 Left: Princess Stephanie with her lover, Fritz Wiedemann, in the United States, January 1941. Wiedemann had been sent by Hitler to San Francisco to be consul general. (Associated Press)

22 Below: Part of the extraordinary FBI memorandum sent in October 1941 to President Roosevelt, in which Princess Stephanie is described as 'intelligent, dangerous and clever, as an espionage agent worse than ten thousand men'. (Franklin D. Roosevelt Library)

October 28, 1941

M E M O R A N D U M

RE: PRINCESS STEFANIE VON HOHENLOHE
     WALDENBURG, with aliases

     Princess Hohenlohe has been a very close confidante of Fritz
Wiedemann, the former German Consul General at San Francisco, and over
a period of time has been suspected by the French, British and American
authorities of being an international spy for the German Government.
She is known to have very close connections with high officials of the
Third Reich, is described as being extremely intelligent, dangerous and
clever, as an espionage agent to be "worse than ten thousand men", to
reputedly be immoral, and capable of resorting to any means, even to
bribery, to gain her ends.

     As Stephanie Richter, Princess Hohenlohe was born in Hungary
in 1891. Her father is described by some to have been a small town
dentist, by others an insignificant lawyer in Vienna, Austria. Her
mother is reportedly a Jewish woman of very low birth.

     Princess Hohenlohe entered the Ballet School of the Imperial
Opera at Vienna around 1906 but did not continue this career after
having met men who supplied her with a means of living. At the early
age of seventeen she was very well known in the circle of wealthier men
and extended her field of action to Berlin and Paris. She became the
lady friend of Archduke Leopold Salvator, through whom she gained acces
to military circles during the World War and many of her "connections"
date from those days. She reportedly forced Prince Hohenlohe Schilling
furst to marry her upon the claim that she was pregnant by him and thus
obtained the title of "Princess", which she still uses. Doubt exists
in the Hohenlohe family that her son, Prince Franz, is in fact a
Hohenlohe. The Almanach de Gotha, 1939 Edition of Justus Perthes,
verifies this information to the extent that it reflects the marriage
of Stephanie Julianne Richter to Francois, Prince of Hohenlohe Waldenbu
in London, England, on May 12, 1914, and the birth of her son in Vienna
Austria, on December 5, 1914. She obtained a divorce in Budapest, Hung
on July 29, 1920.

23 Annabel Wilson and Jack Kruse at their marriage at New York City Hall, April 1924. In London society and in the south of France they were known as a 'golden couple' – rich and influential. (Courtesy of Jan Kruse)

24 Lord Rothermere was fond of Annabel; she and her husband were part of his close circle. It was Annabel who brought Princess Stephanie and the press baron together. (Courtesy of Jan Kruse)

25 Part of Jack Kruse's iconic collection of cars at Sunning House in the mid-1920s. (Courtesy of Jan Kruse)

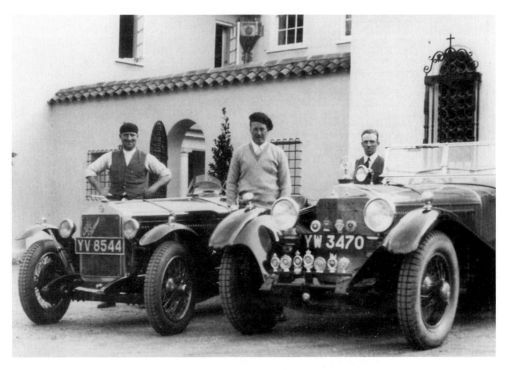

26 Jack Kruse with two of his three chauffeurs. His aim was to own the most competitive sporting model of the 'Roaring Twenties'. (Courtesy of Jan Kruse)

27 Jack and
Annabel Kruse.
One commentator
described them as
'dazzlingly rich, a
couple who would
have been at home in
the pages of a novel
by F. Scott Fitzgerald'.
(Courtesy of Jan
Kruse)

28 Post-War Black
List, dated June 1945,
barring Princess
Stephanie from
entering Britain
again: part of the MI5
files on the princess.
(National Archives
UK)

Emerald Cunard was Wallis Simpson's greatest supporter. She kept her guests in thrall using her waspish and frequently cruel tongue; stimulating provocative conversation in support of the National Socialist views she passionately espoused. Chips Channon was another regular at Lady Cunard's celebrated soirées. His diary records: 'Much gossip about the Prince of Wales' alleged Nazi leanings; he is alleged to have been influenced by Emerald Cunard (who is rather eprise with Herr Ribbentrop) through Wallis Simpson.' Channon went on to note the Prince of Wales had made an extraordinary speech to the British Legion advocating friendship with Germany; 'If only the Chancelleries of Europe knew that this speech was the result of Emerald Cunard's intrigues, themselves inspired by Ribbentrop's dimple!' To which Channon might have added, 'and Princess Stephanie's duplicity'.[5] According to a Metropolitan Police Special Branch report, it was at one of Lady Cunard's parties in January 1935 that Edward, then Prince of Wales, first met Oswald Mosley.

The prince showed keen interest in the Blackshirts and questioned Mosley on the strength and the policies of his British Union of Fascists. He was later to comment that Mosley would make a first-rate prime minister.[6] Edward was never much worried about expressing indiscreet views in public. In July 1933 Sir Robert Vansittart, a diplomat and socialite, recounted in his diary that at a party where there was much discussion about the implications of Hitler's rise to power, 'The Prince of Wales was quite pro-Hitler and said it was no business of ours to interfere in Germany's internal affairs either re- the Jews or anyone else, and added that dictators are very popular these days and we might want one in England.'[7] In March 1935, with scarcely concealed motives, the January Club became the Windsor Club; its members for the most part well-connected right-wingers.

Princess Stephanie was being referred to openly in reports in newspapers abroad, circulated by the International News Service, as 'Europe's Number One secret diplomat' and 'Hitler's mysterious courier'. The *New York Mirror* described how she was exerting her influence in London:

Her apartment has become the focus for those British aristocrats who have a friendly stance towards Nazi Germany. Her soirees are the talk of the town. Prominently displayed in her drawing room is a huge portrait of Hitler. So it was only natural that her efforts on the Führer's behalf would also bring her into contact with the 'Cliveden set' whose members include some of the most important statesmen of the British Empire.[8]

Stephanie was a regular weekend guest at Cliveden, the home of Lord and Lady Astor, as notes she wrote herself confirm. The Astors' house parties became notorious for attracting members of aristocratic society supportive of Hitler and his policies, and for enthusiasts of appeasement. Lord Astor owned both the *Observer* and *The Times*; Geoffrey Dawson, editor of *The Times*, was another of Princess Stephanie's acquaintances and also regularly attended at Cliveden. The house parties were therefore fruitful occasions for Stephanie to work her brand of subtle propaganda: persuasive, clever conversation which traded heavily on her personal contacts with Hitler. She was to later write, in an effort to distance herself from her energetic dissemination of Nazi propaganda in London in the 1930s: 'It is true that at Cliveden a number of recurrent guests were those in favour of appeasing the new Germany, but appeasement was by no means a bad word at that time.'[9]

Ribbentrop, a regular visitor to London even before he was appointed Hitler's ambassador to Britain in October 1936, became one of the most sought-after party guests in the capital. He was a natural social climber, and dressed to give the impression of being the perfect English gentleman. He liked nothing more than rubbing shoulders with royalty and aristocrats, and was frequently seen in London's most fashionable circles with ardent pro-Nazis like Emerald Cunard, Lord and Lady Londonderry and others in Wallis' and Princess Stephanie's circles.

Princess Stephanie's work with others who agreed an alliance with the new German regime was the way forward, and led to a campaign to form influential organisations, working within British society, who were sympathetic to the Nazis. Prominent names stand out as having common connections or membership with several of these organisations. The Link, which received financial backing from Berlin, included many members of the Cliveden set and of the Anglo-German Fellowship, though on a more modest scale also encompassed members from the Cliveden and London house parties. Stephanie and Ribbentrop were both regulars at Cliveden weekends, and in a report to Hitler on Anglo-German relations written in December 1937, Ribbentrop described the Cliveden set as a group trying hard to impress on Chamberlain the need to really understand Germany and Nazi policy. But he said they were being sidelined by unconditional opponents of Germany, in particular from hostility within the Foreign Office.[10]

The Link was overtly pro-German and expressed strong anti-Semitic and fervent pro-Nazi views. It had been founded by Sir Barry Domvile, a retired admiral who had also been a one-time director of naval intelligence. Domvile was another prominent figure in British society with whom

Stephanie had forged a friendship. The Link's membership spanned both the upper and middle classes. It included a number of retired military officers and businessmen, but there was also an important element of the aristocracy among its ranks. They included Lord Redesdale, father of the Mitford girls; Lord Semphill and the Duke of Westminster – all of them friends with Hitler's 'dear Princess'. By the middle of 1939 The Link had around 4,300 members.[11] Significantly, The Link's founder, Sir Barry Domville, is picked out in MI5's files as a particularly close contact of Princess Stephanie and with him she seems to have been one of the prime movers in the organisation's creation. Domville was among those interned by Churchill as a threat to national security under the 18B orders in May 1940. The Duke of Westminster, one of the richest men in England, joined The Link as late as 1939 when even some of its most ardent supporters were beginning to have second thoughts about Hitler's Third Reich. It was said one of his motives for joining was to try to prevent Hitler dropping bombs on London, because he owned so much of it!

The other prominent pro-German organisation was the self-consciously elitist Anglo-German Fellowship, established in 1935 with the outward aim to promote 'good understanding between England and Germany and thus contribute to the maintenance of peace and the development of prosperity'. The Fellowship worked closely with its counterpart in Berlin, the Deutsch-Englische Gesellschaft. Although it sought to suggest that membership did not necessarily imply approval of National Socialism, in reality the Fellowship operated – as Princess Stephanie wanted it to – as a tool of Nazi propaganda. There is also evidence to suggest that there were links between the Fellowship and the Nazi intelligence-gathering organisation the Auslands-Organisation, or more cryptically, AO, which operated in countries outside Germany.

A leading member of the Fellowship was the merchant banker Ernest Tennant, who had been a guest of Rothermere and Stephanie at the dinner in Berlin the press baron hosted during his first trip to meet Hitler. Tennant had also arranged the Fellowship's financial backing. Another prominent member was T.P. Conwell Evans, who had been instrumental in organising visits to meet the Führer for several pro-German aristocrats, including Lord Lothian. Membership overwhelmingly demonstrated wealth and influence.

MPs, generals, admirals, businessmen and bankers figured on its membership list. Both the governor of the Bank of England and the chairman of the Midland Bank were members.[12] A number of financial institutions were corporate supporters together with some leading industrial firms, including Unilever and Dunlop. Directors of companies as prominent in British life as ICI, Tate & Lyle and the Distillers Company were private members. The Fellowship's chairman was Lord Mount Temple, a former Conservative minister and father-in-law of Lord Mountbatten. Although the Fellowship was not as passionately pro-Nazi as The Link, Sir Barry Domville was a welcome member. Once again, in what MI5 observed was Stephanie's closeness to Domville, there are multiple links between her and the Fellowship's membership.

The Fellowship grew rapidly. By the end of 1936 it numbered some 450 people. By now the aristocratic element of its membership read like a substantial roll-call of the House of Lords: Lords Abedare, Airlie, Arbruthnot, Arnold, Barnby, Brocket, Douglas Hamilton, Ebbisham, Eltisley, Hollenden, Londonderry, Lothian, McGowan, Mottistone, Mount Temple, Nuffield, Nutting, Pownall, Rice, Redesdale, Semple and Strang, the Earl of Glasgow and later the Duke of Westminster. In July 1936 the Fellowship held a glittering dinner in London to honour the kaiser's daughter, the Duchess of Brunswick, and her husband, at which guests sat at tables decorated with swastikas. In December the same year the Fellowship threw another grand dinner in honour of Ribbentrop.

The Nazis regarded these Anglo-German societies as propaganda platforms where prominent Germans could meet and influence sympathetic audiences. They also formed part of Ribbentrop's intelligence network of 'listening posts', which fed back reports to the German Embassy on the state of British public opinion. In 1935 a rival to the Anglo-German Fellowship was formed called the Nordic League. It was set up by Nazi agents sent to London by the Abwehr and the SS to rival the Ribbentrop-orientated Fellowship. The Nordic League was an offshoot of the Nordische Gesellschaft run in Berlin by Alfred Rosenberg, an acquaintance of Prince George, Duke of Kent. It was regarded as the British branch of international Nazism and too extreme even for Mosley, who refused to get involved in it, although some of his lieutenants were founder members.

It was widely believed in society circles that Wallis Simpson was having an affair with Ribbentrop because of his constant visits to her apartment at Bryanston Court. Before he was appointed ambassador in the UK and was a foreign affairs adviser to Hitler, Ribbentrop routinely arranged to have a bouquet of seventeen red roses delivered to Wallis Simpson's flat whenever he was in London. It was an open secret in the city's social and diplomatic circles that Ribbentrop was infatuated with her, or perhaps it was a politically inspired infatuation?[13] Even Hitler teased Ribbentrop about his methods of gaining the lady's attention. Rumours began to circulate and the friendship between

Ribbentrop and Edward's mistress made Wallis a positive security risk. The FBI informed MI5 that the reason Ribbentrop sent seventeen flowers was because each bloom represented an occasion they had slept together. MI5 were probably not convinced by that, but nevertheless, they kept Bryanston Court under surveillance and noted the salacious gossip circulating about Wallis. It was easy for them to do so – they were already monitoring Stephanie's apartment in the same building! The scandalous tales so annoyed Mrs Simpson, however, that in 1937 she gave an interview to an American journalist strongly denying she was being used as a tool by the Nazis.

Yet stories continued to emerge, suggesting that Ribbentrop was paying Wallis to influence the king with funds coming directly from Berlin.[14] There were fears in some official circles that crucial information from state papers relating to the international situation, sent by government departments in red boxes for the king's eyes only, was finding its way to Berlin. Edward was easily bored by official paperwork and was careless with state papers. Wallis was thought by many to be the source of these leaks. So concerned were officials in the Foreign Office that they began screening documents to ensure nothing highly secret was included before being sent to Buckingham Palace or Fort Belvedere, Edward's private home. Sir Robert Vansittart, Permanent Under-Secretary at the Foreign Office, was convinced Wallis Simpson was the person responsible for passing information to the German government, and conveyed his fears to Prime Minister Baldwin. Within a few months of Edward becoming king, Foreign Secretary Anthony Eden restricted all confidential documents from the king's eyes. Eden had no time for Edward, and the feeling was mutual. Behind the scandal of the king's mistress, the government were well aware of a growing danger that had nothing whatsoever to do with the question of an unsuitable royal marriage, and everything to do with the king and Wallis Simpson's Nazi sympathies.

In their biography of Stanley Baldwin, Prime Minister at the time of Edward's abdication, authors Keith Middlemas and John Barnes describe the scandal:

> About Mrs. Simpson greater suspicions existed ... she was under close scrutiny by Sir Robert Vansittart and both she and the King would not have been pleased to realise that the Security Services were keeping a watching brief on her and some of her friends. The Red boxes sent down to Fort Belvedere were carefully screened by the Foreign Office to ensure that nothing highly secret should go astray. Behind the public facade, behind the King's popularity, the Government had awakened to a danger that had nothing to do with any question of marriage.[15]

A member of the German Foreign Office staff, Paul Schwarz, in his biography of Ribbentrop, confirmed that secrets from the British government dispatch boxes were being widely circulated in Berlin and he strongly implied that Wallis was the source.[16] Then in 1939, three years after the abdication, a secret FBI report to President Roosevelt stated:

> It has been ascertained that for some time the British Government has known that the Duchess of Windsor was exceedingly pro-German in her sympathies and connections, and there is a strong reason to believe that this is the reason why she was considered so obnoxious to the British Government that they refused to permit Edward to marry her and maintain the throne ... Both she and the Duke of Windsor have been repeatedly warned by representatives of the British Government that in the interest of the morale of the British people, they should be exceedingly circumspect in their dealings with the representatives of the German Government.[17]

Collin Brooks noted in his diary, on 18 November 1936, what informed comment in London was saying about Edward: 'the suggestion has been made in many quarters that he could, if he wished, make himself the Dictator of the Empire.'[18] Chips Channon said he was 'pro-German', and Ribbentrop noting Edward's sympathies called him 'a kind of English national socialist'.

Mosley's British Union of Fascists, unlike the fascist dictators on the Continent, identified strongly with the monarchy, and Mosley himself saw the possibilities of achieving political power if he and his policies could win royal support. 'He who insults the British Crown thus insults the history and achievements of the British race' was the popular BUF message for which Mosley cunningly sought to win support.[19] The Blackshirts saw no impediment in Edward's relationship with Wallis Simpson. 'The King,' Mosley declared, 'has been loyal and true to us. My simple demand is that we should be loyal and true to him.'[20] He stated that the king deserved, after many years' faithful service as Prince of Wales, the right to live in private happiness with the woman he loved. Mosley, like Hitler, had much to gain in trying to ensure Edward remained king. He knew perfectly well the king was covertly sympathetic to his right-wing views. Stephen Dorril, in his book *Blackshirt*, says that Mosley had a number of close contacts with the king and he claimed to have had secret correspondence with Edward.[21]

Collin Brooks, confiding in his diary, thought the king might do anything in the face of growing pressure on him to renounce his mistress – even the extreme act of dismissing Prime Minister Baldwin and sending for Mosley to attempt a fascist coup d'etat.[22] There were government ministers, too, who seriously believed this could happen. Certainly Mosley was planning and scheming to bring about such a situation, and it was an open secret to many who were close to the palace that Edward had expressed sympathy with the concept of dictatorship. He was greatly impressed with fascism as a modernising and patriotic force, one that could solve the problems of unemployment he had publicly agonised over as Prince of Wales. Many fascists regarded the new king as one of 'them'; a member of the younger generation who had been held back by the politicians of an older era. The Blackshirts tried hard to rally public opinion with a vociferous 'Save the King' campaign involving leaflets, canvassing public support through meetings and a campaigning newspaper which sold many thousands of copies on the streets, particularly in the capital.

Princess Stephanie, still seeking to fulfil Hitler's wish, was the person who originally floated the concept of a morganatic marriage as a solution to the king's dilemma. She, like the diplomats in the German Embassy, was desperate to find a means of keeping Edward and Wallis in power in Buckingham Palace.[23] The device of a morganatic marriage, she explained, would have allowed Edward to marry Mrs Simpson, but on the condition that she would merely be his consort and would not take the title Queen of England. It was very much in Hitler's interests that a way should be found out of the constitutional maze which threatened to force Edward off the throne. Princess Stephanie quoted, in support of her suggestion, the example of the marriage of the heir apparent to the Austrian throne. Had the royal couple not been assassinated in Sarajevo in 1914, Crown Prince Franz Ferdinand would have become emperor, but his wife would not have been given the title empress, nor would any children of the marriage have inherited any rights to the succession. The ploy suggested by Stephanie was backed by some supporters of the king, notably Stephanie's employer Lord Rothermere. At Stephanie's suggestion the press baron arranged for his son, Esmond Harmsworth, to lunch with Wallis at Claridge's and to urge her to accept the idea of a morganatic marriage and abandon any thought of ever becoming queen. She would have accepted the idea, but there was never any hope of such a device being adopted, by either Parliament or the dominions. Under English law, such an innovation would have required a special Act of Parliament, and it would also have needed the full support of countries throughout the empire. Edward himself, like Wallis, would probably have accepted this solution, but Baldwin had to inform the king that neither the dominions nor Parliament would countenance the idea. In any case, the Prime Minister had warned the king he himself would resign if Edward married Wallis Simpson.

On the night of his abdication, 10 December 1936, 500 Blackshirts shouting support and giving the Fascist salute gathered outside Buckingham Palace chanting, 'We Want Edward'. The next day, at a BUF rally in Stepney, Mosley demanded the question of the abdication be put to the British people in a referendum. When the abdication statement was read out in both the Commons and the Lords, Unity Mitford, Hitler's friend and admirer who had just returned from Berlin, exclaimed: 'Oh dear, Hitler will be dreadfully upset about this. He wanted Edward to stay on the throne.'[24] In Germany, on Hitler's express instructions, Goebbels ordered the media to make no mention of the constitutional crisis raging in Britain. He noted in his diary: 'He [Edward] has made a complete fool of himself. What's more it was lacking in dignity and taste. It was not the way to do it. Especially if one is king.'[25] In contrast, Rothermere's newspapers came out with banner headlines such as, 'God Save the King'. Edward had reigned just 325 days.

Having decided that his only course was to abdicate, Edward sent a message to Mosley thanking him for his offers of support and explaining that he felt unable to take advantage of them.[26] The king's decision undoubtedly avoided an even greater political and constitutional crisis. It seems highly probable that the pressure on Edward was exerted by Baldwin and others as much because of Edward's known sympathies with Hitler, his autocratic tendencies, his advocacy of a close alliance with Germany and the distrust and downright suspicions that surrounded his mistress and her political leanings, as because of the scandal of his romantic entanglement with a twice-divorced American woman and a commoner to boot. Both Baldwin, as premier, and Ramsay MacDonald, as a former Labour Prime Minister, shared the opinion that Edward had acquired dangerous views and an unconstitutional and potentially dangerous interest in foreign affairs.

One senior civil servant close to Baldwin went on record as saying that it became obvious Ribbentrop had been 'stuffing Hitler with the idea that the Government would be defeated and Edward would remain on the throne'. A message from Ribbentrop to the Führer attempted to explain the abdication as being the direct result of 'the machinations of dark Bolshevist powers against the "Führer-will" of the young King'. He blamed a conspiracy of Jews, plutocrats and reactionaries in the British Establishment opposed to Germany.[27] He needed an excuse to explain why German diplomacy in London had singularly failed to keep a Nazi-leaning king and his mistress in office. For his part, Hitler said that if Edward had remained on the throne there would have been no differences and no war between England and Germany. The king had been deposed because he wanted Anglo-German rapprochement.

Ribbentrop was intrigued by Stephanie and her closeness to the Führer, but he became suspicious when he realised that she was the mistress of Fritz Wiedemann, Hitler's closest adjutant. Wiedemann was at that time nearer to the Führer than Ribbentrop himself; he was persuasive and had the Nazi leader's ear. Ribbentrop's dislike of Wiedemann was mutual. Wiedemann could not stand Ribbentrop; he hated the man's vanity and his self-importance, and he was contemptuous of Ribbentrop's overwhelming subservience to Hitler. Among most of the top leaders of the Third Reich, below the Führer himself, mutual detestation was not uncommon. But one thing united them: they nearly all despised Ribbentrop.[28]

In 1936 Ribbentrop became Hitler's ambassador to Britain. He was installed in office in time for the coronation of George VI, in May 1937. When he presented his credentials to the new king, he performed the Nazi salute with such a display of fascist formality, rigour and clicking of heels that it caused something of a scandal. The king's courtiers were furious, whilst the press gave huge prominence to the story of embarrassment at court. They characterised Ribbentrop with tabloid humour as 'Herr Brickendrop'.

To mark the accession of George VI, the new ambassador, ever pleased to curry favour in society, threw a lavish party for 1,400 guests at the opulent, newly restored German Embassy in London. Fritz Wiedemann was among the official German delegation, but to her dismay Princess Stephanie was not on the guest list, and she took this as a direct snub from Ribbentrop.[29] Rothermere had asked her to interview the head of the delegation, Hitler's personal representative, the then Reich Minister for War Werner von Blomberg, for an article in the *Daily Mail*. Stephanie was not to be bypassed in what she regarded as such an insulting fashion by Ribbentrop. She asked her lover Wiedemann to request Hitler to speak directly to Ribbentrop about it. Hitler did so, insisting Ribbentrop apologise to the princess, which eventually he grudgingly did.

The grand party was a major social event in London, attended by royalty in the person of the king's younger brother, Prince George of Kent. It was the first time Hitler's personal adjutant and the princess had been seen in each other's company in England, a fact that did not go unnoticed in social, diplomatic and political circles. Nor did it escape the attention of British intelligence, who had already been informed by the French security service that she was the mistress of the Führer's close friend and aide-de-camp.[30] Writing years later, Princess Stephanie recorded her impressions of Ribbentrop, and they were still bitter:

He considered himself the one and only infallible political authority on England in the Third Reich, and anyone who did not agree with him that the English were hopelessly decadent, that they would never stand up to fight the Germans, and that their world empire had reached its zero hour, was a personal enemy of his. Leading Nazis like Hitler, Goering, Hess, Goebbels, Streicher, and Himmler had never been to England and could neither speak nor read English, in Ribbentrop's eyes I was an arch fiend, a subversive meddler, a pestilential intruder.[31]

For Ribbentrop and his master in Berlin, the abdication was the end of a dream of a British king and his consort both sympathetic to the Nazi regime and both playing a key part in working for a rapprochement between Britain and Germany.

Although no longer on the throne and in exile, Edward was still potentially valuable to the Nazi cause. Princess Stephanie set to work with other Nazi agents to keep alive the hope that, ultimately, a Nazi sympathiser might return to the British throne. Following his abdication, Edward and his mistress had to wait until Wallis' divorce proceedings had been legally completed before they could pursue their intention to marry. While she waited in France, Wallis engaged a lawyer to look after her interests. The man she turned to, Armand Gregoire, was a Nazi activist whose political sympathies were well known to French intelligence. The Sûreté Nationale described him as 'one of the most dangerous of Nazi spies', despite his outward position as a prominent lawyer with offices in Paris' Place Vendôme, and his and his wife's socially high-flying lifestyles.[32] Intelligence archives in Paris and Washington contain bulky files on Gregoire's activities as a leading Nazi agent, and as lawyer for Ribbentrop and Otto Abetz (later to become the Nazi ambassador to Paris and an acquaintance of Princess Stephanie). At the end of the war the French put him on trial, accused of collaboration with Nazi Germany, and he was sentenced to hard labour for life.

Edward and Wallis Simpson eventually married in France in June 1937. The ceremony took place at the sixteenth-century Chateau de Cande in the Loire Valley, owned by multi-millionaire Charles Eugene Bedaux, another man long suspected of being an agent of the Germans. Bedaux was a fascinating character. Born in Paris, he was a stocky figure with black hair, jug ears, the face of a prize-fighter and the slightly bow-legs of a racing jockey. Having dropped out of school, he had amassed a fortune in the United States as one of the leading pioneers of scientific management – time and motion study. The FBI and American Military Intelligence had kept him under surveillance when he was in the United States during the First World War. Later, after a time spent back in Europe, he reappeared in America in the 1920s. By 1925 he had established nineteen offices worldwide with 600 industrial clients, most of them big household names like Campbell's Soup, Kodak and General Electric. He became a US citizen and made a considerable fortune pushing the new philosophy of mass production and business efficiency through a series of companies he created across the US and Europe. In the States he worked with leading industrialists, including Henry Ford, and companies of the status of General Motors, ITT, DuPont and Standard Oil – companies that, when the Second World War broke out in Europe, became members of a loosely connected group in the States dubbed 'The Fraternity'; all of them firms that while aiding the United States' war effort, also aided Nazi Germany's.[33]

After moving back to Europe in 1926, Bedaux became closely involved with some of Germany's biggest and most successful companies. He knew many leading Nazis, not least Dr Hjalmar Schacht, head of the Reichsbank and Hitler's future Minister of Finance. In 1938 Bedaux was appointed by Fritz Wiedemann – acting on behalf of the Nazi leadership – to the post of head of commercial operations for I.G. Farben, the industrial giant which later notoriously produced the gas used in the Holocaust concentration camps. In that role he worked on behalf of The Fraternity in Europe, and collaborated closely with the Vichy government in France as a special adviser to his friend, the Nazi Ambassador Otto Abetz. As well as his chateau in the Loire, Bedaux also owned a villa at Berchtesgaden within sight of Hitler's mountain retreat on the Obersalzberg. It was from there that he wrote offering the Chateau de Cande as the venue for the wedding of the Duke and Duchess of Windsor. The ceremony naturally attracted huge interest across Europe, and among the gifts that arrived for the couple were expensive presents from both Hitler and Mussolini. The Windsors honeymooned in Austria at an Alpine castle owned by Count Paul Munster, who had dual British and German citizenship and was a member of the Windsor Club. Sir Robert Vansittart at the Foreign Office had compiled a security file on the Windsors' dubious links and contacts with fascists, and Munster was one of those associated with the duke and duchess under observation as a known backer of Mosley.

One of the first public engagements the new Duke and Duchess of Windsor undertook, following their marriage, was a visit to Nazi Germany – a visit Princess Stephanie had played a key part in planning. She made the arrangements together with Bedaux and Wiedemann. It gave Edward and Wallis the opportunity to meet Hitler face to face at his mountain retreat at Berchtesgaden with the spotlight of the world's media upon them. Officially, the duke and duchess were guests of the head of the German Labour Front, Dr Robert Ley, and as it was regarded as an official state visit, the trip was paid for by the German government. It was publicised as a study trip to learn about German institutions, but for the Reich leadership it was an opportunity to bring strong influence on the man who they hoped they could eventually return to the British throne.

The occasion gave Hitler a huge propaganda coup, to the anger of the British government and King George VI. The Foreign Office and Buckingham Palace issued instructions to the British ambassador in Berlin, specifically to ensure the duke and duchess would not be treated as having any official status. 'You should not attend yourself,' the British ambassador was told, 'send a secretary or junior diplomat.' Despite the British view, the Nazi regime set out to give the duke and duchess the full red-carpet treatment of a royal visit. They were driven everywhere in a large, open-top Mercedes-Benz with black-uniformed SS guards standing to attention on the running boards. When they were taken to factories, well-drilled workers shouted 'Heil Windsor' and greeted the couple with the Nazi salute. The duke was not slow himself in returning the tribute, rigidly extending his arm like any convinced Nazi. On the first night of the trip the Windsors were entertained at a dinner party at which fellow guests included Hess, Ribbentrop, Goebbels and Heinrich Himmler. A few days later they were invited for tea at Goering's mansion, Carinhall. The duke and duchess were impressed by the lavish hospitality. Wallis, deprived in Britain of the title 'Her Royal Highness', was delighted to be given such a high-level reception and treated as royalty. Another event took them to the training school for the Death's Head Division of the Elite Squad of the SS. Here they were greeted by an SS band playing the British National Anthem.

Not to be outdone, Ribbentrop hosted a splendid occasion at the famous Restaurant Horcher in the German capital. Goebbels noted in his diary that the duke was 'a nice friendly young man clearly equipped with sound common sense'. The duchess, he noted, is 'unassuming but distinguished and elegant, a real lady. Magda is charmed by them.'[34] The climax of the visit was a trip to Hitler's mountaintop retreat, where the duke and duchess were in the Führer's company for several hours. Wiedemann met them at the railway station and after a short walk along the shore of Lake Königssee, he drove them to the Berghof where Hitler greeted them warmly, taking them to his vast reception room with its wall of glass looking out on a stunning mountain panorama. The duke is reported to have expressed the couple's gratitude for the moral support Germany had shown to them during the Abdication Crisis.

If any record of the talks between the former British king and the Führer survive, they are almost certainly among papers captured after the war and now held securely in the royal archives in Windsor, beyond the reach of Freedom of Information laws. However, the duke, in an article published in the *New York Times* in December 1966, recalled part of the discussion: 'Hitler was then at the zenith of his power,' he wrote. 'His eyes were piercing and magnetic. I confess frankly that he took me in. I believed him when he said that he sought no war with England … I thought that the rest of us could be fence sitters while the Nazis and the Reds slogged it out.'[35] As the couple left the Berghof, Hitler gave them a formal Nazi salute, and the duke in turn extended his arm to salute the Führer. The duke appeared impressed by what he had seen in Germany.

The Nazi press was fulsome in its praise, but in Britain, France and the United States reports were much more critical. The *New York Times*, in an editorial commenting on the Windsors' visit, said:

> The Duke's decision to see for himself the Third Reich's industries and social institutions, and his gestures and remarks during the last two weeks, have demonstrated adequately that the abdication did rob Germany of a firm friend if not indeed a devoted admirer on the British throne … The Duke is reported to have become very critical of English politics as he sees them and is reported as declaring that the British Ministers of today and their possible successors are no match for the German and Italian dictators.[36]

The British ambassador to Germany, Sir Ronald Lindsay, said the duke's reception by Hitler could only be construed as a willingness to lend himself to fascist tendencies. The duke, he said, was trying to stage a 'come-back' and his friends and advisers were semi-Nazis. Suspicions of the motives and loyalties of the Duke and Duchess of Windsor persisted after the outbreak of war. During the 'Phoney War', when the duke was attached to the British Military Mission in France in the rank of major general, there were allegations of injudicious or careless talk across the Windsors' dinner table in Paris – where Bedaux was a regular supper guest. Some in senior positions in London strongly suspected that the Windsors were a security risk.[37]

Hitler's blitzkrieg – as first Denmark and Norway were overrun in April 1940, followed a month later by the Low Countries – led to major concerns in Whitehall and at Buckingham Palace for the duke and duchess' safety in France. There were fears that they could be captured, allowing the Nazis to use them as immensely valuable pawns – which is just what the Germans would have wished to do. As the German Army advanced on Paris, Edward fled to the south of France. He and the duchess stopped briefly at their residence at Villa La Croe near Cap d'Antibes, hoping they could at least find a temporary sanctuary and some comfort there. But when the Italians declared war on 10 June, with both the Germans and Italians closing in, they once again had to flee. Not, as military orders stipulated, returning directly to England, but heading for the Spanish frontier. They crossed into supposedly neutral Spain and by 23 June were in Madrid.

Fears in London were matched by concerns in Berlin. There was still everything for the Nazis to play for by enticing the former British king to reach an understanding with them; if Germany successfully invaded Britain, this would result in Edward being restored to the throne, with Wallis as queen. The Germans were convinced that in Britain this might well prove a popular move. Ribbentrop, by now German Foreign Minister, was well aware from his many meetings with the former king of Edward's National Socialist sympathies, and of his view that war was unnecessary. Since the Fascist government of General Franco was aligned with Berlin and the Axis powers, though still nominally neutral, Ribbentrop reasoned it was in Germany's interests to detain the duke and duchess in Spain. The Nazis made strenuous efforts to ensure the couple remained there, where Germany could continue to exercise influence on them. The Abwehr, German military intelligence, had some 1,500 agents throughout Spain, many of them German émigrés. Intelligence poured into the Abwehr's Madrid headquarters adjoining the German Embassy. As long as the duke and duchess remained in Spain, Germany was well placed to plot to keep them there under constant surveillance.[38]

Ribbentrop persuaded the Spanish government to offer the couple hospitality and a palatial residence, to encourage them to remain in the country. He was conscious of the ongoing conflict between the British government, Buckingham Palace and the duke and duchess over the refusal to grant Wallis HRH status, and the reluctance of the British Establishment to welcome the Windsors back to the UK for fear of destabilising the position of the new king and queen. The Germans even undertook, at the duke's request, to arrange for the Windsors' Paris home and all its contents, and their villa at Cap d'Antibes, to be safely looked after for the duration of the war.

A German plot to ensure the Windsors remained under Nazi control was hatched and the Gestapo leader of counter-intelligence, Walter Schellenberg, was dispatched by Ribbentrop to take control of the plans. Churchill, conscious of the acute and growing danger of the king's brother being influenced or even abducted by the Nazis, instructed the duke and duchess to cross into Portugal forthwith. Portugal was a more reliable neutral country than Franco's Spain, and Churchill's instructions were that the couple should go straight to Lisbon where they could be picked up by a British flying boat and flown out of reach of Nazi agents. But the duke and duchess played for time. Edward outrageously, given that the British government was at war, tried to negotiate guarantees that if the couple returned to Britain they would be given full royal treatment, and the title of HRH conferred on the duchess. Churchill, who had far more important things to worry about with Britain facing a threat of imminent invasion, was fast losing patience with his former monarch. He knew that Spain was a hotbed of German intelligence and he insisted the Windsors move at once to Lisbon to shake off German conspiracies. Churchill even resorted to issuing threats that if Edward disobeyed government instructions, as a senior British officer still under military authority, he would be subject to court martial.[39] The duke and duchess finally succumbed to the mounting pressure from London. They moved to the Portuguese capital on 3 July, a week before the start of the Battle of Britain. There they took up residence with a wealthy banker, Ricardo Espirito Santa Silva, a close friend of the German ambassador to Portugal and a man who was under suspicion by British intelligence for his pro-German views and activities. Ribbentrop maintained the momentum of his campaign to entrap them. First he sent emissaries to Lisbon to flatter and cajole the couple, with promises to return Edward to the British throne when Germany had defeated and occupied Britain; then he dispatched a senior SS officer with instructions to force them back into Spain where it would be far more difficult for the British to exercise influence or, as a last resort, even to kidnap them.

At Buckingham Palace a senior courtier, Alec Hardinge, made a note on an intelligence report: 'Germans expect assistance from Duke and Duchess of Windsor. Latter desiring at any price to become Queen. Germans have been negotiating with her since June 27th.'[40] The issue of the Windsors, and how to get them away from German influence, was becoming more and more urgent for Churchill and for King George VI. If Edward and Wallis fell into German hands, either willingly or by force, the impact on British morale and the future conduct of the war would be disastrous. Churchill hit on the idea of removing the couple far from the reach of Nazi agents by offering the duke the post of the governorship of the Bahamas; a post where they would be free of Nazi influence and where they could do the least harm. Although his brother and the rest of the royal family were initially not enthusiastic, the Windsors reluctantly had to agree to it. As King George VI put it, 'it was imperative to get him away from Lisbon'.[41]

Had George VI known what was passing between the German ambassador to Portugal and Ribbentrop, he would have been even more alarmed about his brother's loyalty. A long report to the Nazi Foreign Minister from the German ambassador, Baron von Hoyningen-Huene, stated that the idea of the Bahamas appointment was to keep Edward out of England because if he returned there it would greatly strengthen the position of a peace party in the United Kingdom. The ambassador went on to say that the duke had been voicing his opinion in Lisbon, stating that if he had remained on the throne there would have been no war, and that he was still a firm supporter of compromise with Germany. Finally, the report said the duke had disloyally – it could be termed treacherously – expressed his belief that 'continued heavy bombing will make England ready for peace'.[42] The duke was careless in his comments to the American ambassador in Lisbon, too, speculating that the Churchill government would fall and a replacement government would then be prepared to negotiate peace with the Germans. In such circumstances Edward foresaw George VI abdicating. He added that if he went back to London to resume the throne and restore his power, he would lead Britain into a coalition with France, Spain and Portugal, leaving Germany free to march on Russia, which in his view was the real threat to Europe.

When he was told what was planned for him and his wife, Edward again played for time, making further selfish demands. He insisted that his former servants should be released from duties in the armed services to accompany him to the Bahamas, and that en route he and Wallis should be allowed to visit New York. Churchill had other more pressing worries and was reluctant to negotiate conditions. He did, however, agree to sanction the discharge from the forces of two of Edward's old servants, but adamantly refused to allow the Windsors to stop off in the United States. He was worried the duke would make more ill-considered and unhelpful public comments in America at a sensitive time for Anglo-American relations, when Britain crucially needed America's assistance in the war.

Edward and Wallis' departure was still not certain. The Germans, through their agents in Lisbon, tried to convince the duke that the British secret service had plans to assassinate him on the voyage to the Bahamas, and that he would be much safer under their protection in Spain. Offers of luxurious accommodation were made if the Windsors would remain in Europe. Arrangements were even put in hand to bribe the duke with 50 million Swiss francs if he was prepared to give some official gesture disassociating himself from the British Crown and the British government.[43] Schellenberg considered removing the Windsors from Portugal and taking them to Spain by force, but British agents and Churchill back in England successfully outmanoeuvred the German plot – although it took a trip to Lisbon by Sir Walter Monckton, former lawyer, close adviser to Edward and now a government minister, to persuade the duke and his wife to take up the governorship of the Bahamas and leave Portugal. Whatever the arguments and threats that were deployed, much to the relief of Churchill and the new king, Edward and Wallis eventually set sail for the Bahamas on 1 August.

There is no way of knowing if Edward would have committed treason by co-operating with the Nazis had an opportunity arisen for his return to the throne following a German invasion of Britain. He was certainly put under severe pressure by the Germans to do so. The considered view of his biographer, Philip Ziegler, was: 'there seems little doubt that he [Edward] did think Britain was likely to lose the war and that, in such a case, he believed he might have a role to play'. But Ziegler concluded that in the event of a German victory in the early 1940s, 'the Duke's belief in the British meant he could not have allowed himself to rule by favour of the Germans over a sullen and resentful people'.[44] That may well be true, but it is certain Churchill had grave fears and was far from confident what Edward's actions would be. Many Nazi agents, orchestrated by Ribbentrop and including Princess Stephanie, had worked hard for an outcome favourable to the Nazis, and Edward and Wallis under German control would have been the propaganda coup that could have changed the course of war.

In his book *Operation Willi*, Michael Bloch wrote:

The Duke unwittingly encouraged Hitler's hopes and illusions concerning him in a remarkable degree; and his presence in Europe, while it lasted, appears to have had a tantalizing effect on Nazi policy. The consequences may possibly have been fateful. Throughout that July, Hitler hesitated to order the attack on Great Britain – Operation Sealion – thus giving the British a chance to regroup their forces and survive. Were Hitler's hopes that the Duke could be persuaded to go along with the plan to restore him as king one of the principal causes of Hitler's hesitation? What one can say for certain is that it was not until August 1st – the day that the Duke finally sailed from Europe – that the Führer issued his Directive No. 17 ordering the Luftwaffe 'to overcome the English Air Force with all means at its disposal and in the shortest possible time'; and it was not until August 2nd that Ribbentrop ordered Eberhard von Stohrer [German ambassador to Spain] to work for Spain's early entry into the war.[45]

Ribbentrop, of course, failed in that ambition, too.

Edward and Wallis remained in the Bahamas until April 1945. From the governor general's residence the duke maintained contact with Charles Bedaux until 1943, when Bedaux was arrested in North Africa where he was supervising the construction of a German pipeline. He was taken back to the United States on a charge of treason and committed suicide in February 1944 while in prison in Miami, awaiting a grand jury investigation into his wartime activities.

The duchess compared her and her husband's enforced stay on the remote British territory to Napoleon's incarceration on Elba. But Edward's appointment as governor general did not stop his flirtation with Nazi Germany. In December 1940, as Britain battled against Hitler's war machine alone and in isolation, an American journalist with close connections to President Roosevelt received an unexpected invitation to the Bahamas. He was invited to conduct a rare interview with the island's governor. Edward was still an officer in the British Army, both as a result of his royal appointments and his war service in France with the British Expeditionary Force. He might have been expected to fly the flag for his embattled former kingdom. Yet he gave Fulton Oursler of the magazine *Liberty* an amazing eulogy to Hitler. The former British monarch told the journalist it would be tragic for the world if the Nazi dictator was overthrown; Hitler was the right man at the right time and the logical leader of the German people. Edward argued for a negotiated peace with Germany. 'It cannot be another Versailles. Whatever the outcome a new order is going to come into the world ... it will be buttressed by police power. When the peace comes this time there is going to be a new order of social justice – don't make any mistake about that.'[46]

As Oursler tried to take in the enormity of what he was hearing, the duke asked him: 'Do you suppose your President would consider intervening as a mediator when and if the proper moment arrives?' The American understood he was being asked to carry a message to the President, but he was unsure of the exact terms. As he was leaving the governor general's residence, the duke's aide-de-camp spelt it out. He instructed Oursler to tell the President that if he would make an offer for intervention for peace, before anyone in England could oppose it, the duke would instantly issue a statement supporting the move. It would start a revolution in England and, the duke hoped, lead to peace.

Roosevelt would have nothing to do with the duke's treacherous scheme. He had already placed Edward and Wallis under FBI surveillance. FBI papers, declassified in 2009, show just how scathing the American authorities' assessment of the duke and duchess was. 'The British government were anxious to get rid of the Duke of Windsor, first and foremost because of his fondness for the Nazi ideology,' the 227-page report concludes. 'The duchess' political views are deemed so obnoxious to the British Government that they refused to permit Edward to marry her and maintain the throne.'[47] The FBI was instructed by the President to tail the Windsors discreetly whenever they made short visits to the United States during their sojourn in the Bahamas. A further FBI report, this time to the FBI chief, J. Edgar Hoover, stated:

> An agent has established conclusively that the Duchess of Windsor has recently been in touch with Joachim von Ribbentrop and was maintaining constant contact and communication with him. Because of their high official position the Duchess was obtaining a variety of information concerning the British and French official activities that she was passing on to the Germans.[48]

Churchill was predictably furious at the *Liberty* article. It threatened to scupper the Prime Minister's plan to bring the United States into the war with all the military power at its disposal. He sent a strongly worded cable to Edward in which he said the former king's words would be interpreted as defeatist and pro-Nazi, and by implication approving the isolationist aim to keep America out of the war.

In Berlin, Hitler's propaganda chief Goebbels noted in his diary: 'The Duke of Windsor has given an interview to a magazine in the USA in which he pretty frankly disclaims all chance of a British victory. We decide not to use it for the present, so as to avoid suffocating this tender seedling of reason.' The following day he noted that the duke's interview had been published in the Italian press, and he added significantly: 'We shall not use it so as to avoid discrediting him.'[49]

In May 1941 Hoover sent a message to President Roosevelt in which he said information had arrived at his office suggesting that the Duke of Windsor had entered into an agreement to the effect that if Germany was victorious, Hermann Goering would seek to overthrow Hitler and install the duke as king. Hoover claimed that this information had come from Allen McIntosh, a personal friend of the duke's.[50]

12

INTRIGUE IN AMERICA AND LONDON

During the 1930s Princess Stephanie undertook several trips to America. As she had done in Europe and in England, she set about making contacts with high-level, wealthy individuals; cultivating friendships wherever she detected the possibility of influence, whatever the sphere, be it industry, the arts or politics. Her contacts included Cathleen Vanderbilt and her stockbroker husband Harry Cushing Jnr; the composer Cole Porter; the art collector John Hay Whitney; and the industrialist Walter P. Chrysler. She was assiduously building a network of powerful acquaintances.

Some of these contacts, particularly those involved in industry and finance, appear in lists of members of the so-called Fraternity, the name Charles Higham, in his book *Trading with the Enemy*, gives to a loosely linked group of Americans whose companies, he alleged, continued commercial and financial relations with Germany even after America entered the war. While aiding the US war effort, they also aided Nazi Germany. It is claimed in 1942, for instance, Standard Oil was shipping fuel to Germany via neutral Switzerland. The Chase Bank in Nazi-occupied Paris was doing millions of dollars' worth of business with Germany – although the bank's head office in Manhattan must have been fully aware this was happening. Ford trucks were being built for German occupation forces in France, as Ford headquarters in Michigan must have known. ITT, the American communications conglomerate, was helping Germany with communications systems and working on remote control devices for V1 and V2 weapons through subsidiaries in neutral countries. They were also assisting Germany to build Focke-Wulf aircraft. Ball bearings, crucial to German war production, were being shipped to Nazi-associated customers in Latin America. At the time of Pearl Harbor, the size of the United States industrial investment in Germany totalled nearly $500 million. Many prominent American companies allowed their German subsidiaries to remain in holding companies in Nazi Germany, operating profitably, but with the profits accumulating there until the end of the war.[1]

In 1937 Stephanie persuaded Wiedemann to join her on a trip across the Atlantic. Hitler gave permission for his adjutant to accompany her and a cable from the American ambassador to Berlin, William Dodd, made it clear to the State Department that, as far as he was concerned, Wiedemann's intention was to discuss political matters with his colleagues at the German Embassy in Washington. The costs of the trip, including the tickets for the princess and her personal maid, were paid for out of the special fund Hitler had put at Wiedemann's disposal to underwrite Stephanie's expenses. The princess' maid, Wally Oeler, had been recruited for her by Wiedemann. She had been in service working for a prominent German family in Berlin. Wiedemann had no difficulty in arranging a permit for her to leave Germany. She was a bright and intelligent young woman. Some suspected she was a Gestapo informer.[2] The American authorities were suspicious that the real reason for Wiedemann's mission was to sound out known Nazi supporters and to encourage growth of the German-American League in the United States. The League consisted of American citizens, many with German family backgrounds, who were largely sympathetic to the Nazi regime. It was in Hitler's interests to expand its membership and its propaganda in support of National Socialism. Moreover, actively expanding pro-Nazi support was very much along the lines of what the princess had successfully achieved in England. Wiedemann was well acquainted with The Fraternity and its members' activities both in the United States and in Europe. It was alleged part of the reason for the trip was to assess the strength of Nazi support in the States and look at ways of expanding pro-German organisations like The Fraternity and the German-American League.

On arrival in New York in November 1937, the princess and her lover were received by the German Consul General, but there was also a hostile crowd at the dockside, some carrying banners reading, 'Out with Wiedemann, the Nazi spy'. The following day the couple travelled by train to Washington, where they stayed at the German Embassy. The ambassador, Dr Heinz Dieckhoff, was adamant that Wiedemann should convey direct to Hitler just how strong a potential military force America represented, and what a potential threat the country posed should the United States ever be drawn into another European war. Among those whom Hitler's adjutant met was Hugh R. Wilson, shortly to take up his post in Berlin as America's last pre-war ambassador to the Third Reich. After Washington, Wiedemann and the princess travelled to Chicago where they made contact with branches of the German-American League, which in the Illinois area was known to be particularly strong and highly pro-Nazi. Finally, Wiedemann travelled across to San Francisco where he had meetings with pro-German contacts and branches of the League based on the west coast.

The princess always had her relationship with Hitler on her mind. In the States she bought a number of expensive books on architecture to send to the Führer as a Christmas present. As his closeness to the architect Albert Speer and his grand plans for buildings in the new Germany indicate, Hitler was fascinated by bold, brutal architecture. Shortly after Christmas, the princess received a personal note of thanks signed 'Adolf', conveying Hitler's 'devoted greetings'. The Führer added he had been told how 'staunchly and warmly' the princess had spoken up on behalf of the new Germany and the country's vital needs in the United States. 'I am well aware this has caused you a number of unpleasant experiences, and would therefore like to express to you, highly esteemed princess, my sincere thanks for the great understanding that you have shown for Germany as a whole and for my work in particular.'[3]

In February and March 1938 the princess was again visiting the United States, once more at the expense of the Nazi regime. During her absence across the Atlantic, her Austrian homeland was appropriated and absorbed into the German Reich, when on 12 March Hitler ordered units of the Wehrmacht to invade in the coup that became known as the Anschluss. By then Hitler had assumed for himself the powers of Minister of War and Supreme Warlord, dismissing many of the aristocratic and military 'old guard' and replacing them with his own appointees. Rothermere's congratulatory letters and telegrams continued to arrive, supporting Hitler's policies, excusing even the worst excesses of Nazi rule. Commenting in a memorandum she wrote later on the dismissal of Hitler's Minister for War, General von Blomberg – along with others of the conservative and moderate element in the Nazi Party – Stephanie noted that Wiedemann had warned her 'the warmongers are now in control and war is now inevitable'. Wiedemann had added: 'If your old fool of an English Lord still supports Hitler after this he is committing high treason.'[4] But the 'old fool', Rothermere, maintained his friendly correspondence with Berlin.

Ward Price, Rothermere's central Europe correspondent, who always accompanied Rothermere and the princess when they visited Hitler, had the reputation of being Fleet Street's most enthusiastic supporter of the Nazis. He was on close terms with all of the leading Nazi hierarchy. He even began affecting the use of a monocle, aping some of the senior Nazis grouped around the Führer. When German troops entered Vienna, Ward Price was there, standing close to Hitler as the Führer addressed the crowds. In Prague he argued that Czechoslovakia should succumb to Germany's demands. He was a welcome guest at Goering's vast mansion, Carinhall, where in 1937 he spent a day with Goering on his estate. Price was even invited to play with the field marshal's huge miniature model railway laid out in the attics at Carinhall. The field marshal, as excited and enthusiastic as a child, knelt to direct the electric-powered model trains deftly around the extensive tracks. In the ceiling above the layout, a system of wires allowed model aeroplanes to fly across the room dropping miniature bombs on the railway below. For Goering it conjured up his own exploits as a pilot in the First World War. Afterwards, on Goering's behalf, Price conveyed a chilling message to the British government. Enquiring why Britain had driven Germany into the ranks of her enemies, Goering had said: 'The sands of possible reconciliation are fast running out.'[5]

The Times' Vienna correspondent, describing the Anschluss in a private message to his editor, took a very different line to Rothermere and the *Daily Mail*. He cabled: 'In my wildest nightmares I had not foreseen anything so perfectly organised, so brutal, so ruthless, so strong. When this machine goes into action it will blight everything it encounters like a swarm of locusts.' He warned that the Nazis' ultimate object was 'precisely the destruction of England ... Their real hatred is for England.'[6] The same newspaper's representative in Prague conveyed a similar warning. He wrote that he was convinced Nazi Germany had a long-term programme which it was determined to carry out. He had little doubt that Hitler intended both the break-up of Czechoslovakia and to challenge the British Empire. 'The Nazis have to be confronted,' he said.[7] But at home, leading politicians remained wedded to a policy of appeasement.

Having returned to England, in the summer of 1938 Princess Stephanie received a highly sensitive private assignment from the Reich Chancellor, asking her to find out if one of his 'intimate' friends could safely visit England to undertake unofficial conversations at senior government level. Hitler was contemplating authorising Goering to travel to England to negotiate on his behalf, but he wanted an assurance that Goering would not be humiliated by being subjected to open insult and demonstrations if he crossed the Channel and stepped onto British soil. Stephanie was summoned to Carinhall, Goering's mansion. It was the first time she had met the flamboyant reichsmarschall. Stephanie recalled the meeting in a memorandum written some years later. Goering, she wrote, was 'the leader of the peace party' among the

Nazi hierarchy. 'But he qualified his policy with opportunism and was certainly not espoused to peace at any price.' This position was far removed from Ribbentrop's, by then German Foreign Minister, who was 'the open leader of an absolute unconditional war movement'. His stance was: 'War against England at any time, at any price, in any circumstances.'[8] Goering, Stephanie wrote, was the economic dictator of Germany – the logical and actual heir presumptive of Adolf Hitler. 'There is no other man of whom the Führer speaks with so much respect, admiration and gratitude.'[9] In complete contrast, Goering's opinion of the new German Foreign Minister, Ribbentrop, was that he was incompetent, stupid and stood in the way of any deal with Britain. Hence the plan for a visit by Goering as negotiator; a visit that needed to be kept secret from Ribbentrop.

Although the princess knew Lord Halifax, the British Foreign Secretary, she recognised how arrangements for such a sensitive visit would need to be handled diplomatically, and so she turned for help to her friend Lady Ethel Snowden, widow of Chancellor of the Exchequer Philip Snowden in the Labour governments of 1924 and 1929. Ethel Snowden was no stranger to Nazi Germany. She had attended the last three Nuremberg Nazi Party rallies in company with the princess. She had also written many articles for the *Daily Mail*, most of them enthusiastically supporting the National Socialists. Moreover, Goebbels admired her; he had written about her in his diary in September 1937, calling her a 'lady with guts'. His diary entry observed that in London her spirit and courage was misunderstood.

Ethel Snowden agreed to help, and used her political contacts to get privileged access. She called on Halifax at his private house in London's Eaton Square early one morning, and personally passed on the message proposing a possible meeting with a highly placed Nazi leader. Halifax told a colleague that Lady Snowden had been approached 'through a personage who was in a very intimate relationship with Hitler and whom I understand to be Princess Hohenlohe'. In his diary for 6 July 1938, Halifax also noted:

> Lady Snowden came to see me early in the morning. She informed me that, through someone on the closest terms with Hitler – I took this to mean Princess Hohenlohe – she had received a message with the following burden: Hitler wanted to find out whether H.M. Government would welcome it if he were to send one of his closest confidants, as I understand it, to England for the purpose of conducting unofficial talks. Lady Snowden gave me to understand that this referred to Field-Marshal Goering, and they wished to find out whether he could come to England without being too

severely and publicly insulted, and what attitude H.M. Government would take generally to such a visit.[10]

A few days before Ethel Snowden's call at the Foreign Secretary's home, Princess Stephanie had received a cable from Fritz Wiedemann summoning her to Berlin. On arrival there she had been immediately driven to Hermann Goering's mansion. Goering told her he was keen to visit Britain. He said Hitler was not bluffing when he threatened war. The one chance he could see of avoiding conflict was if he could speak with the British Foreign Secretary in London. He asked Stephanie to make all the urgent arrangements necessary for the high-level meeting. He genuinely believed war could still be avoided, but only if he could get some time alone, face to face, with Lord Halifax. Wiedemann, he said, would travel in secret to London to prepare the ground, and that Ribbentrop must know nothing about the proposed meeting. The German Foreign Minister was no friend of either Wiedemann or the princess, as Hitler well knew, and Goering was an arch-rival of Ribbentrop's in foreign affairs within the Nazi hierarchy.

Halifax was concerned and somewhat suspicious of the unorthodox nature of the approach, and he privately noted that Wiedemann and Princess Stephanie were not the go-betweens he would have chosen to deal with. He described the princess as a 'well known adventuress, not to say blackmailer'.[11] Halifax had good reason to be suspicious. The previous year Sir Walford Selby, the British ambassador in Vienna, Stephanie's birthplace, had warned the Foreign Office that she was an 'international adventuress' who was 'known to be Hitler's agent'.[12] However, having weighed up the prospect, and sought permission from Prime Minister Chamberlain, Halifax agreed to meet Wiedemann – but only on the strict understanding that the sole purpose of the meeting was to discuss the visit of a high-ranking Nazi figure for wide-ranging talks on Anglo-German relations. Halifax intimated that he understood the emissary he would be meeting would be Field Marshal Goering. But if Goering did come, Halifax said, there was no way his presence in England would remain secret. The flamboyant Goering was an unlikely figure to be 'smuggled' into London without the press finding out. In any case, that was not the way Goering would have been prepared to act. He would have wanted the status and the red-carpet treatment that he would have considered were his due.

The meeting between Halifax and Wiedemann took place on 18 July at Halifax's private residence in Belgravia. Wiedemann confirmed he had come with Hitler's knowledge to explore the possibility of a very senior Nazi leader entering into a full discussion on Anglo–German relations. Halifax gave a cautious welcome in principle, but he said the timing of such a visit would need to be carefully chosen as it would inevitably attract wide public attention and comment. He added that there was a danger that a face-to-face discussion might do more harm than good. Wiedemann assured Halifax that Hitler had always regarded England with admiration and friendship, but he also felt that on a number of occasions Hitler's friendship had been rebuffed and this had caused serious resentment in Germany.[13] Halifax told Hitler's adjutant that the present time might not be altogether favourable, unless there was a peaceful resolution of the position of Czechoslovakia. Was Wiedemann in a position to give him any assurances on that, he asked? Wiedemann initially said he had not been charged with a political mission, and therefore was not in a position to discuss Czechoslovakia or to negotiate. When he saw Halifax was put off by this response, Wiedemann changed tack and gave a solemn undertaking that the German government was not planning any kind of action involving force, unless they were given no option to act through some unforeseen incident. The brief meeting ended on good terms, with Wiedemann recalling his time in the trenches during the Great War as Hitler's senior officer.

Halifax noted in a memorandum:

> The Prime Minister and I have thought about the meeting I had with Capt Wiedemann. Of especial importance to us are the steps which the Germans and the British might possibly take, not only to create the best possible relationship between the two countries, but also to calm down the international situation in order to achieve an improvement of general economic and political problems … Our hopes have recently been shattered by the conduct of the German press, which it seems to us, has not hesitated to incite public opinion in a dangerous manner over every incident that occurs in Czechoslovakia or on the frontiers.[14]

Although the Foreign Office was cautiously optimistic about the visit, the low-profile episode quickly rebounded on the British Foreign Secretary. Wiedemann had been spotted by journalists arriving at Croydon airport. The next day the *Daily Herald* came out with a banner headline revealing the secret meeting. Once the news was out, there were diplomatic responses across Europe. The French government said the idea of Wiedemann being received by Lord Halifax had been 'cooked up' by Princess Hohenlohe, who was extremely well known to the secret services of all the 'Great Powers'. While 'pretending to serve the interests of Britain', she was actually 'chiefly committed to the interests of Germany'.[15] The Czech ambassador in London wrote to his government in Prague:

> If there is any decency left in this world, then there will be a big scandal when it is revealed what part was played in Wiedemann's visit by Steffi Hohenlohe, née Richter. This world-renowned secret agent, spy and confidence trickster, who is wholly Jewish, today provides the focus of Hitler's propaganda in London.[16]

Sir Walford Selby, British ambassador to Austria, warned the government that the princess' suite at the Dorchester Hotel in London had become a base for Nazi sympathisers and an 'outpost of German espionage', and that she had been behind much of the German propaganda circulating in London since she had first moved to England.[17] A rather different view came from Herbert von Dirksen, Germany's ambassador in London in 1938. In his autobiography he recalled what he described as the most important political event of the summer of 1938:

> It was an attempt at rapprochement, undertaken from the German side which sheds the brightest of lights on the methods of Hitlerian diplomacy – its multi-tracked approach, its by-passing of official channels, its dishonesty and lack of consistency, as well as the complete inability to attune itself to the mentality of the other side.

He wrote that the motivation for the London mission had come from two sources: Goering's desire for prestige and his wish to maintain peace through an understanding with Britain; and an initiative by a clever woman.[18]

Ribbentrop, who had been purposely kept out of the loop, reacted with fury when news of the meeting reached Berlin. He protested vehemently about this interference in foreign affairs that had been arranged entirely without his knowledge, and it appears he succeeded in changing Hitler's mind about pursuing a high-level Anglo-German meeting. When Wiedemann returned to Berchtesgaden to report back to Hitler, he was kept waiting at the Berghof for several hours while Hitler entertained Unity Mitford. Later, Wiedemann was given just five minutes in Hitler's presence, during which Hitler angrily ruled out a visit by Goering to London and refused to discuss the subject further. Wiedemann was ordered to compile a lengthy report for Ribbentrop. In it he made the extraordinary claim that Halifax had asked him to convey to Hitler that before he (Halifax) died, he would like to see, as the culmination of his work, the Führer entering London at the side of the English king, amid the acclamation of the English people.[19] It is hard to believe Halifax could have made such a comment to Wiedemann, but Halifax's biographer records that in 1957, when the *Manchester Guardian* enquired about the incident, Halifax, then aged 75, 'decided to absent himself from his Yorkshire home for the day and consistently refused to take calls from the press about it'.[20]

Wiedemann's mission caused a flurry of speculation in the press. The *Daily Express* came out with a full-page article examining Wiedemann's background, particularly the curious situation Wiedemann and Hitler had found themselves in among the muddy trenches of Flanders. 'The orderly of Lieutenant Fritz Wiedemann was Lance-Corporal Adolf Hitler,' the writer C.A. Lyon recalled. 'Adolf Hitler saluted Lieutenant Wiedemann, clicked his heels, ran across the desert of shell-holes with the message and came back, reported, saluted and clicked his heels again. There was no friendship, that would have been impossible, but there in the trenches Hitler must have conceived an unforgettable respect for his officer.'[21] Now the boot was on the other foot. 'Hitler's thoughts' after he achieved supreme power, the article continued, 'always turned to the man whose errands he had run and whom he admired ... It was now the captain who ran the messages and clicked his heels to the lance-corporal.' Wiedemann was recruited by Hitler as his closest adjutant and promoted to be his 'listening-post, his contact man, negotiator, a checker-up, a man with a job without a name and without a parallel'. Wiedemann was trusted and Hitler continually found him new jobs to do.

A few months after his abortive trip to London, Fritz Wiedemann was sent to San Francisco to take up the appointment of Consul General. Was this punishment for the failure of his and Princess Stephanie's mission to establish high-level talks in order to achieve an alliance between Britain and Germany? It certainly seemed like it – but perhaps there were other, more covert reasons.

13

CHATELAINE OF SCHLOSS LEOPOLDSKRON

The award of the Nazi Party Gold Medal was not the only reward Princess Stephanie received 'for services she rendered to the Führer'. After the Anschluss Hitler directly commanded the Nazi government to put at her disposal one of Austria's most magnificent mansions: Schloss Leopoldskron, a historic national monument in the southern district of Salzburg, dating from 1736. It is a vast rococo palace famous for its elaborate stucco work, which is regarded at its finest in the castle's chapel and its vast ceremonial hall. The building had been confiscated by the Gestapo from its owner, the world-famous theatre director Max Reinhardt, on the grounds that he was 'a person hostile to the people and the state'. He was in fact a Jew.

Reinhardt was among Germany's greatest actors and theatre directors. He was a co-founder in 1920 of the Salzburg Festival and he used the castle as a glittering location for some of his most lavish stage productions. He used the whole building as his stage, with the audience moving from room to room as the production proceeded. Reinhardt had bought the mansion in 1918 and Leopoldskron was central to the lively social side of the famous festival with numerous patrons from all over Europe. It became a prominent gathering place for writers, artists, composers and designers. Reinhardt spent twenty years renovating the building and its famous Great and Marble Halls, and creating a library, a Venetian Room and also an outdoor theatre in the extensive gardens. In 1933 the Nazis offered Reinhardt 'honorary Aryanship', probably because Hitler admired great theatre. But Reinhardt vehemently rejected the offer. In October 1937, having criticised Hitler and been the victim of a bomb attack at Leopoldskron, he left his homeland and travelled to America as an immigrant. The grounds of the schloss, which have magnificent views to the Alps, were in the limelight again in 1965 when they featured in the film *The Sound of Music*.

Following its confiscation by the Nazis, the castle and its estate were offered personally by Hitler to the princess for use as a home and a 'political salon'. She was given the task of transforming it into a guest house for prominent artists of the Reich, and as grand reception accommodation convenient to Hitler's home at the Berghof, some 10 miles away. The intermediary, who made all the actual arrangements on behalf of the Nazi leadership, was the princess' lover. The actress Helene Thimig, who later married Max Reinhardt in the United States, when she heard of the gift to Stephanie, wrote in fury: 'What a macabre joke: Reinhardt's creation – now a palace for the Nazis! And this Aryanised palace has been placed under the management of the Jewish Princess von Hohenlohe.'[1]

Despite the care and money Reinhardt had lavished on it, Princess Stephanie, as the new chatelaine and using Nazi funds, had extensive works carried out to match her own needs and to make it more suitable for the use the Nazis now required. She planned to hold large receptions there which would enable her to continue her work of lobbying and manipulating influential people from across Europe in support of Nazi policies even more effectively. To do this, extravagant catering facilities were installed. Also, to allow her to pursue her passion for tennis, she had a court built, and the castle's extensive gardens remodelled. The considerable costs of all this were paid by the central government in Berlin. Wiedemann, who was agent for payment of the bills, commented that the Führer had said the renovations would increase the value of the schloss, and contribute to the tasks he wanted Stephanie to fulfil. As the mansion was now state owned, Hitler felt it was money well spent. In 1939, when Wiedemann had left Germany for his posting to San Francisco, the Reich Party Leader, Martin Bormann, took over as intermediary, paying all the bills at the princess' request.

Princess Stephanie was by now not the most popular person in Austria, the country of her birth. After the Anschluss her fellow countrymen judged her critically, knowing her background and her close friendship with Hitler. She was not well liked in Salzburg, particularly after being installed as the chatelaine at Schloss Leopoldskron. To help her gain the support of the local authorities, and to demonstrate that she had powerful friends in Berlin and was carrying out Hitler's direct orders, Wiedemann gave her an official note, signed 'Adjutant to the Führer'. Dated 10 June 1938, it read:

Princess Stephanie von Hohenlohe is personally known to the Führer. She has at all times stood up for the new Germany abroad in a manner worthy of recognition. I therefore ask all German authorities concerned with domestic and foreign affairs to take every opportunity to show her the special appreciation that we owe to foreigners who speak up so emphatically for today's Germany.[2]

Whenever she was at Leopoldskron, Stephanie invited a number of French, British and American guests with a view to winning them over to Hitler's regime, particularly by impressing them with the cultural and artistic events Salzburg offered. Goebbels was at pains to ensure that the famous Salzburg Festival should become a cultural pilgrimage dedicated to Hitler's Reich, and the schloss was an important symbol of this. It fulfilled the role of luxury guest house for important visitors whose support and influence the Nazi state wished to win. It was conveniently close to Hitler's and Goering's Bavarian mountain homes on the Obersalzberg, just over the border in Germany. During the long, hot summer of 1938 numerous guests were entertained at the mansion: princes, European aristocracy, statesmen, bankers, and many from the worlds of music and the theatre. The princess was in her element as hostess and the Führer's ambassador.

Among those she entertained were the famous American conductor Leopold Stokowski, the theatre critic Philip Carr and the wife of a prominent New York art dealer, Mrs Carroll Carstairs. Others who enjoyed her hospitality included Charles Bedaux, who, it will be recalled, had been instrumental with Stephanie in organising the visit to Germany of the Duke and Duchess of Windsor. Stephanie revelled in having charge of the schloss, with its extravagant furnishings and spacious grounds. It suited the style she loved to portray and it certainly impressed all those who visited her there, but she was disappointed Hitler himself never came to visit her at the mansion the Nazis had stolen from its legitimate owners. Germany's ambassador to Britain, Herbert von Dirksen (after Ribbentrop he became Hitler's Foreign Minister), did however visit the princess there on several occasions. He was a well-travelled man, skilled in diplomacy and an expert in foreign affairs, having also been the German emissary in Tokyo and Moscow.

While she was at Schloss Leopoldskron, Stephanie was primed by the Reich Chancellery to influence the British politician Lord Runciman. In 1938 he had been appointed by the British government as its official mediator in the dispute between the Czech and German governments over the Sudetenland. The western border regions of Czechoslovakia were largely

populated by ethnic Germans. Under the pro-Nazi Sudeten leader, Konrad
Henlein of the Sudeten German Party, serious civil unrest had been provoked
in the Sudetenland. Hitler saw this as the perfect pretext to invade the territory and later to annexe the whole of Czechoslovakia. The dispute was
dangerous; it was escalating fast and threatened to be the flash point leading
to war. Runciman was sent by the British government to sound out the situation. It was suggested by Nazi authorities in Berlin that Princess Stephanie
should invite Runciman to the schloss. After hours of tiring negotiations in
Prague, trying to solve the Sudetenland problem amicably, Runciman and his
wife were keen to escape at the weekends and visit some of the castles of the
Austrian nobility. Runciman had a penchant towards the aristocracy.

Stephanie was not able to attract Runciman to Schloss Leopoldskron, so
instead she used her connections to meet him at another Austrian schloss.
Here she used the meeting to steer him towards a resolution that favoured
the Nazi cause. The princess subtly spun him the pro-Nazi line, as she was
so competent in doing, and the British government's representative seems to
have largely accepted her arguments. In America, *Time Magazine* described
the affair:

> Titian haired, 40 year old Stephanie Juliana Richter Princess Hohenlohe-
> Waldenburg-Schillingsfürst, confidante of the Führer and friend of half of
> Europe's great is scheduled to sail from England to the US this week. Since
> the fall of Austria, Princess Stephanie, once the toast of Vienna, has lent her
> charms to advancing the Nazi cause in circles where it would do the most
> good. As a reward the Nazi government 'permitted her to take a lease' on
> the sumptuous Schloss Leopoldskron near Salzburg, taken over from Jewish
> Max Reinhardt after Anschluss. During the Czecho-Slovak crisis she did
> yeoman service for the Nazi campaign. When Mr. Chamberlain sent Lord
> Runciman to gather impressions of conditions in Czechoslovakia Princess
> Stephanie hurried to the Sudetenland castle of Prince Max Hohenlohe
> where the British mediator was entertained.[3]

When he went back to London, Runciman reported to the British government that the Sudetenland wanted to be taken over by Germany and ethnic
Germans there were desperate to be returned to their homeland. Stephanie
had done a good job, but her efforts did not stop there. She was also involved
in preparing the ground for the Munich Conference in September 1938, a
summit between Britain, France, Italy and Germany which decreed – without Czechoslovakia even being present – that the Czech government must

hand over the Sudetenland to Germany in return for vague promises of an international guarantee of integrity for the rest of Czechoslovakia. Hitler gave his assurance at Munich that the Sudetenland was his last territorial claim, but secretly he had resolved to 'smash the rump of the Czech State'. It was this that eventually led, inexorably, to Hitler's designs on Poland that proved to be the direct cause of the Second World War. The piece of paper Chamberlain brought back from Munich proved useless in the face of Nazi ambition. Fourteen months later, in the High Court in London, a judge was to hear that 'it was the princess' groundwork that made the Munich Agreement possible'.[4] The day after Chamberlain returned in triumph to London with the paper bearing his and Hitler's signatures, and declared 'Peace with honour – peace for our time', Rothermere sent a telegram addressed to Reichskanzler Adolf Hitler in Berlin. 'Frederick the Great was a great popular figure in England, may not "Adolf the Great" become an equally popular figure? I salute your Excellency's star which rises higher and higher.'[5]

From the Hotel Adlon in Berlin, at the end of the dramatic diplomatic exchanges that surrounded the Munich Agreement, the princess wrote to Hitler:

> There are moments in life that are so great – I mean, where one feels so deeply that it is almost impossible to find the right words to express one's feelings – Herr Reich Chancellor, please believe me that I have shared with you the experience and emotion of every phase of the events of the last weeks. What none of your subjects in their wildest dreams dared hope for – you have made come true. That must be the finest thing a head of state can give to himself and to his people. I congratulate you with all my heart.

She signed it, 'in devoted friendship'.[6]

In 1938 Hitler began to reveal the true horrors of Nazism and National Socialism. When the year began, apart from the reoccupation of the Rhineland and Saar – portions of Germany temporarily wrested from the Fatherland after the First World War – Hitler had not yet grasped any vital chunks of European territory likely to pitch the Continent to the edge of war. By the time the calendar was counting down to the end of the year, the picture was totally transformed. Hitler, by bullying, bravado and guile, had occupied both his and his princess' Austrian homeland, together with the Sudetenland – the ethnically German border region of Czechoslovakia – reducing the rest of the Czech territory to a virtually powerless morsel ripe for the swallowing. In Germany, the mass pogroms of Kristallnacht had signalled the way for the

Holocaust; and Germany's armed forces were ready for what now seemed imminent and all-out war. He had outwitted and demoralised his enemies; Europe lay at his feet. Much of his success had been to impose his will on ministers throughout the chancelleries and embassies where the Continent's fate was decided. That was an environment in which Princess Stephanie moved with ease, where her title gave her access to people with influence and where she was adept at promulgating Hitler's cause.

All this did not escape the notice of British intelligence. Her file notes: 'Schloss Leopoldskron is only an hour's drive from Hitler's home and she is frequently summoned by the Führer who appreciates her intelligence and good advice. She is perhaps the only woman who can exercise any influence on him.'[7] The secret service, through the Home Office, issued a further warrant authorising the opening of all letters and telegrams addressed to the princess, both at her London address and those originating in England addressed to her at the schloss. The reason given to justify this action was stated: 'Her connections with highly placed members of the Nazi Party and the fact that previous warrants had yielded results of considerable interest.' It was urgently desired in the public interest, MI5 recorded, to find out more about how far the princess' activities reached.

14

COMIC OPERA
IN THE HIGH COURT

The highlife Stephanie was enjoying at Schloss Leopoldskron was destined to come to an abrupt end as questions started to be asked in Berlin about her and her lover, Fritz Wiedemann. Their enemies amongst the Nazi hierarchy, particularly Ribbentrop, seemed intent on stirring up trouble for them, and now it looked as if Hitler himself was beginning to take the allegations about Stephanie's Jewish origins seriously.

Aware she faced questioning and probably considerable danger, the princess and her mother, who had been staying with her for the last few weeks, left the mansion in a hurry at the end of January 1939. Hitler had fallen out with his long-time adjutant and friend, probably over the plan hatched up between Wiedemann and Goering for talks in London with the British Foreign Secretary. Dismissing him from his inner circle on 19 January 1939, Hitler had appointed him to the post of German Consul General in San Francisco. Hitler told his former close colleague: 'I have no use for men in high positions, and in my immediate circle, who are not in agreement with my policies.'[1] In his diary in the autumn of 1938, Goebbels noted that the Führer had intimated he would have to get rid of Wiedemann: 'During the Munich crisis he apparently did not perform well and lost his nerve completely ... When things get serious he has no use for men like that.'[2]

Another factor weighing with the Nazi leader was Wiedemann's close relationship with the princess. Hitler told his adjutant he must break off the association immediately, since Princess Stephanie was 'under suspicion'. Goebbels, closely observing what was happening in the Führer's immediate circle, again noted in his diary:

Princess Hohenlohe now turns out to be a Viennese half-Jewess. She has her fingers in everything. Wiedemann works with her a great deal. He may well have her to thank for his present predicament, because without her around he probably would not have made such a feeble showing in the Czech crisis.[3]

The SS was gathering information about the princess and her racial origins were being closely re-examined at the highest level. A member of Adolf Eichmann's Department for Jewish Affairs gave his verdict to Himmler, having thoroughly researched her background in Vienna, that the princess was certainly 'half Jewess'. The Nazi military intelligence service, the Abwehr, were also taking an interest in Wiedemann and his mistress, and Ribbentrop, who had been no friend of either of them, was happy to use the situation to his advantage. In his memoirs, Wiedemann stated that when he took his leave from the Führer, on his appointment as Consul General, Hitler had warned him against Princess Stephanie, saying he had come to the conclusion that she could not be relied upon and alleging that various anti-German articles published in the foreign press could be traced back to her.[4] Wiedemann said he told Hitler that he could vouch absolutely for the princess' integrity and loyalty to the Third Reich, and that he could prove that the princess had had a decisive influence on the attitude of Lord Rothermere and the *Daily Mail*, and the impact this had had, in turn, on furthering Nazi propaganda in Britain and in London society.

Another woman who had made a deep impression on Hitler, the actress and film producer Leni Riefenstahl, is said to have commented that Wiedemann's 'relationship with Hitler became more distant because of his half-Jewish girlfriend'.[5] At the end of January 1939, *Time Magazine* in the United States was highlighting Wiedemann's new role on behalf of the Nazi leadership:

Adolf Hitler's Man Friday, big, burly, 47 year old Captain Fritz Wiedemann, who has carried out many a delicate mission in Europe as the Führer's personal adjutant, was last week assigned to another. He will serve as Consul General at San Francisco, replacing the unpopular Baron Manfred von Killinger, recalled to the Reich to report on the bombing of a Nazi freighter in Oakland Estuary, two months ago. Capt. Wiedemann's mission: to smooth ruffled US-German relations and sell the Nazi regime to an unsympathetic US.[6]

The *Time Magazine* report went on to record that the princess was supposedly the daughter of Jewish parents and that many of the Führer's British friends, particularly Unity Mitford, had protested that a Jewess, however valuable, was no friend for Hitler to be associated with. The Führer had assured Unity some months ago, *Time Magazine* told its readers, that he would investigate the princess' parentage. What Hitler had found had not been revealed, but his portrait, inscribed 'To my dear Princess', still adorned the desk of the princess' London flat.[7]

Given the suspicions that were now surrounding her, stirred up by her enemies in the Nazi Party, the princess' flight from Leopoldskron to London in January 1939 is understandable. She had strong reason to fear the consequences if she remained in reach of those Nazis opposed to her. Although this did not entirely blunt the princess' loyalty to the Führer, it did finally poison her relations with Ribbentrop. 'He began to sense angrily illegitimate outside influences,' she wrote. 'He must have traced back – rightly or wrongly – some such occasional scepticism of his leader to me and thus I became an arch-fiend in his eyes.'[8] After her reluctant abandonment of the schloss it became the residence of the local Nazi gauleiter until the American Army reached Salzburg at the end of the war, at which point it was returned to the Reinhardt family from whom the Nazis had stolen it. Before leaving Salzburg, virtually overnight, Stephanie tried but failed to get permission for her aunt Olga, her mother's younger sister, to accompany her and her mother. Olga was instead arrested soon after. She died in the Theresienstadt concentration camp in September 1942.

The British intelligence service quickly picked up on the fact that the princess had fallen out of favour in Berlin and, as a result, Nazi funds paying the rent for the schloss had been stopped. MI5 files contain a memorandum to Sir Robert Vansittart at the Foreign Office, which speculates that her relations with Wiedemann had led to disclosures of Nazi secrets through indiscretions committed by them both. British agents on the Continent were keeping a close eye on developments. 'We have independent evidence, of a very delicate nature, to the effect that the affair between Wiedemann and this lady is still going on,' her file notes. 'We also know from a very secret and delicate source that Wiedemann has advised her to recommend her creditors to apply to Major-General Bodenschatz, chef de Minister antes to Field Marshal Goering, for settlement of her debts.'[9] Bodenschatz was one of Goering's principal lieutenants who had been in London on various occasions, notably in November 1938.

Hitler's change of mind over Princess Stephanie cut off any money she was receiving for working on behalf of the Third Reich. She returned to London badly in need of a new source of finance. Rothermere had paid her a final cheque for the services she had undertaken as his so-called go-between a year earlier, in January 1938. At that point he had made it clear that he did not want her to carry out any further commissions for him. Writing to her on 19 January 1938 he had told her:

> My mission to create a better feeling between Britain and Germany has largely succeeded. Mine was a lone voice in the wilderness four years ago but now it is generally accepted by almost every political party in this country that good relations between Britain and Germany are essential for the peace of the world. You have helped much to achieve this better understanding. I do not wish to be considered an international busybody![10]

In a bid to revive the remunerative contract, Stephanie wrote to Rothermere from the Hotel de Paris in Monte Carlo on 2 February 1938, saying:

> It is important to know what is currently going on in Germany. The Germans are going through a serious crisis. Changes are taking place, which are of the greatest importance for the future of Europe. All the conservatives are being thrown out and only extremists are keeping their jobs or being recruited. You must be very careful in future. I do not see how it will be possible for you, under these new conditions, to continue to support Hitler in future and at the same time serve the interests of your own country.

She added, clearly with an eye to clear her name with the British authorities should she need to do so: 'Hold on to this letter, so that it will be evidence of how accurately I have kept you informed. I'm serious; don't throw this letter away.'[11] Nonetheless, Rothermere took little notice of Stephanie's advice and was not willing to renew her contract. He also persisted with his ongoing correspondence with Berlin and his letters to Hitler continued to eulogise the Führer despite the princess' warning. Until Wiedemann was dispatched to the United States in March 1938, the princess, through her lover, continued to be informed of the letters that were still passing between Rothermere and Hitler.

As late as the summer of 1939, Rothermere continued to write to the Führer and to others in the Nazi leadership, paying them glowing compliments and appealing to them not to provoke a war. 'Our two great Nordic countries should pursue resolutely a policy of appeasement for, whatever anyone may say, our two great countries should be the leaders of the world,' he told Ribbentrop in early July.[12] There were other eyes eager to read this correspondence. As Foreign Office papers now in The National Archives indicate, British intelligence was intercepting Rothermere's telegrams. Rothermere's letters to Hitler, Goering, Goebbels and Ribbentrop – some of them extremely compromising – were being monitored in Whitehall with rising concern. One note from a senior official that has survived, written in the summer of 1939, comments: 'The fact that Lord Rothermere is a Privy Councillor makes it in the opinion of [name blanked out] most significant.'[13] Significant for what? That a privy councillor was expressing views disloyal to his country, or because it made it difficult for the authorities to do anything to stop it? Perhaps the authorities valued the chance to read the views of the Nazi leaders in correspondence that was not on a government-to-government footing.

At the end of June 1939 Rothermere wrote direct to Hitler: 'My dear Führer. I have watched with understanding and interest the progress of your great and superhuman work in regenerating your country.' He assured Hitler that the British government had 'no policy which involves the encirclement of Germany, and that no British government could exist which embraced such a policy'. He added: 'The British people now like Germany strongly rearmed, regard the German people with admiration as valorous adversaries in the past, but I am sure that there is no problem between our two countries which cannot be settled by consultation and negotiation.'[14] If Hitler worked to restore 'the old friendship', Rothermere said, he would be regarded by the British as a popular hero, in the same way they regarded Frederick the Great of Prussia. Rothermere appealed to the Nazi leadership to convene a conference to sort out what he called 'the misunderstandings' – concerns about Germany's intentions, particularly with regard to Poland. Within weeks of Rothermere writing these words, Germany invaded Poland and triggered the start of the Second World War.

To ease her increasing financial problems, Stephanie decided, rashly, to sue the press baron for what she alleged was breach of contract. She protested that Rothermere had entered into an agreement to pay her an annual sum of £5,000 (the equivalent of £200,000 today) to act as his special foreign-political representative in Europe, and she understood that this contract was ongoing, if not for the rest of her life. In a move that smacked strongly of blackmail, she made it clear that should she lose the case she would not hesitate to publish her memoirs in the United States, which would put Rothermere in the worst possible light over his political connections with Hitler and other leading members of the Nazi Party. She intimated she had been offered a sum of £25,000 (around £1 million today) in America to publish her story in which Lord Rothermere's relationships with women much younger than himself, and in particular with her, would be alluded to. Princess Stephanie further alleged in her writ that Lord Rothermere had failed to implement promises to vindicate her reputation by exposing the falsity of libellous statements and comments inferring she was a spy and an agent of the Nazis, published in the foreign press in Europe in 1932.

To make these allegations so publicly displayed considerable nerve on the princess' part. She was embarking on a case which could cost her a substantial sum, particularly as she hired one of the most fashionable law firms in London, Theodore Goddard & Partners; the solicitors who, in 1936, had handled Wallis Simpson's notorious divorce case. Correspondence amongst her papers now in the Hoover Institution Archives makes it clear that even before the case began she was struggling to meet her lawyers' bills. The consequences of taking such a sensational case to the High Court, with the inevitability that her reputation and Lord Rothermere's would be exposed mercilessly in cross-examination, were obvious. In Berlin Goebbels followed these events with interest. He realised what the outcome might be and noted in his diary that all kinds of embarrassing details would come out if the case went to court – not only about Rothermere's letters to Hitler, but also about the princess and her sexual relationship with Hitler's adjutant.[15] It is clear the princess was banking on Rothermere being so alarmed at the public exposure of the flattering letters he had written to Hitler, that he would call the case off and pay up. As was later said in court by Rothermere's counsel, the princess was indulging in naked blackmail.

Meanwhile, Britain's secret intelligence services were stepping up their surveillance of the princess. Referring to her friendship with a number of society figures, the MI5 file particularly mentions Lady Asquith (wife of the former Liberal Prime Minister) and Lady Snowden (wife of a Labour chancellor of the exchequer). The princess' correspondence was being routinely intercepted and monitored, and the implications of her friendships in British society with rich and influential people were being carefully recorded. A further note in her MI5 file says:

> Princess Hohenlohe has given us a great deal of work owing to the fact that she is frequently the subject of denunciation to the effect that she is, or has been, a trusted political agent and personal friend of Herr Hitler; that she is a German political spy of a very high order; and that she was given the Schloss Leopoldskron by Herr Hitler for signal services rendered for him.[16]

In March 1939, as the certainty of war in Europe loomed closer, MI5 began taking an interest in the forthcoming court case between the princess and

Lord Rothermere, which had the potential to rapidly turn into a public scandal if the supportive letters that had passed between Rothermere and Nazi leaders were exposed in open court. A passport control officer at Victoria Station intercepted Stephanie's Hungarian lawyer, Erno Wittman, as he arrived in the British capital. He was carrying correspondence relating to the case, and it included a bundle of the deeply incriminating letters from Rothermere to Hitler, and from him to others in the Nazi leadership. These were copies of Rothermere's letters Berlin had passed to the princess to help her in her case – and stir up the maximum trouble within Establishment and political circles in Britain. The correspondence was of substantial interest to the British government and it confirmed just how extensive, and, in the eyes of some, downright disloyal, the contact had been between Rothermere and the highest levels of the Nazi leadership. The passport control officer wrote: 'This was astonishing; it appeared to be copies of documents and letters which passed between Lord Rothermere, Lady Snowden, Princess Stephanie, Herr Hitler and others.'[17]

This considerable bundle of letters was secretly circulated within the intelligence services and to senior civil servants in key government ministries. Among them was a highly indiscreet communication to Hitler from Rothermere congratulating the Nazi leader on his annexation of Czechoslovakia – Hitler having sent his troops into the Czech capital earlier in 1939 in breach of the 1938 Munich Agreement. Rothermere's note urged Hitler to follow up this 'triumph' by sending his troops into Romania.[18] Nothing could be more revealing of the press baron's continued support of the Nazi Führer as the inevitable conflict drew closer, but it appears MI5 shied away from actually taking action against the press baron. Certainly there is nothing in the derestricted files to indicate whether Rothermere was warned to cease his correspondence with Berlin, though some information in the files still remains undisclosed. The Foreign Office could easily have brought pressure personally on Rothermere to be more discreet via his powerful friends with close contacts in Whitehall. The MI5 file makes it clear that the secret service had warned the government that copies of this correspondence would be produced in open court, which would embarrass not only Rothermere but also a number of other notable members of the British aristocracy, and that these disclosures would shock the British public.

In September 1939, ten days after Britain had declared war on Germany, alarm bells were set ringing anew when the head porter at London's Dorchester Hotel called at a West End police station to give what he described as important information to the War Office. What he had to say was rapidly in the hands of MI5. Princess Stephanie's MI5 case officer recorded that the porter suggested it would be worthwhile for the police Special Branch to interview the princess' Austrian maid, Anna Stoffl. The porter had been speaking to Miss Stoffl, who had alleged her employer was operating in Britain as a very active and dangerous agent for the Nazis. The princess met many influential people in Britain, the maid had told him, and regularly reported back to Hitler's agents. She had direct access to the highest authorities in Germany. The police informed MI5 that the maid was very embittered against the princess, and if she was approached discreetly by a British intelligence officer she would be willing to give details of the princess' contacts in Britain.[19]

The maid was duly interviewed. Her mother and sisters were still in Austria and she was fearful they would suffer if it was known that she had spoken against the Nazi regime. Although she still held a German passport, she told the intelligence officer that she was anti-Nazi. The file records:

> Miss Stoffl is in no doubt Princess Hohenlohe was acting as a German agent. She had lived with her for about a year in this country and travelled with her on the Continent. For a time she had lived with the princess at a castle in Salzburg, placed at her disposal by the German authorities. During that time there had been a good deal of entertaining. The princess had paid a visit to Berlin when she was at the castle and had told the maid she had had an interview with Hitler.[20]

The maid added that the princess was always careful to keep as much from her as possible. When visitors were expected, the princess generally sent the maid out of her apartment. She was in no doubt that Princess Stephanie was engaged in deep intrigue, and that visitors were giving her information which she then passed straight on to Berlin. The MI5 officer recorded in the secret file:

> At the time of the German entry into Czechoslovakia the princess had expressed disapproval of the Nazi action. Wiedemann, Hitler's former confidant and friend of the princess, had taken a similar line. The maid understood Wiedemann's fall from grace and his transfer by Hitler to San Francisco were the result of his attitude on the Nazi coup.

Shortly after these revelations to the British authorities by the princess' personal maid, there is a note in Stephanie's MI5 file stating that a letter had been sent to the Home Office recommending that the princess' stay in the United

Kingdom should be curtailed in view of her close contact with leading Nazis. It is followed by a detailed biographical document on her background marked 'most secret'. It noted that she had first come to the attention of British intelligence as far back as 1928, three years after Annabel Kruse had introduced her to Rothermere. The intelligence services had taken an interest in her because of the considerable influence she was exerting on the press baron. MI5 revealed that a man named Andre Rostin, 'not of good repute and strongly suspected of being a German secret agent', had been involved in helping to engineer the princess' introduction to Rothermere. The file gives no indication of the exact role Rostin played.[21]

It is possible that on instructions from Berlin, Rostin had 'used' my great-aunt, an unsuspecting friend of Princess Stephanie, to ensure the crucial introduction took place. It is unlikely Annabel Kruse was in any way knowingly complicit in a German plot. The British intelligence service's records throw no light on the mystery. But the reference to Rostin as a German agent strongly suggests that Rothermere was targeted, and that the meeting over the gaming tables in Monte Carlo was not as innocent and unplanned as it appeared at the time.

MI5's biographical notes go on to record that the princess had been on the most intimate terms with Lady Snowden since 1928, and since 1933/34 she had become acquainted with Lady Oxford and Lady Cunard; through them she had infiltrated society circles in London. Among her friends, the file details, were Lady Austin Chamberlain, Lord and Lady Londonderry, Sir Barry Domville and Sir Horace Rumbold. Sir Horace had been British ambassador in Berlin at the time of Hitler's rise to power. 'On her visits here she has always lived in a most expensive way, staying usually at the Dorchester or taking a flat in Mayfair,' the file continues.

> She gives extravagant presents of dresses and jewellery to her friends. Princess Hohenlohe has acted as a link between Nazi leaders in Germany and society circles in this country. At Schloss Leopoldskron she has entertained prominent Nazis and introduced them to English friends. She had also played a part in arranging meetings between Lord Runciman and the Sudeten Nazis.[22]

The file then records that at the end of 1938, or the beginning of 1939, she had been in Syria with a Wilhelm von Fluegge, where both were suspected of working as German agents. She had also been reported as mixing with German and Italian contacts in Istanbul. MI5 goes on to record that: 'Hitler counts on the help of Princess Hohenlohe, his Vienna born friend and talent spotter. He appreciates her intelligence and advice.'

As the international situation began to move inevitably towards war, further intelligence began to be whispered into the ears of MI5 officers. And at this point the name of Kruse re-enters the story. The princess' MI5 file records that, in response to a telephone tip-off, an officer met with an unnamed source who had a great friend called 'Capt. J.F.C. Kruse' (Jack Kruse), living at Ridge House, Sunningdale; a former private secretary to Lord Rothermere:

> Kruse is very friendly with the princess and had known her for a number of years. On 26 June 1939 Kruse saw the princess who showed him a letter from a contact writing from the Hotel Bieux Dolen in the Hague, that stated the Führer had told Ribbentrop he must make it plain to the British prime minister that a gesture from Britain must definitely be made very soon, independent of the Cabinet if necessary, and that he must permit Germany to occupy Danzig.

Kruse told MI5 officers that since Wiedemann's transfer abroad, the princess' contact with the Nazi leadership was via Ribbentrop. Princess Stephanie, it was alleged, now intensely disliked Hitler – perhaps because of the way he had treated her lover – but although now anti-Hitler, she was emphatically not anti-German.[23]

With these revelations reaching the Home Office it is not surprising there were further moves inside government to expel her from Britain. 'In view of this women's record and known activities,' wrote one nameless senior civil servant, 'there seems no real reason why we should give ourselves the trouble of looking after her and allowing her to pay such frequent and extensive visits to this country.' But with the High Court case now pending, it was decided the government would have to allow her to remain in the UK for about six months to enable the hearing to take place, although, it was stressed, she would remain under continuous covert surveillance.

Meanwhile, the virtual certainty that, when the case eventually went to the High Court, details of the indiscreet letters between Rothermere and the Nazi high command would come out, was starting to seriously worry Rothermere and his advisers. The letters, if disclosed in court, would be highly embarrassing, if not incriminating. They undoubtedly would call into question the press baron's loyalty to his country and his motives in conducting the lengthy relationship with the Nazis. The letters were capable of revealing Rothermere as someone who, despite exercising considerable influence on the public through his newspapers and in government circles, had been actively and, arguably treacherously, working against British interests. In a confidential report, dated 25 September 1939, three weeks after the declaration of war with Germany, Rothermere's lawyers attempted to have the legal action stopped. A member of his law firm, Charles Russell & Co., went to the Home Office to say that Rothermere had finally reached the conclusion that the princess was a German agent and she had probably been double-crossing him well before he had terminated his contract with her towards the end of 1937. Lord Rothermere had also come to the view that it was undesirable for the princess to remain in the UK.[24] Belatedly for the press baron, the truth had sunk in. The approach by his lawyers appeared to be as much a device to protect Rothermere as it was a move to act in the interests of the public.

The press baron's lawyer subsequently argued to Home Office officials that it would not be in the public interest for the case to proceed. It was certain to receive huge publicity; it could undermine public morale and it was inappropriate it should be heard openly in the High Court when Britain was officially at war. The lawyer urged the Home Office to approach the Attorney General and obtain his fiat that the case should be stopped. The Home Office came to the conclusion that it would be improper to intervene, however, and the case finally reached the High Court, before Mr Justice Tucker, on 8 November 1939. It lasted for six days in a packed courtroom in the King's Bench Division, and attracted huge press interest. In Berlin, watching what was going on with some mischievous satisfaction, Goebbels wrote in his diary on 15 November with evident delight: 'In London a legal wrangle is in progress, Rothermere against the Princess Hohenlohe concerning an allowance that this "lady" is demanding from his lordship. All kinds of painful revelations, including some to do with Wiedemann!' Goebbels added: 'Nevertheless, I don't believe that the Hohenlohe woman has been spying. It is true that she has intervened in our favour on many occasions.' Spy, agent, intriguer, manipulator, adventuress – the label differed whether you were in Berlin or London.[25]

Sometime before the court hearing began, Princess Stephanie rang my father in Norfolk. What the exact purpose of the call was is by no means clear. How my father could have been associated with the allegations which formed the basis of her claims against Rothermere is a mystery. But the telephone call was significant enough to be brought up in cross-examination early in the hearing. I guess it was something to do with publishing the princess' story in an effort to bring pressure on Rothermere to drop the case. She knew that at one point in the early 1930s my father had worked for an agency in London which specialised in representing writers and journalists. Questioned about the phone call by Sir William Jowitt KC, Rothermere's barrister, the princess denied the call had been anything to do with Rothermere. She said it was to do with a publicity job she thought my father might be able to undertake for someone she had met. She denied she had told my father that the matter was of great interest and she wanted to discuss it with him. She even said she had no idea my father was managing a property in Norfolk for Lord Rothermere. All of this rang as hollow as her comment to Sir William that her understanding of the contract with the press owner was that she would be paid £5,000 a year for life by Rothermere, whether she was working for him or not.[26]

The telephone call from the princess – who by then, because of all the press commentary, was well known as a notorious pro-Nazi, a close friend of Hitler and had been exposed as guilty of working as an agent of the Nazi regime – must have been highly embarrassing for my father. The exchanges in court received prominent publicity not only in the London newspapers, but also in the pages of the *Eastern Daily Press* in Norfolk. It led to some unfortunate, hurtful and damaging finger-pointing at my father by those keen to unmask pro-German sympathisers, fifth-columnists and even possible spies at a time when Britain was at war. People were happy to assume that someone who had fairly recently moved from London, was obviously known to the princess and was now living in relative isolation on a remote North Norfolk farm, fitted the bill.

In court the princess' case was that in 1932, when Rothermere had promised to engage her as his European political representative on an annual salary of £5,000, she had understood the engagement was ongoing. She made it clear to the judge that if she lost the case she would not hesitate to accede to requests to publish her memoirs in America, giving prominence to the political activities she had carried out on behalf of Rothermere, their implications for relations between Britain and Germany now the two countries were in a state of war and Rothermere's alleged numerous, often indiscreet, liaisons with women.

Gilbert Beyfus KC for the princess said the contract she had with Rothermere was a 'general hiring', requiring twelve months' notice for it to be concluded. Rothermere, he said, had been corresponding with the ex-kaiser, the ex-Crown Prince of Germany, Hitler, Ribbentrop, Goering and others as though he himself was a sovereign power dealing with them on equal terms. The princess denied suggestions she had been a spy. She denied that in the early 1930s a blank cheque and secret correspondence had been discovered by French intelligence agents in a secret drawer of a bureau in her

Paris flat, which had led to her being gravely libelled in European newspapers as a spy. Asked what effect the alleged libels had had on her, Princess Stephanie said that 'people did not want to have anything more to do with me. They cut me off and I was excluded from functions which I was entitled to attend – it was a humiliation.' She said there had been innumerable instances of hurtful allegations since the slanderous reports had appeared in some European newspapers several years previously. Lord Rothermere's attitude to the libellous reports, she claimed, seemed to point to him sacrificing her interests and her reputation to protect his own.

Sir William Jowitt asked the princess if she had used the services of Wiedemann to put pressure on Lord Rothermere to pay her a large sum of money. Princess Stephanie replied: 'I have not.' The court heard that Wiedemann had written a letter to Rothermere in which he said Hitler greatly appreciated the work done by the princess, adding that it had been carried out with 'great ability, astuteness and tact', as Rothermere well knew. The princess told the court she had handed a short statement of her case against Rothermere – together with all the correspondence between Rothermere, Herr Hitler and others in the Nazi leadership – to the Führer's adjutant. She said she felt it was important to get Herr Hitler's permission if the Führer's private letters were to be read in an English court. Sir William quoted an extract from Wiedemann's letter to Rothermere, which said: 'You know that the Führer greatly appreciates the work the princess did to straighten relations between our countries … it was her groundwork which made the Munich agreement possible.' 'Is that true?' Sir William asked. To which the princess replied: 'Yes.' Sir William went on to say that Wiedemann's letter stated Hitler was prepared to act with chivalry and magnanimity and would grant any help needed to re-establish Princess Stephanie's honour, although it could be very unpleasant for him. 'Why would it be unpleasant?' Sir William asked. 'Because he hates publicity, he does not like journalists or newspapers. Because he has been treated, shall I say, unkindly,' she replied.

For his part, mindful of the potential damage to his reputation and the possible consequences he himself might face with war now a reality, the press baron was at pains to make clear that his campaign for friendship with Germany had been before, as he put it, 'Hitler had run amok', and that he had simply been working for peace between the two countries. When he was asked if the princess had acted as his ambassador, Rothermere, who had engaged a legal team of seventeen to mount his defence, frostily told the judge, 'I am not a sovereign state, yet!' He said it was preposterous that he had agreed to support Princess Stephanie 'for the rest of her life'. Between 1932 and 1938 he had paid her considerably more than £51,000 (almost £2 million in today's money) and added testily, 'there was no opportunity of "giving" her money because she was always "asking for it" ... she was always pestering and badgering me, so I sent here away to Budapest and Berlin'. But wasn't that a little hard on Hitler? the princess' counsel enquired. 'Oh, I'm sorry,' Rothermere replied, 'Hitler richly deserved it.'

Sir William Jowitt said the decision to fight the case had required very grave consideration on the part of Lord Rothermere's legal advisers and not a little courage by Lord Rothermere himself. It was perfectly easy for Lord Rothermere 'to pay all, and more than all, this lady desires. He has deliberately not taken this course because the view which he seeks to present to the court is that the claim this lady is making is not an honest claim.' It was shocking, Sir William told the court, that 'this lady' had had his client's letters photocopied behind his back by the Special Photographic Bureau of the Department of the German Chancellor. In his summing up, Sir William referred to the fact that Britain was at war. 'Who can say,' he asked, 'whether if Lord Rothermere had succeeded in the endeavours which he made, we might not be in the position in which we are today.'

After six days of legal argument, under the intense spotlight of the press and in the unreal circumstances that relations between one of the most powerful newspaper proprietors in Britain and the Führer and his Nazi agent were being picked over, just as the two countries had entered a disastrous war, Mr Justice Tucker ruled against the princess. He said her claim that Rothermere had promised her a lifelong retainer for acting as his special foreign-political representative in Europe was entirely without justification. There was no evidence to support her contention. The judge added that Lord Rothermere had never contractually undertaken to vindicate the princess in relation to the damaging press reports in foreign newspapers.

As the court case closed, Princess Stephanie realised that she was now facing substantial costs which threatened to ruin her.[27] Her reputation in London was already in tatters. *Time Magazine* in America reported on just one incident of many where she was publicly abused as a spy. When she walked into the Ritz, four society ladies – the Duchess of Westminster, Lady Dufferin, Lady Stanley and a Mrs Richard Norton – saw her and a loud remark was directed at her: 'Get out you filthy spy!' Other newspapers described her as 'a spy, a glamorous international agent and a girl-friend of the Führer'. Aristocratic friends who had welcomed her in the past now shunned her and wanted nothing more to do with her. But some still stood by her. The day before the court case began, Margot Lady Oxford sent her a consoling note. It read:

Dearest Stephanie, We are all with you. I have always told you Rothermere is no good. I respect you for having challenged him. Never mind the outcome. He is finished here. I know what I am saying. The most important things in life are: 1. To love and to be loved. 2. To be trusted. Rothermere has neither![28]

Soon after the trial finished, Rothermere, desperate to draw a line under the whole affair and limit the damage to his own reputation, used Lady Snowden as an intermediary and sent the princess a message to say he would meet all her costs if she undertook to get out of the country and return to Europe. The reply came back via Lady Snowden that Princess Stephanie would accept Rothermere's generous offer, but she and her mother would go to America. This was not what Rothermere had in mind at all. In America, the princess could use the offers she had received from the press to publish and further blacken Rothermere's name. He was adamant she should not set foot in the United States. He fulfilled his promise to pay her legal bills, but refused any further funds to enable her to travel to America. Nevertheless, Stephanie found the funds herself to buy tickets to travel to the States. It is possible the money came from Berlin or via Wiedemann in San Francisco. Within weeks the princess and her mother were on a liner heading for New York. As *Time Magazine* commented: 'The curtain fell swiftly on the comic-opera lawsuit of Her Serene Highness Stefanie Hohenlohe-Waldenburg-Schillingfurst [sic] versus Viscount Rothermere.'[29] But British intelligence certainly weren't laughing.

MI5 were aware of her intention to go to the States, well before the court case had started. An entry on her file, dated 13 October 1939, recorded that she had applied for permission to go to America where, she claimed, her son was seriously ill. British intelligence was not convinced that this was the true reason. The case officer noted that they were inclined to believe her objectives were to see Wiedemann, whose mistress she had been for a considerable time, and to get out of the country before the security services could place her under internment as a Nazi agent. They speculated that a third reason might have been to get an American lawyer to help her blackmail Rothermere from the other side of the Atlantic. 'She could very well threaten him with all sorts of publicity in the US,' the officer noted. 'Of course,' the MI5 record went on, 'it is also possible someone [Rothermere perhaps?] had offered her a considerable sum to leave the country.'[30] For the time being, it was decided by the British authorities that she would not be given a permit to travel. That might be reviewed later, her file noted, but any permission granted should make it clear that it was a one-way ticket. Any return to the United Kingdom was strictly ruled out.

When that 'no return' permit came to be issued to her, the decision to grant it became a matter of discussion in the House of Commons. The MP for Wolverhampton East asked the Home Secretary, Herbert Morrison, why she was being allowed to leave the country. He asked if the minister knew that 'this woman is a notorious member of the Hitler spy organisation'. The Home Secretary replied that he needed notice of the question, but in any case she had been granted only a 'no return' permit; there were no circumstances in which she would be allowed to return to Britain. The Wolverhampton MP was clearly outraged. With Britain at war, he felt someone who had been so instrumental in spreading Nazi propaganda and who had worked as an agent of the Third Reich should be arrested and tried for espionage. 'She is a political intriguer and adventuress of the first water and should be treated with the utmost suspicion,' he declared.

15

EXILE

In the summer of 1939, shortly before Germany invaded Poland with sixty of her divisions, Rothermere wrote to Churchill predicting that, with the approach of war, his old friend's time for greatness was approaching. If Churchill was aware of the private words of praise Rothermere had heaped on Hitler in his correspondence with Berlin as the war-clouds gathered, it might have taken the shine off those warm words from the newspaper owner. Once again, Rothermere showed remarkable foresight. He told Churchill: 'I can very well see a great responsibility may be placed upon you at an early date.'[1]

When war was finally declared on 3 September 1939, the British ultimatum over Poland having expired, just as Rothermere had predicted Churchill was recalled to the Admiralty. Seven months later, in May 1940, as invasion of Britain appeared imminent, Churchill replaced Chamberlain as Prime Minister. One of his first acts was to appoint Max Beaverbrook to the new Cabinet post of Minister for Aircraft Production. It was an appointment that reflected another prediction Rothermere had long been making, and had campaigned for vigorously for years: Britain's need to build up meaningful air defences against the inevitable blitz to come from a powerful German bomber force.

Rothermere's concern at the devastation German bombers could inflict in this new and terrible kind of air warfare that would strike indiscriminately at civilians, women and children alike, moved him to ensure at least two families could leave London for the relative safety of the countryside. Ever since 1932 Rothermere had had his country estate at Stody in North Norfolk. Having purchased the extensive arable and sporting estate, he spent a considerable sum rebuilding Stody Lodge after the previous house had been gutted by fire. He also laid out the famous azalea and rhododendron gardens that have remained ever since a distinctive feature of the grounds at Stody, and he improved the glasshouses and gardens. In 1938, obsessed by the dangers of aerial blitzkrieg in the war he now thought was inevitable (in spite of his continued pro-Nazi correspondence with Hitler), Rothermere offered his close colleague and confidant Collin Brooks the opportunity to leave London and move with his young family to The Mount, a large house on his Norfolk estate. At the same time he made my father a similar offer. My father's job as company secretary of Rothermere's cigarette factory, originally established at the time the *Daily Mail* was looking favourably on Sir Oswald Mosley and his Blackshirts, had ended. The project had been wound up and Rothermere suggested my father and his family should move to another house on his Norfolk estate, Hole Farm at Hempstead. My father was to take the tenancy of the farm and run it, as well as establishing a business breeding traditional Norfolk black turkeys for the Christmas market.

It is clear from Collin Brooks' diaries that Rothermere made these offers to give both families, and particularly the children concerned, the opportunity to escape the devastation from the air which he believed would obliterate large sections of the capital. He himself had suffered the loss of two of his sons in the First World War and had never fully recovered from the pain. He wanted to protect two families from suffering similar pain. But what Rothermere had not considered, if Hitler succeeded in overrunning France and the Low Countries, was a German invasion along the east coast. Parts of the east coast, notably in the vicinity of the North Norfolk village of Weybourne, were favourable for a beachhead landing. In conjunction with a force striking across the Channel, such a manoeuvre would have enabled the Germans to mount a pincer attack on London. In May 1940 this possibility was taken so seriously that eighteen east coast and south-east coastal towns, together with areas inland up to 10 miles from the coast, were subject to strict control orders resulting in the evacuation of nearly 50,000 children. Rothermere offered Brooks The Mount in March 1937, but it was not until September of that year that Brooks accepted the offer. In a letter to Brooks, the press baron wrote: 'I can't bear the thought of your children being bombed in London.'[2]

My parents, brother and I arrived at Hole Farm in the summer of 1938. It must have been a huge shock for my mother to leave a modern, well-equipped suburban house in Surbiton, and move to an isolated farmhouse which had neither electricity nor mains drainage and, until a bathroom was installed when we moved in, only the traditional outside brick-built privy in the garden. Water came from the original farm well and had to be pumped by petrol engine up to a storage tank in the roof. My father was 28 and had never farmed in his life. He had to learn fast to make the venture a success. Agriculture had gone through hard times in the 1930s, but with war now almost certain, it was clear that British farming would have to face the challenge of feeding the nation. The threat that Hitler's U-boats would cut off supplies by decimating Britain's merchant fleet was real and potentially devastating. I remember Rothermere visiting us just before Christmas 1938 bearing lavish presents for my brother and myself. It was the press baron's last Christmas at his beloved Norfolk retreat. If Rothermere seemed unaware of the dangers of invasion, should Hitler's armies break through to threaten Britain's shores, my father certainly recognised the possibility. He equipped himself with a six-chamber revolver to go alongside the more familiar farmers' arsenal of a 12-bore shotgun and 2.2 rifle.

The day after Beaverbrook was appointed to his role as Minister for Aircraft Production, in May 1940, Rothermere sent his fellow press baron a telegram saying he was overjoyed that the government had found some use for the 'Beaver's ... glittering abilities'. It was the appointment Rothermere had been campaigning for, and he offered Beaverbrook his help for the dura-tion of the war.[3] Beaverbrook replied the same day, saying that he would value Rothermere's services in America in helping to negotiate practical aid from the States, in particular helping to provide the essential materials which would be required by the aircraft factories in the rush to rapidly expand the RAF's squadrons. Rothermere claimed Beaverbrook had asked him to make arrangements at once to travel to the States. When Foreign Secretary Lord Halifax objected to Rothermere being recruited to undertake an official mission of this nature, given his record of dealing with Hitler now clearly exposed in the very public High Court hearing, Beaverbrook countered by saying he thought Rothermere was already in the States.

Collin Brooks was also anxious to play his part, giving tangible help to the war effort. He was already working in a key role for the National War Savings Scheme, but he jumped at the chance when Rothermere asked him to accompany him on a rearmament mission to America. Brooks had played a vital role in the establishment of the National League of Airmen, and was as committed as his employer to the cause of a strong air defence. The two left for the States by transatlantic liner on 25 May 1940. But it soon transpired that the 'mission' was not as official as Brooks had thought, and Rothermere had led him to believe. In his journal Brooks recorded:

> After a few days at sea R gradually let me know that what had really happened
> was that when he heard of Beaverbrook's appointment he had wired his con-

gratulations and had said 'I am going to America almost immediately, can I be of use to you there?' The Beaver had wired back saying that he might well be of use in America. Morison [Rothermere's assistant] then told me that he believed that the Beaver had consulted Esmond Harmsworth [Rothermere's surviving son] and that the whole thing had been fixed so that R should have a good excuse for being out of the country. (It is possible that they, like R himself, feared that his friendship with Hitler and his known defeatist attitude might bring him under arrest). So the mission was not really a mission at all. I was angry, having been taken from War Savings on false pretences.[4]

In the final months before war was declared, Brooks had been under pressure from Rothermere to help him prepare three books he had written for publication: *My Fight to Rearm Britain, Warnings and Predictions* and *My Campaign for Hungary.* All three were published in 1939 against a very tight publishing deadline. There is strong evidence Rothermere and Brooks worked to place in these books, in the best possible light, all that had passed between Rothermere and the Nazi leadership during the years in which Princess Stephanie was his go-between; when she was engineering the meetings, the correspondence and the propaganda with Hitler and his Nazi colleagues.

In a careful entry in his journal for 3 December 1939, written when he was at Stody in Norfolk, Brooks recorded:

I wish I had time to log here the machinations of the Princess and the full reasons for the urgent haste of this new book – begun on Monday and sent to press in seventeen days. In going over the files I found one letter which might be awkward if she published her photostats.

The letter Brooks referred to was one in which Rothermere had written, 'You know I have always been a fervent admirer of the Führer'. In war, Brooks commented, the populace get angry with fervent admirers of the 'arch-villain'.[5]

The Times, reviewing Rothermere's book *My Fight to Rearm Britain*, gave Rothermere the benefit of any doubts it may have had about his relationship with the Nazis. 'Wisely or unwisely, it must be left to readers of his correspondence to decide, but obviously with complete sincerity he made personal approaches to the Nazi leaders Hitler, Goering and Ribbentrop, right up to the eve of war in his efforts to effect a peaceful settlement.' Referring to Rothermere's rearmament campaign, *The Times* said: 'Some of his efforts might not win full approval but there is little doubt of the value of his services to the cause of national safety.'[6]

What would the attitude of the British government have been had Rothermere stayed in Britain? Would he have been interned, as Mosley and his wife and many of his Blackshirt followers were? Or would friends in high places, Churchill in particular, have shielded him? It is impossible to know, but clearly the possibility of arrest and internment was on Rothermere's mind when he decided to take flight across the Atlantic. When intelligence files were published in 2005 it became clear that Rothermere was sending supportive telegrams to Nazi leaders just weeks before the outbreak of war, messages that were routinely intercepted by British agents. At the same time, he was also appealing to Hitler not to provoke war, and was writing to Rudolf Hess, Hitler's deputy, calling for an international conference 'to settle outstanding problems'. Nevertheless, Rothermere might have seen that war was inevitable. In correspondence with Ribbentrop just before war was declared, he wrote: 'I have never known the British people more warlike than they are today ... They are talking as they did at the outbreak of the Great War and the Boer War.'[7] Ribbentrop's reply a few days later gave an even stronger threat:

> If these two countries should ever clash again, it would this time be a fight to the very end and to the last man. And this time every German conscious of the tremendous power of these 80 million people behind one man and of Germany's powerful allies, is convinced that this war would end with a German victory.[8]

When war was declared the *Daily Mail* printed a powerful patriotic leader, but it had an ironic ring given the views its owner had been expounding in his private correspondence to Berlin. 'No statesman, no man with any decency could think of sitting at the same table with Hitler or his henchman the trickster von Ribbentrop, or any other of the gang,' the *Daily Mail* declared. 'We fight against the blackest tyranny that has ever held men in bondage. We fight to defend and to restore freedom and justice on earth.'[9]

In New York, in late October 1939, Rothermere was having cash problems and said he needed to move to a sterling area. He travelled by liner from New York to Bermuda. Several days after his arrival there he became seriously ill and was taken to the King Edward VII Memorial Hospital. He partially recovered, but during the following months his health gradually deteriorated again and he died on 27 November 1940. He was buried in the churchyard of St Paul's in Paget, Bermuda, the following day. Meanwhile, in the United States, the FBI, alerted by their colleagues in British intelligence, were closely monitoring Princess Stephanie's movements there, aware that had she not fled to seek asylum in America she would have undoubtedly been imprisoned in Britain.

16

TRAILED BY THE FBI

On 11 December 1939 Princess Stephanie, accompanied by her mother and both travelling under false names, boarded the Dutch liner SS *Veendam* at Southampton for the journey across the Atlantic to the safety of a country that was still neutral. She did not wait long enough to discover if the British government would imprison her for espionage, her close relationship with Hitler, her espousal of his Nazi policies and the persuasive way she had worked to influence people in Britain to support the Third Reich. Lady Snowden had arranged for an MP to put down a question in Parliament enquiring whether it was the government's intention to expel her. In response, the Home Secretary made it clear that as the princess had already left of her own volition, no further action was necessary. But, he added, she had better not try to return to Britain, because he guaranteed that entry would be refused.

Stephanie arrived in New York, elegantly dressed and bedecked in her usual array of expensive jewellery. A report in the *New York World Telegram* described her as having her auburn hair combed straight back and wearing a silver-fox turban with a 'provocative pink rose perched on it'. She wore a three-quarter-length silver-fox fur coat, a black silk jersey dress and black kid Perugia sandals with very high heels and sky-blue platform soles. Expensive diamond ear-clips and a scintillating diamond brooch gave the finishing touches to an outfit designed to make an impression.[1] She possessed only a visitor's visa, but the 106 pieces of luggage she brought with her, and the knowledge that she could never return to England, suggested that she thought she was in America to stay. MI5 had made sure the FBI were waiting for her. Ever since Fritz Wiedemann's arrival to take up his diplomatic appointment in San Francisco, the FBI had been told to track her movements if she should ever try to join him in the United States.

Predictably, the first phone call Stephanie made was indeed to Wiedemann in San Francisco. She asked him not to travel to New York to meet her. She calculated that it would not be wise for her to be seen so soon in the company of probably the most notorious Nazi in the country. Instead, she stayed some time in New York, having well-publicised meetings with literary agents and publishers who wanted articles about her close relations and first-hand knowledge of Hitler, his intentions in starting a war in Europe and his character – although it appears from letters from some of these publishers, now among the princess' papers, that Stephanie was loathe to tell her story as truthfully and openly as the press wanted, perhaps for fear of incriminating herself. She was more concerned with painting herself as innocent of the label of spy, confidante of Hitler and political intriguer, than telling the real story of her relationship with the Nazis. Her lover, Wiedemann, was also concerned about his own position. A letter from Hearst Magazines Inc. made the point:

> She will have to go a little bit more into some of the legend in order to explain that it is not true. She must explain the true story of the activities that brought her so much uncalled for publicity. She says that up to 1932 she was a private citizen and cannot understand why she has become so celebrated and misunderstood.[2]

The journalists thought she was concealing the real story in order to protect herself. In March 1940 Wiedemann was writing to her about the possibility of her publishing her memoirs: 'Certain information you have could only have been received from me and you must consider my position. Only something outstanding and sensational will interest the public – for that sort of thing your name is too good.'[3] Wiedemann knew publicity would damage the covert work he was intent on pursuing in America.

In January 1940 an article appeared in the *New York Times* under a headline referring to the princess' role in Nazi 'diplomacy'. It said the princess was a star among a whole group of female members of the former German aristocracy who had been recruited by Hitler for a wide variety of operations, many of a secret nature. The newspaper described these people as 'political spies, propaganda hostesses, social butterflies and ladies of mystery'. The publicity all this attracted probably persuaded her that she needed the support only her lover could give her, but it also enhanced her glamour and notoriety. The idea of a Nazi princess electrified some in society and she was invited to many social events which only enhanced the opportunities for her to spread a pro-Nazi message in America. Her loyalty to Nazism and Germany remained strong, despite Hitler's suspicions of her.

In late March 1940 Stephanie decided to travel to California to meet Wiedemann. The reunion took place in the holiday resort of Carmel, 90 miles south of San Francisco. Both of them must have been aware they were likely to be watched by the FBI, but they probably had no idea that they would be under the intense 24-hour observation the FBI had put them under. The pair clearly realised they needed to be discreet, because their next meeting took place in an obscure hotel in Fresno, where Princess Stephanie booked in under the name of Mrs Moll. She received a telephone call in her room and the agents listening in picked up the arrangement for Wiedemann and the princess to meet and dine at a nearby restaurant. As they dined the princess' hotel room and her possessions were searched. Agents then watched them as they later drove to the General Grant National Park, and from there to the Sequoia National Park, where they rented a chalet under the name of Mr and Mrs Fred Winter from San Francisco. Finally, they drove on to the San Francisco suburb of Hillsboro, where the German Consul General's residence was located. Wiedemann and the princess had clearly agreed any further efforts to cover their tracks and to escape surveillance would be futile. The princess and her mother moved into 1808 Floribunda Avenue, the German Consul General's official residence, where they stayed, perhaps rather surprisingly, with the approval of Wiedemann's wife, whose forbearing in the face of her husband's passionate romantic attachment to the princess must have sorely strained her Nazi loyalty.

It may have seemed to some in Berlin that Hitler had completely fallen out with, downgraded and sidelined his old friend and personal adjutant by dispatching him to the relatively obscure post of Consul General in San Francisco, California. But the truth appears to be very different. Wiedemann's mission was of the greatest importance to the Nazi high command. His role, as the American *Time Magazine* reported in January 1939, was to calm US-German relations and to sell the Nazi regime to an unsympathetic America. *Time Magazine* had described him as Hitler's 'Man Friday'; burly and competent, with black wavy hair and chiselled, handsome features. He is shrewd, the report said, intelligent and seemingly popular in society.[4] The US Treasury secretary, Henry Morgenthau Jnr, received a report on 2 January 1940 that said the German Consul General in New York had intimated that Wiedemann had indeed been given the job of keeping America out of the war, and that his posting to San Francisco should not be taken that he was persona non grata with Hitler, as had been suggested.[5]

A significant percentage of Americans wanted nothing to do with a new European war. In their view, America's entry into the First World War had been a costly mistake, and neutrality and isolationism was a more sensible position for America to take. Any threat lay 3,000 miles away. Wiedemann, the Nazi hierarchy calculated, had fertile ground on which to work. Goebbels had noted in his diary that public opinion in the US was in a state of ferment and the isolationists were very active.[6] It was not difficult in the circumstances for Wiedemann to encourage the spread of anti-war feeling, and, where there were pro-German activists, to go even further by cultivating positive support for the Third Reich.

He achieved it partly through the Auslands-Organisation, which was referred to cryptically by its adherents as AO; this was the foreign arm of the Nazi Party which embraced all Germans and pro-German supporters abroad. Although this was kept carefully concealed, the organisation was under the direct control in Germany of Walter Schellenberg, the Nazi Gestapo counter-intelligence boss, and Ernst Bohle, a Secretary of State at the Nazi Foreign Ministry, who had been born in Bradford. In England, MI5 concluded that AO was a 'ready-made instrument for intelligence, espionage and ultimately for sabotage purposes'. The leading agents for AO in the States were Wiedemann and now Princess Stephanie.[7] With the support of Himmler and backed by money from I.G. Farben, the huge Nazi industrial trust, Wiedemann and Stephanie were the key figures helping to knit the organisation together in the States, travelling across the country to build and widen support.

As Consul General in San Francisco, Wiedemann was head of a network that covered not just the US but the whole Pacific basin and included countries in South America. Between them the couple's social position enabled them to exercise influence on prominent figures, and with their support persuade others to sympathise with the Nazi cause. With war now raging in Europe, the most important task of AO was to keep America out of the conflict and unite German-American businesses and industrial companies to the Fatherland. To do this Wiedemann established the German-American Business League. Among its rules were that member companies would purchase only from Germany, they would strictly boycott Jewish firms and employ only Aryans. The organisation spread to enrol the owners of over 1,000 small companies. The network stirred up anti-Jewish feeling, paid for radio airtime supporting German propaganda and publicised German goods. Just after the outbreak of war in Europe, Wiedemann gave a speech to the League in which he told members:

You are citizens of the United States, which has allied itself with an enemy
of the German nation. The time will come when you may have to decide
which side to take. I would caution that I cannot advise you what to do, but
you should be governed by your conscience. One duty lies with the Mother
country, the other with the adopted country. Blood is thicker than ink ...
Germany is the land of your fathers and regardless of the consequences, you
should not disregard the traditional heritage which is yours.[8]

There were other damaging allegations circulating. A woman employed
by Wiedemann, Alice Crockett, the divorced wife of an American general,
accused him of being head of the Nazi espionage network in the USA.
Wiedemann, trusting in her friendship and loyalty, had arranged for her to
undertake an official trip to Berlin on his behalf in May 1939 to meet Hitler
and Himmler. It was on her return that she made the sensational allegations,
reporting Wiedemann's secret activities to the FBI.[9] Crockett alleged that
the Nazi regime had transferred a massive sum of over $5 million to fund
espionage and set up a spy ring across the United States. She further claimed
that among those employed in this intrigue was Princess Stephanie and that
Nazi networks existed on the east coast controlled by an office in New York.
The FBI may well have been aware of some of these allegations, but Alice
Crockett's visit to Berlin opened their eyes to the extent of German influence
that Wiedemann and his colleagues were masterminding, and some of the
details she brought back were a shock to Edgar Hoover, the FBI boss.

From his residence in California, Wiedemann made many trips to Mexico.
It was suspected one of his tasks was to discover ways of gaining the support
of Central American states to block the Panama Canal to American shipping in the event of America being drawn into the war. The Germans were
not alone in establishing an espionage network in the United States, however. With Britain standing alone and vulnerable, Churchill was desperate to
involve American strength and arms in the war. Britain set up a rival network
to the Nazis with a view to engineering a situation where America would
be drawn into the conflict. Covert initiatives such as false rumours and the
creation of false documents were employed. A document emerged purport-
ing to show secret Nazi plans to invade South America and therefore pose an
immediate threat to the United States.

Foremost among those working on behalf of British intelligence was
a Canadian citizen called William Stephenson, known by the codename
'Intrepid'. A personal friend of Churchill, he had been mentored by Sir
William Wiseman who had led British intelligence in the US during the First

World War. He operated his secret network, known as BSC (British Security Co-ordination), from offices in New York's Rockefeller Centre.[10] A prime aim was to organise American public opinion in favour of aid to Britain, and ultimately to get the United States into the war so Britain was no longer alone in facing Nazism. One of his fellow agents was none other than Ian Fleming, creator of James Bond, who we have already met in connection with Jack Kruse and his 'Stately Super-car'. The trigger, which some commentators have suggested persuaded Hitler to declare war on the United States on 11 December 1941, was a forged document which 'Intrepid' is credited with planting into Hitler's hands; it purported to show that Roosevelt was planning a pre-emptive strike against Germany without a formal declaration of war by the US Congress.[11] In 1945 Stephenson was knighted at the request of Churchill for his secret work in both North and South America. He also received the highest US civilian award, the Presidential Medal for Merit, having been credited with a key role in the creation of the CIA.

Princess Stephanie, it will be recalled, in London in 1938 had tried, with Wiedemann's help, to arrange a peace mission direct with the then British Foreign Secretary, Lord Halifax. Now, two years later, another meeting was being set up to trigger new negotiations and Lord Halifax was again a key player. Despite Churchill's determination as Prime Minister that Britain would never surrender, there remained an element inside the British Cabinet that were prepared, even now, to attempt to negotiate for peace if the time and terms seemed right. Among them was Foreign Secretary Halifax. Lothian, the British ambassador in Washington, was also one of the peace plotters and had opened up a dialogue with Hans Thomson, the German charge d'affaires in Washington. On 6 June 1940 Sir William Wiseman, a former Cambridge boxing blue, lunched with Halifax in London. Wiseman had been sent by the first director of the Secret Intelligence Service, Mansfield Cumming, to establish the agency's office in New York during the First World War. He had acted as a liaison link between President Woodrow Wilson and the British government, and was referred to by those 'in the know' as the President's 'confidential Englishman'. He was a man who always seemed to move mysteriously in international circles and was widely credited with playing a major role in getting the US into the First World War. Wiseman remained living in the States after the Armistice and had joined Kuhn, Loeb & Co., the second greatest US private banking house, but he retained his British passport, his family titles and his connections to British intelligence.

Halifax briefed Wiseman to assist Lothian and help him to find some way of starting peace negotiations that would be effective. Before the outbreak of war a substantial number of the British Establishment (prime movers in political, aristocratic and financial circles), many egged on by the princess' activities, were totally opposed to the coming conflict. When, despite their efforts, war broke out, these people continued to believe that it should be resolved as quickly as possible through a negotiated peace. This belief did not necessarily make them pro-Nazi, although some certainly were. In November, as the Blitz was hitting Britain hard and the Battle of Britain had just been won, Wiseman, now back in the States, was contacted by Princess Stephanie. They had two meetings. The second and most important took place in Wiseman's suite at the Mark Hopkins Hotel in San Francisco on 27 November 1940, at which Wiedemann was also present. The three had a lengthy conversation which lasted from 7.30 p.m. until the early hours of the following morning. The FBI was suspicious of Wiseman's activities and had him under surveillance. Edgar Hoover, the FBI boss, had received a note from Brigadier General Sherman Miles which inferred Wiseman was a member of the same group of Englishmen in America who had attempted to negotiate with the Nazis in the past.

Unknown to Wiseman and the princess, the FBI had bugged Wiseman's apartment and recorded the entire conversation, which amounted to a detailed discussion of possible peace negotiations. Stephanie promised she could get any proposals direct to Hitler, and Wiseman made it clear he represented a group of Englishmen who believed a satisfactory peace arrangement could still be concluded between Britain and Germany. The next day Wiseman met Wiedemann and disclosed that Halifax, the British Foreign Secretary, represented a group which had members in both Houses of the British Parliament and felt strongly that a negotiated peace was both possible and desirable. The FBI leaked the contents of these undercover meetings to British intelligence. The result was that Wiseman lost the backing he had originally had from influential sources in London.

At the Wiseman meeting, Princess Stephanie had put forward an audacious plan. She said she was prepared to travel to Berlin via Switzerland to intercede directly with Hitler. She was sure the Führer would meet her given the affection in which he had held for her in the past. If she failed to see Hitler, she would negotiate with Himmler. Stephanie believed that if her talks in Berlin were successful it would be possible for a Nazi emissary to see Lord Halifax, in London or in a neutral city, to confirm arrangements for a ceasefire and an alliance between Britain and Germany. The princess had not changed her allegiance. It was her firm conviction that a pact between Britain and Germany against communism and the Soviet menace was in the best interests of Germany and the surest way of furthering Hitler's objectives. Among comments overheard by the FBI were those of Sir William Wiseman saying Hitler needed to know that the amount of damage the Nazis could do to America was nothing compared to the damage the Americans would inflict on Germany if they were provoked to enter the war. Following this meeting, Hoover ensured the FBI kept tight surveillance on all three participants and he sent a summary of what had occurred at the Mark Hopkins Hotel to President Franklin D. Roosevelt.[12]

The FBI informed the President that during the meeting the princess had done most of the talking. She said Hitler was genuinely fond of her and would listen to her. She thought she could impress on the Reich Chancellor that at the opportune time, if he aligned himself with Britain, such an alliance would bring lasting peace. She considered there were several powerful arguments that would convince the Führer: that Hitler had not been able to defeat Britain in the air (the Luftwaffe had failed to destroy the RAF in the Battle of Britain) and the planned invasion of Britain had been postponed; the alliance with Russia and Italy could deliver little in comparison to an alliance with Britain; and finally, the overwhelming military and economic strength of America should stand as a warning to the Third Reich, if it too was drawn into the war. Anyone who supposed the German Reich was stronger than the United States was fooling themselves. She pointed out that America had already technically breached its neutrality by providing Britain with fifty destroyers, and Churchill was pressing the American President for further financial and material assistance.

The discussions between Stephanie, Wiedemann and the former British intelligence chief came to nothing. In any case, their proposals were never likely to gain the support of Churchill and the majority of the British Cabinet. Following that meeting, when the princess phoned Wiseman to elicit further help, in particular to get him to provide an affidavit to support her bid to have her American visa renewed, Wiseman was very keen to sever the relationship.[13]

After the Wiseman talks the FBI stepped up their monitoring of the princess' movements and her attempts at further intrigues. A remarkable memorandum compiled by the FBI, and sent to the President's office at the end of October 1941, said Princess Stephanie had been suspected by the French, British and American authorities of being a spy for the Nazis. She was known to have very close connections with high officials of the Third Reich, and it described her as 'extremely intelligent, dangerous and clever'. As an espionage agent, the memorandum concluded, she was 'worse than ten thousand men'. The FBI said she was reputedly immoral and capable of resorting to any means, including seduction and bribery, to achieve her ends. That opinion was absolutely accurate, as was soon to be proved.[14]

When the princess' temporary visa expired in November 1940, an extension was blocked by Hoover and she was told she had to leave the US within four days. FBI agents listening in to her phone calls heard her begging Wiseman to assist her in getting an extension to her visa. There was nothing he could or would do to help. The authorities would not have listened to a British resident, however distinguished, particularly when he was under suspicion for the discussions over a deal with Hitler. But the Hungarian Embassy did take up her case – legally she was a Hungarian citizen and still possessed a Hungarian passport – and she won a temporary postponement for a maximum of twenty days until 11 January 1941. When that expired she was told she would have to sail from New York to Lisbon, but the princess was still refusing to give up. She wrote a remarkable personal letter to President Roosevelt, pleading to be allowed to stay. With her tongue firmly in her cheek, she asked for the same privileges that 'this land of freedom' would grant to anyone who was not guilty of an unjust or disloyal act. 'Please spare me the humiliation of having to leave this country under such oppressive circumstances as though I were a criminal,' she wrote.[15]

Her pleas to the President fell on deaf ears. Roosevelt had been made amply aware by FBI reports of her background and of the dangers she posed. She was informed by her lawyer that she would be forcibly deported. Her reaction was to make a dramatic threat of suicide. When the hearing for the enforcement of the deportation order was held, she made a show of being too ill to face the court and insisted on arriving in an ambulance on a stretcher. It was all to no avail. On 7 March 1941 the President himself gave a direct order to the US Attorney General: 'That Hohenlohe woman ought to be got out of the country as a matter of good discipline,' his direction read. 'Have her put on a boat to Japan or Vladivostok. She is a Hungarian and I do not think the British would take her.' It was signed, 'FDR'.[16]

The following day Stephanie was arrested on the orders of Major Lemuel Schofield, head of the United States Immigration and Naturalisation Service. A few days later Schofield, who was obviously intrigued by her, visited the princess at the detention centre. As she had done so successfully so often before, she switched on her undoubted sexual charms and flirted with her captor. Schofield was hardly a handsome 'catch'. He was obese with large, ugly features, but he had authority and influence. Despite his senior position of trust in the American immigration service, Schofield succumbed willingly to the princess' seductive wiles. In the way so many influential men had done before him, he found he could not resist her. On 19 May, in a move which directly contradicted the President's specific order, Schofield released her on $25,000 bail on condition she informed the immigration service of where she was living; made no contact whatsoever with Wiedemann in San Francisco; or had any contact with any other foreign government; and gave no interviews nor made any public declarations.[17] Dropping the deportation proceedings, Schofield explained to a journalist that while in custody the princess had co-operated with the Department of Justice and given information of national interest. Her release would not pose a threat to the interests of the United States and she had promised her continued co-operation. Newspapermen saw Major Schofield personally escort her to a luxury apartment in Palo Alto. She was elegantly dressed in chic black crêpe with a stylish white collar, white gloves and a black-and-white hat. Schofield was quizzed on the information the princess had provided. To all questions he refused to give any detailed answer beyond that it was 'interesting information for the authorities', though it is clear from FBI records that the authorities had no knowledge of what Schofield claimed she had revealed to him. Her release from detention, surprisingly, did not provoke much of a public outcry – but the *New York Sun* expressed a view many others might have echoed: 'If 130 million people cannot exclude one person with no legal right to remain here, something seems wrong.'[18]

Meanwhile, the princess and her mother had moved into the Raleigh Hotel in Washington DC where, conveniently, Schofield was also staying. Stephanie was frequently seen visiting 'Lemmy' Schofield in his room and on most occasions staying there all night – she was clearly resorting to sex to ensure her protection, but she was in serious financial difficulties.[19] Her next ploy to try to secure permission to remain in the United States was to offer, via Schofield, to work for the American authorities; putting to use her intimate knowledge of Hitler and his policies. In late July 1941 Schofield wrote to the newly appointed US Attorney General Francis Biddle, saying the princess had personal experience, extending over six years, of the way Hitler operated:

> She can describe his treachery, his deceit, and his cunning ... She can portray him not as a daring conqueror but a sly and cunning trickster who doesn't shun to use the lowest methods to accomplish his aims and who only strikes when he is assured of an absolute superiority when he has check-mated his opponent morally and physically.[20]

Stephanie had put forward a number of ideas on how her first-hand knowledge could be put to use in America's interests. She had suggested, for instance, that she could participate in short-wave radio propaganda broadcasts transmitted to Germany and the countries under Nazi occupation, using her fluent language skills – a kind of 'Lord Haw-Haw' in reverse.

The message from Schofield was sent in secret to the Attorney General, but the chief of the FBI, Hoover, was tipped off about it and was predictably furious. He again demanded to know, in the national interest, exactly what information on Nazi espionage in the US the princess claimed she was in a position to provide. The princess and her mother moved to a house in the Washington suburb of Alexandria, but it did not take long for the FBI to track them down. All they needed to do was follow Major Schofield, who by this time was totally smitten with Stephanie and called on her frequently for sexual encounters in her room. The princess regarded him as an insurance policy for her continued stay in the United States. He had fallen hopelessly for her charms, as is clear from one of the letters he sent her. In it he wrote:

> Everything about you is new and different and gets me excited. You are the most interesting person I have ever met. You dress better than anyone else, and every time you come into a room everyone else fades out of the picture … Because of you I do so many crazy things, because I am mad about you.[21]

In mid-June 1941 Roosevelt ordered that all Nazi consulates in America must be closed. Wiedemann was told to leave the country by 10 July 1941. The night after that order was given, neighbours of the consulate in San Francisco noticed smoke pouring from the chimneys of the building and flakes of burned papers blowing around the area. It was clear incriminating papers were being hastily burned. Other documents were taken out of the country aboard German ships. Having been ordered out of the States, Wiedemann travelled to Berlin via Lisbon where he reported to Himmler and Ribbentrop on his espionage and his pro-Nazi activities in the States. In September he was en route to Argentina where the Nazis also had extensive links. From there he went on to Rio de Janeiro to confer with the Gestapo leader in South America, Gottfried Sandstede. A Brazilian newspaper, *O Globo*, put a photograph of him on its front page with the headline, 'Number One Nazi of the Americas'. Brazilian police secretly searched Wiedemann's hotel room in Rio and discovered in his luggage a list of Nazi agents based in California.[22] On 8 September 1941 he was in Chile making arrangements to sail for the Japanese port of Kobe. A significant stop-off perhaps, in view of what was soon to happen. From Japan, Wiedemann travelled on to China to take up the new post he had been assigned as German Consul General in Tientsin.

On 8 December 1941, the day after Japan carried out its devastating surprise attack on the US Pacific Fleet at Pearl Harbor, Stephanie and her mother, who were staying with friends in Philadelphia, made a visit to the cinema. As they were leaving at around 10.20 p.m. they were surrounded by FBI agents and the princess was arrested. She was bundled into a car, while her 89-year-old mother was left on the pavement screaming abuse at the agents. At a police station the princess was fingerprinted and photographed. She endeavoured to call Schofield, but failed. She was taken to the Gloucester Immigration Centre in New Jersey and placed in solitary confinement. Elsewhere across the country, German, Japanese and Italian nationals were also being arrested. America was at war.

The *New York Journal*, reporting on the round-up of enemy aliens, said federal agents had confiscated many samples of Nazi literature, records and other data, which indicated a far-reaching underground network of German propaganda and espionage. Among these items were powerful short-wave radios and expensive cameras – both items were forbidden to enemy aliens under federal order. The radios led officials to believe that agents of the Gestapo were, until the recent raids, in close co-operation with persons in America. The report added that other Nazi paraphernalia included huge photo-enlargements of Hitler, swastika armbands and German victory banners. German uniforms, flags, guns, badges and identification cards were also seized.[23]

Within weeks the Attorney General had signed an order citing that Princess von Hohenlohe-Waldenburg-Schillingsfürst was a potential danger to public security and peace. Meanwhile, Hoover ordered the search of her home. In the house they found the Gold Medal of the Nazi Party Hitler had conferred upon her.

17

THE PRESIDENT'S ANGER

Wiedemann fulfilled his duties in Kobe, Japan, Germany's Pacific ally, before the Japanese launched their infamous attack on Pearl Harbor, Hawaii, on 7 December 1941. By the time of the attack he had moved on to China where he joined another German agent, Klaus Mehnert, who, significantly, had been Professor of Anthropology at the University of Hawaii in Honolulu until shortly before they met up in China. Mehnert had undertaken extensive studies of the US Navy's weaknesses in their Pacific bases and had concluded that if the Japanese could exploit these vulnerabilities they could wage a successful campaign in the Pacific. From his base in San Francisco, Wiedemann had been responsible for German intelligence and espionage activity on America's west coast. That included the Hawaiian Islands, so he would have been aware of the undercover work in which Mehnert was involved and he may well have known that as a result of Mehnert's intelligence reports, Japan was about to launch its unheralded attack. Perhaps the reason Wiedemann stopped off in Japan on his way to his posting in China was to discuss Japan's military intentions and her imminent entry into world war.[1]

Hitler now had other work for Wiedemann. As Consul General he ran Nazi intelligence in occupied China for the rest of the war years, and remained there until September 1945 when, some weeks after the Japanese surrender, he was taken prisoner by the US Army. He tried to claim diplomatic immunity, but the Americans knew his background and eventually he was taken back to Washington. *Time Magazine* reported his return to the States in 1945:

Captain Fritz Wiedemann, Hitler's company commander in World War 1, German consul general in San Francisco for two stormy years and spy extraordinary for the Third Reich, was back in the US for a brief stay. Newsmen who remembered Wiedemann as a tall, black-haired fashion plate scarcely recognised the baggy-suited, greying, unshaven man who de-planed from an Army transport at California's Hamilton Field. Hitler's onetime personal adjutant was to be a star witness at war crimes trials of top Nazis.[2]

Under interrogation about his time as German Consul General in San Francisco, Wiedemann admitted his espionage role in the US on behalf of the Nazis, and that he had received a great deal of secret information and help during that time from his friend and lover Princess Stephanie.

To return to 1941, the princess was finding the conditions in the internment centre where she was held far from the lifestyle she had been used to. In letters to her mother she described conditions as appallingly unhygienic. There were, she said, twenty women living in the filthy room in which she was held, and the prisoners she was interned with included prostitutes and 'sluts with venereal disease'.[3]

In February 1942 Princess Stephanie's son, Prince Franz Hohenlohe, was also arrested and interned. Initially he was held at Ellis Island. Subsequently, he was taken to internment centres in Oklahoma and Texas. He was finally released on parole in February 1944 and finished the war in the US Army as a member of the American occupation force in Japan.

Despite the orders he had received from the highest authorities, Major Lemuel Schofield refused to break off contact with the princess. When President Roosevelt heard about this gross insubordination, he dispatched a furious letter to the head of the FBI, Hoover: 'Once more I have to bother you about that Hohenlohe woman. This affair verges not merely on the ridiculous, but on the disgraceful.'[4] The President followed this up with a letter to the Attorney General demonstrating his growing anger and frustration:

If the immigration authorities do not stop once and for all showing favour to Hohenlohe, I will be forced to order an inquiry. The facts will not be very palatable and will go right back to her first arrest and her intimacy with Schofield. I am aware that she is interned in the Gloucester centre, but by all accounts she enjoys special privileges there. To be honest, this is all turning into a scandal that requires extremely drastic and immediate action.

It was signed personally by 'FDR'.[5]

The Attorney General took immediate action. He transferred the princess to a more remote internment centre, Camp Seagoville, near Dallas in Texas. The authorities had underestimated Stephanie's extraordinary hold over her lover Schofield, however. Amazingly, still in an authoritative position in the immigration service, he gave the governor of Camp Seagoville instructions that the princess was to receive special privileges, including the use of a telephone outside the camp and permission for her mother to visit outside official visiting hours. Not surprisingly, the pressures on Major Schofield from his superiors became so great that he was forced to resign his post, and he returned to his former career as a lawyer in a successful New York practice. An FBI agent reporting in November 1943 said he had found the princess distraught and emotional. But he felt she was 'a consummate actress' and her emotions were 'artificial and designed to win my sympathy'.[6]

In March 1944 a review hearing took place to consider the princess' continued detention. The outcome was a recommendation that she should be paroled. Stephanie conducted her own defence and it appears, against the odds and in defiance of the records secretly held by the FBI, she successfully argued her innocence and that she had renounced all her Nazi sympathies. That outcome beggars belief and raises the question of whether the three-man tribunal was in possession of any papers recording the facts of her background in either the States or in Europe. The hearing ended in a statement which said: 'We are convinced that her position is one of determined and unqualified opposition to Hitler, and that she earnestly supports the Allied cause. It is our view that, once she is at liberty again, she will do everything in her power to further our war effort.'[7] But wiser councils prevailed. Hoover held up her release for several weeks and finally President Roosevelt overruled the board. He ordered she should not be released for the duration of the war. When VE Day came, on 9 May 1945, she was the last detainee to leave the Seagoville Camp. Major Schofield welcomed her back with open arms.

On the other side of the Atlantic, the British were not so forgiving. In September 1945 the princess was included on an official post-war blacklist of persona non grata. Her file, which was still being maintained by MI5, describes her as 'a notorious intriguer who had in the past had extremely close relations with the Nazi leaders. She must still be regarded as a highly dangerous person.'[8] British intelligence continued tracking her movements until September 1949, when a memo to the chief inspector of the Immigration Branch at the Home Office described her as being no longer of security interest, but that certain other ministries in Whitehall still had grave concerns about her.

18

JUST DESSERTS?

With Europe plunged into world war, what happened to the extraordinary cast of characters involved in this story?

Lord Rothermere had died in Bermuda in November 1940, as his predictions of a bombing blitz on London were becoming horrifically true – although history was to show that the Allied bombing of German cities far surpassed, in civilian deaths and in the devastation caused, anything the Luftwaffe achieved in their attacks on London. The greatest air armadas in history, of the type Rothermere had feared, flew from English airfields bearing RAF and USAAF roundels, not Nazi swastikas.

Having been told the news of Rothermere's death in a telephone call from Hitler's favourite journalist, Ward Price, Collin Brooks, Rothermere's confidant and colleague, wrote in his diary that he felt conflicting emotions:

> Chief of them was grief and self-pity. Grief that Rothermere should have died in Bermuda virtually alone; and self-pity that I no longer have the resort to his good humour, his sagacity, his kindness that has been mine for over five years … I remember only his great heart and his loneliness and his affection for me and me for him.[1]

What had Rothermere himself believed his relationship with Princess Stephanie had been all about? Certainly until very late in the day he had no idea of the magnitude of the deception that had been practised against him, and he had been confident in his own actions by wooing the Nazi leadership. In January 1938 he had written to the princess saying:

My mission to create a better feeling between Britain and Germany has largely succeeded. Mine was a lone voice in the wilderness four years ago, but now it is generally accepted by almost every political party in this country that good relations between Britain and Germany are essential for the peace of the world.

He added with unintentional irony a tribute to the princess: 'You have helped much to achieve this better understanding.'[2]

A more objective view was expressed by a leader in the *Yorkshire Post* in November 1939. Referring to Rothermere's lengthy dealings with the Nazi leaders, revealed by the notorious court case, the paper said:

The danger of these negotiations was two-fold. There was first the danger that Lord Rothermere might unwittingly give the Nazis a misleading impression of the state of opinion in this country; and there was also the danger that Lord Rothermere might – again unwittingly – allow himself to be used as a vehicle for the extremely subtle manoeuvres of Nazi propaganda ... discussions with heads of foreign governments are best left to persons whose status is on both sides clearly understood. A newspaper owner has great responsibilities towards the public of his own country; he should be particularly chary of placing himself in situations liable to misinterpretation, or abuse, abroad.[3]

Princess Stephanie had fled to the United States to join her lover Fritz Wiedemann and, as told in the last chapter, she spent the rest of the war in internment there regarded as a dangerous alien; a spy for the Führer. The princess then manipulatively switched on her seductive charms to corrupt an official of the American government in an effort to protect herself. After her death, documents released in Washington suggested that during her internment the American Office of Strategic Studies had called on her experiences with the Nazi leaders to provide insights into the character of Hitler and others in the Nazi hierarchy.

Wiedemann, Stephanie's lover, was thrown out of the United States and dispatched by Hitler to what was termed as a diplomatic post in China, but was almost certainly more to do with espionage than diplomacy.

What of the woman who was the catalyst in the princess' and Lord Rothermere's 'flirtation' with Hitler and his Nazi high command? American-born Annabel Kruse, my great-aunt, having tasted the peaks of 1930s highlife in Britain and on the Continent, had fallen victim to one of the deadly addictions to which some of the stylish super-rich of the period were attracted – heroin. Amongst the very wealthy, use of the drug was not uncommon. From 1933, six years after that fatal introduction of Princess Stephanie to Rothermere, Jack and Annabel were searching desperately for a cure for her drug-induced illness. They sought advice from specialists in London, New York and Paris. When more orthodox cures from qualified medical experts failed to relieve Annabel's suffering, she turned in desperation to faith healers and 'quacks'. It cost the couple a great deal of money, but to little effect. Annabel was sinking into a half-world, detached from much of what was going on around her. She was cared for by nurses and by her sister-in-law Lilian Kruse, languishing for days at a stretch in her antique Renaissance bed surrounded by antique furniture, Dresden mirrors and priceless tapestries.

The Wall Street Crash of 1929, followed by the Depression years of the early 1930s, seriously damaged the Kruses' finances. In the early 1930s Sunning House was sold to Rothermere, and the couple also had to give up their apartment at the Grosvenor House Hotel, the permanent suite they kept at Claridge's and a mansion on Egham Hill standing in 50 acres of parkland. They had been forced to reduce the standard of super-rich living to which they had become accustomed, but they were still able to afford a fifty-room mansion, Ridge House, close to the Women's Golf Course at Sunningdale. Before Annabel succumbed completely to her heroin-induced illness, she was able to furnish Ridge House in fairly lavish style.

By the mid-1930s Jack was virtually retired, although he was then only in his mid-40s. Encouraged by Rothermere's campaigning, his interests had moved from expensive cars and Alpine touring to aviation and, in particular, the need for the country to build up its air defences. He, like Collin Brooks, took to lobbying through the National League of Airmen. He was an avid writer of letters to *The Times* on rearmament and the enlistment of men from the empire into the British Armed Forces. Kruse was well informed, too. He had travelled widely and, as a director of one of Rothermere's newspaper companies based in Paris, he was extremely well briefed on European affairs. As the dictators and their National Socialist ideas gained ground, he took a much more balanced view than his employer. On the one hand he disliked Churchill's hawkish anti-appeasement policy, but on the other he was appalled by Rothermere's cosy relations with Hitler. How he judged the role Princess Stephanie was playing in that relationship, and her real motives, is unrecorded. He maintained his friendship with her, but to an observant man her deceptions must have been pretty clear.

Kruse was spending more and more time in North Yorkshire at Moor Top, his bolt-hole and the place he loved perhaps more than anywhere else. His last 'exotic' car, purchased in 1937, was a Buick saloon. Despite returning frequently to Moor Top, Kruse still travelled extensively. He became friendly with a Russian woman, Tamara, who ran a vegetarian guest farm in the Pyrenees. As Annabel became more and more detached in her own uncomprehending world, Jack sought comfort in his friendship with Tamara. By this time Annabel, who had worshipped Jack ever since they had first met in New York, was incapable of recognising him. In the late 1930s, worn down and distraught at Annabel's illness, he went to live at Tamara's apartment in the Avenue des Baumettes in Nice. Sadly, his family never saw him again.

When war broke out and the German invasion of France looked inevitable, Jack and Tamara attempted to escape back to England. They hitched rides to Paris, but the fall of France overtook them and they were forced to turn back and try to find a route out via Spain. They never made it. They were caught and interned in Grenoble, and it was there, on 8 February 1943, that Jack was taken ill with heart disease and died at the age of 51.

As for Annabel, she languished in her 'half world'. Through the first two years of the war she was looked after by her sister-in-law. In 1940 Ridge House was hit by a German bomb. Although it was not damaged beyond repair, Annabel and Lilian moved to Great Copse House at Eversley in Hampshire. With Jack's money gone and his assets on the Continent confiscated, Annabel was living chiefly off the proceeds raised by the sale of her jewellery. She died at Great Copse House on 22 March 1941.

John Kruse, Jack's son by his previous marriage who had been brought up to regard Annabel as his mother, was called up for military service on the outbreak of the Second World War. He served as a liaison officer in India and the Middle East, and returned to England at the end of hostilities to find his home bombed, Annabel and his father dead and no family business. All the wealth, luxury and classic cars he had known as a child had disappeared. He had to earn a living and he did so by driving a tar lorry for the local council during the day, and using his talent as a storyteller to write short stories at night. He succeeded in supporting his wife and young child, and embarked on a flourishing literary career which was to span four decades.

After quitting his lorry driving to take a job as clapper-board operator at Pinewood Film Studios, he quickly rose through the ranks to cameraman. The whaling scenes in Moby Dick were shot through his lens. Meanwhile, his short stories developed naturally into film scripts. His first feature film, Hell Drivers, in 1957, featured a young Sean Connery among its cast. Then television beckoned, and soon John was scripting some of the most-watched TV series of the 1960s and '70s, including *The Avengers, Shoestring, Colditz* and *The Persuaders!*. His work culminated in the classic *The Saint* series, starring Roger Moore, for which he was principal writer. After leaving England with his family in 1981 to live in Spain, John wrote three novels, including the bestseller *Red Omega*. He then turned to another artistic talent: painting. Over the years his artistic output was seen by thousands of people in bars, restaurants and exhibitions in the area of Spain in which he lived. John Kruse died in 2004.

With the death of Lord Rothermere in November 1940, the Stody estate in Norfolk and the press baron's other assets passed to his only remaining son and heir, Esmond Harmsworth. Collin Brooks was obliged to give up The Mount which proved to be a point of conflict between Esmond and Brooks. Before Rothermere had left England, he apparently signed ownership of The Mount over to Brooks. However, Esmond sought Brooks' eviction. Brooks confided in his diary that, aside from sentimental attachment, 'it's going will be a blessing for my diminished income cannot keep paying for its upkeep'.[4] The Stody estate was put up for sale by the new Lord Rothermere and purchased in the early 1940s by George Knight. He appointed my father as agent for the whole estate, and my father remained in that role throughout the war years until the early 1950s.

Collin Brooks became chairman and editor of *Truth*, a magazine aimed at political and society issues. He was a prolific writer with over fifty books to his name. He also appeared in many BBC programmes, including being a member of the original 'Any Questions' team and frequently taking part in the BBC's *Brains Trust*. He died in 1959 and his long-time friend, the distinguished poet T.S. Eliot, gave the address at his memorial service in the Fleet Street church of St Bride's.

As for Princess Stephanie's female rivals for Hitler's attention, the Mitford sisters: Unity was shattered by the outbreak of war between the two countries she loved. She could not bear to live with her loyalties so torn and a few hours after the war broke out she sat on a park bench in Munich's Englischer Garten and put a bullet through her head. For days she lay unconscious in hospital in Munich, her life hanging in the balance. Eventually, Hitler arranged for her to be moved to a hospital in Switzerland, which remained a neutral country. The Führer was personally shocked and full of regret at her fate. 'She lost her nerve just when for the first time I could really have used her,' he was recorded as saying. In January 1940 her mother and one of her sisters, Deborah, Duchess of Devonshire, travelled to Switzerland to bring her home. She could not walk, and could only talk with difficulty. Above all, she appeared to her family as a stranger, a totally changed personality and in need of constant care. Unity never fully recovered and died in 1948.

Her sister Diana, wife of Sir Oswald Mosley, was interned with her husband for much of the duration of the war. MI5 believed there was evidence that Mosley thought he would be able to seize power if Hitler successfully carried through with Operation Sealion, the Nazi plan to invade Britain. Had this happened the British authorities feared the Germans would have put into action Operation Willi: replacing George VI with the Duke of Windsor as king, his wife Wallis as queen and Mosley as prime minister. Goebbels, writing in his diary in January 1940, expressed that hope: 'The Mosley people keeping their heads down at the moment. Their only, but perhaps their big chance.'[5] But that opportunity never came.

Sir Oswald lived on after the war and formed yet another new party, the Union Movement, which failed to gain anywhere near the support he had achieved with the BUF in the 1930s. He and Lady Mosley took up residence in France, only a few miles from the Windsors' home, and all four became close companions, dining together twice a week. Sir Oswald died in December 1980. His wife Diana survived for more than twenty years longer, dying in Paris in 2003 in her 90s, still sticking to her fascist views. In an interview in 1986 she was insistent that from the 1930s right up until their deaths, the Windsors shared her and her husband's views on politics.

Hitler's adjutant and former senior officer, Fritz Wiedemann, having been captured by the Americans following the Japanese surrender, was interrogated and then held in detention. He was moved back to Germany under guard and required to give evidence at the Nuremberg War Crimes Tribunal in October 1945. But the extensive FBI file on Wiedemann and Princess Stephanie was never considered at Nuremberg. It was never asked for by the trial authorities. Wiedemann was credited with being part of the plot in which the chief of the Abwehr, Admiral Franz Canaris, had hoped to remove Hitler, which enabled Wiedemann to escape much of the evidence that he might have been confronted with. The tribunal hearings over, he was kept in detention until May 1948, one of only 6,656 Nazis who faced conviction for crimes following the fall of the Third Reich. He died at the age of 78 in Fuchsgrub in January 1970.

Wiedemann's lover and co-conspirator, Princess Stephanie, outlived him by two years – but of all this cast of extraordinary characters she was the survivor. After her release from internment by the American authorities at the end of the war, she set about totally reinventing herself. As she had succeeded in doing all her life, she clawed her way back into high society in the States. She used a series of wealthy male friends, whom she either charmed or seduced, as her source of funding, and she exploited her title and her notoriety as her entry ticket to American society. First she had to contend with continuing newspaper criticism and attempts by the American immigration authorities to eject her. In March 1947 she was living in New York with her lover, Major Lemuel Schofield, who had remained infatuated with her throughout the time she was held in internment as an enemy alien. Yet her past refused to fade. In July 1947 *The San Francisco Examiner* published a story saying that she was being feted in Long Island and Connecticut society. 'The Princess is pretty well known locally,' the newspaper reported. 'Not favourably. She was once an ardent and well-subsidised Nazi good-will ambassador. She still is an outspoken admirer of certain Nazis. How forgiving and forgetful we get!'[6]

She was trying to live down her colourful past and reinvent herself, but it was short-lived. A leading newspaper columnist, Robert Ruark, with a column syndicated throughout the States, noted in March 1947 that the princess – who by then was playing a not-insignificant role in New York society – was the same Princess Hohenlohe who had been released from one of America's 'top security prisons for spies'. His column went on to remind his readers that she had been a close friend of Hitler and 'his most trusted female spy'. She had arranged the famous meetings between the Führer and Lord Rothermere, and had set up the Sudetenland talks between Viscount Runciman and the German gauleiter in Czechoslovakia, Konrad Henlein, the outcome of which was the 'glowing fuse before the world blew up'. The column continued that in Nuremberg the Allies had strung up a number of 'her old buddies' for similar misdeeds, and it suggested she was a legitimate candidate for similar treatment. Finally, Ruark asked how New York society could nurture a one-time member of the Nazi hierarchy to its bosom. After this attack she was seen dancing at the classy New York Stork Club which prompted Ruark to publish another jibe. Soon American society would see Ribbentrop parading in similar circumstances, he wrote. Although, of course, Ribbentrop had paid the price with his life at Nuremberg.[7]

After that public attack, the princess sought refuge out of the public eye on Schofield's farm, Anderson Place near Phoenixville in Pennsylvania, although she retained an apartment at the Barclay Hotel in Philadelphia. They lived on the farm as man and wife until Schofield died in 1954. She must have felt her reinstatement into American society was complete when in 1953 she was named by the New York Dress Institute as one of the Ten Best Dressed Women in America. The Philadelphia *Sunday Bulletin* described her as dividing her time between fashionable society in Paris and Salzburg when not in her apartment at the Barclay Hotel on Rittenden Square, Philadelphia.[8]

Stephanie's new image was shattered some months after Schofield's death, however, when sensational claims were printed in the *Philadelphia Inquirer* in August 1955, headlined: 'Wealthy Princess filed no Tax Returns for Three Years Agents Find'. The report described her as 'a resident alien and international cosmopolite who occupies a sumptuous suite at the Barclay'. The princess' apartment, the news report said, could be called a 'royal suite ... Its walls are hung with priceless tapestries and paintings by famous artists, among them those of Thomas Gainsborough.'[9] The newspaper was wrong about Princess Stephanie's tax returns, but right about her late lover's tax debts. Schofield had failed to file returns for the last six years of his life, leaving a tax and penalty liability that approached $1 million, effectively wiping out his entire estate.

In the early 1950s Stephanie applied to become a US citizen. In a letter to the authorities, Schofield had written: 'There never was a scintilla of evidence that her presence in this country was hostile or adverse to the best interests of the United States.'[10] Her persuasive powers produced a sworn affidavit in support of her bid for naturalisation, in which she was described as 'a person of great education, intelligent and of exemplary moral character'. Before the death of her lover she made a couple of trips with him to her old haunts in Europe, visiting France, Austria, Germany and Italy. On one of these she could not resist revisiting Schloss Leopoldskron to recall the days she had spent there as chatelaine courtesy of Adolf Hitler. In Germany she also renewed her friendship with Fritz Wiedemann, no doubt to talk over past memories of the Third Reich and the Führer.

With her financial support and her home gone, and little or no benefit from Schofield's estate, Princess Stephanie did what she had proved she could always do in a crisis – she seduced another wealthy man. This time it was multi-millionaire Albert Monroe Greenfield, the richest man in Philadelphia. She went to live with him at his ranch at Cobble Close, New Jersey, and his riches and reputation gave her new opportunities to be welcomed in American society. In 1957 she was guest of honour at the influential Women's Press Club of New York.

In 1959 she moved back to Europe, settling in Geneva in an apartment with a living room that looked out in one direction on Lake Geneva and on the other to Mont Blanc. There she signed a contract with the magazine *Quick* to act as a consultant, much as she had done years before for Rothermere, setting up contacts with important and newsworthy people, using her title and her network of friends to open doors. She became a personal friend of President Richard Nixon and, using her influence, her contacts and her fatal charm, she arranged interviews with successive American Presidents John F. Kennedy and Lyndon B. Johnson. In an extraordinary turnaround from Nazi spy to American socialite, she was even invited to Johnson's presidential inauguration ceremony in Washington in January 1965.[11] An ex-prisoner of the United States, denounced as a danger to democracy and to American liberty, she was now an honoured guest of the President.

Two years later she signed a contract with *Stern* magazine in Germany – which became Europe's highest-selling magazine – to develop story opportunities. In this role she arranged high-profile interviews with President Johnson, Vice-President Hubert Humphreys and Supreme Court Judge Earl Warren, who had been in charge of the commission investigating the assassination of President Kennedy. Further interview successes followed, notably with Grace Kelly when she became Princess Grace of Monaco, the wife of the Shah of Iran and Lady Bird Johnson, wife of the US President. She also worked for another influential publisher, Axel Springer, who owned, among other publications, the tabloid newspaper *Bild* and the broadsheet *Die Welt*, two of the most influential organs in West Germany in the 1960s. Perhaps fittingly, given Stephanie's own Jewish heritage, Springer was intent on making a significant contribution towards reparation of the terrible wrongs done to the Jews in Europe under the Nazis. The princess reverted to the role she had played so successfully between Rothermere and Hitler, as fixer, go-between and manipulator. But this time the part she played did not include, as had been the case in pre-war Europe of the 1930s, the role of spy.

It took longer for the British government to forgive. In 1962 the British Consulate in Geneva refused her application for a visa to return to Britain. At that time Sir Frank Soskice, a friend of the late Lord Rothermere and one of the law team who represented him in the celebrated court case in 1939, was Home Secretary. In 1966, twenty-seven years after she had left England on the understanding she would never be granted permission to return, she wrote from Geneva to Soskice's successor, Roy Jenkins, begging for the opportunity to explain personally why the ban on her returning to London, if only as a visitor, should be lifted. Her letter asked him not to pay any attention to her MI5 file. 'It is made up for the major part,' she wrote, 'of newspaper stories, gossip, hearsay and a great deal of deliberate distortion.' She said she did not want to return to England to reside but 'merely to clear up this humiliating matter once and for all'.[12]

In a postscript to the letter to the Home Secretary, she wrote: 'At the outbreak of war, on 20 December 1939, my mother and I left London for the United States. In other words we lived in war-time London for a full three months with the British authorities' knowledge and consent unlike so many other foreigners who were immediately interned.' (She failed to say that the only reason she was allowed to stay was because of the court case against Lord Rothermere.) Her postscript went on: 'A year later Mr Esmond Harmsworth came to New York and asked Sir William Wiseman to do everything in his power to prevent publication of my memoirs.' A fortnight later she was informed by the Home Office that she was free to apply for a British visa, if she chose to do so. After over a quarter of a century, the ban on her never returning to England had been lifted.

Three months before her 81st birthday, Princess Stephanie Hohenlohe-Waldenburg-Schillingsfürst died in a private clinic in Geneva. She was buried in the village cemetery at Meinier, in the mountains above the town. Among those who attended the funeral were the Consul Generals of Austria, the country of her birth, and Germany, the country she served under the Third Reich; and the wife of the American ambassador, the country that first interned her and then embraced her as a socialite. She had played an extraordinary role during her life and had lived in an extraordinary and colourful, if duplicitous, way. The deception she practised in life even followed her to her death. The small plaque on her grave records the year of her birth as 1905 – fourteen years later than her actual birth as a Jew in Vienna in 1891!

Finally, as a postscript and as testament to how close my father was to Rothermere and to Jack Kruse, my late brother was given Conrad as one of his three Christian names, from Captain Jack Frederick Conrad Kruse. I received as one of mine the name Harold, after Harold Sidney Harmsworth, 1st Viscount Rothermere.

NOTES

Public Record Office, Kew: Two British intelligence files record Princess Stephanie Hohenlohe's activities. The first (PRO KV2/1696) covers the years 1928–39. The second (KV2/1697), covering 1939–47, is chiefly concerned with her application to leave the UK for America and subsequent steps to ensure that she did not return.

Hoover Institution Archives, Stanford University, California: 'The Prinzessin Stephanie zu Hohenlohe-Waldenburg-Schillingsfürst Papers', consisting of nine boxes of letters, telegrams, documents and biographical notes.

1 Twice Wed in New York

1 PRO KV2/1696
2 Memorandum re Princess Stephanie von Hohenlohe, New York, 28 October 1941: Franklin D. Roosevelt Library
3 PRO J77/1933/483 & J77/2004/2811
4 S.J. Taylor, *The Great Outsiders: Northcliffe, Rothermere & the 'Daily Mail'*, p. 253
5 Princess Stephanie Hohenlohe Papers (Box 5): Hoover Institution Archives

2 Rothermere and Churchill

1 Obituary, *The Times*, 27 November 1940
2 Churchill Papers: Churchill College
3 S.J. Taylor, *The Great Outsiders: Northcliffe, Rothermere & the 'Daily Mail'*, p. 191
4 Obituary, *The Times*, 27 November 1940

3 The Golden Couple

1 PRO J77/1820 Marriage Certificate
2 Martin Pugh, *We Danced All Night: Britain Between the Wars*, p. 352
3 National Motor Museum, Beaulieu
4 'Court Circular', *The Times*, 1920
5 Tom Clarke, *The Flying Lady*, 2001/2: National Motor Museum
6 Rolls-Royce Owners' Club

7 S.J. Taylor, *The Great Outsiders: Northcliffe, Rothermere & the 'Daily Mail'*, p. 256
8 Ibid., p. 253
9 Ibid., p. 257

4 Throw of the Dice
1 Martha Schad, *Hitler's Spy Princess*, p. 214
2 Princess Stephanie Hohenlohe Papers (Box 5)
3 Ibid.
4 Ibid.
5 PRO KV2/1696
6 Princess Stephanie Hohenlohe Papers (Box 5)
7 FBI Memorandum to President Roosevelt, 24 October 1941: Franklin D. Roosevelt Library

5 Whose Go-between?
1 Memorandum re Princess Stephanie von Hohenlohe, New York, 28 October 1941: Franklin D. Roosevelt Library
2 PRO KV2/1696
3 Prince Franz Hohenlohe, *Steph: The Fabulous Princess*, p. 37
4 Princess Stephanie Hohenlohe Papers (Box 5)
5 Ibid.
6 Ibid.
7 Ibid.
8 *Daily Mail*, 21 June 1927
9 Princess Stephanie Hohenlohe Papers (Box 4)
10 PRO KV/1696
11 Hohenlohe, *Steph*, p. 49
12 Letter from Prince Wilhelm to Lord Rothermere, 20 June 1934

6 A Friend in Berlin
1 *Daily Mail*, 24 September 1930
2 Princess Stephanie Hohenlohe Papers (Box 2)
3 Ibid.
4 Ibid.
5 Ibid.
6 PRO KV/1696
7 Memorandum re Princess Stephanie von Hohenlohe, New York, 28 October 1941: Franklin D. Roosevelt Library
8 PRO KV2/1696
9 Princess Stephanie Hohenlohe Papers (Box 1)
10 Prince Franz Hohenlohe, *Steph: The Fabulous Princess*
11 *Daily Mail*, 10 July 1933
12 N.J. Crowson, *Fleet Street, Press Barons & Politics: The Journals of Collin Brooks*
13 Princess Stephanie Hohenlohe Papers (Box 5)
14 Ibid. (Box 2)
15 Ibid. (Box 5)
16 Letter from Hitler to Lord Rothermere, 7 December 1933
17 Hohenlohe, *Steph*, p. 68

7 Threat from the Sky
1 Viscount Rothermere, *Warnings and Predictions*, 1939
2 Ibid.
3 *Daily Mail*, 7 November 1933
4 Stanley Baldwin speech, November 1932
5 Martin Pugh, *We Danced All Night: Britain Between the Wars*
6 *Daily Mail*, 3 April 1936
7 Rothermere, *Warnings*

8 Enter the Blackshirts
1 S.J. Taylor, *The Great Outsiders: Northcliffe, Rothermere & the 'Daily Mail'*, p. 294
2 'Hurrah for the Blackshirts', *Daily Mail*, 8 January 1934
3 Christopher Andrew, *The Defence of the Realm: History of MI5*, p. 192
4 Stephen Dorril, *'Blackshirt': Sir Oswald Mosley and British Fascism*, pp. 269–70, 285, 330, 337
5 *Daily Mail*, 8 January 1934
6 Princess Stephanie Hohenlohe Papers (Box 4)
7 PRO KV3/53
8 *Daily Mail*, 25 April 1934
9 PRO Home Office 144 20140/674216
10 *Daily Mirror*, 22 January 1934
11 N.J. Crowson, *Fleet Street, Press Barons & Politics: The Journals of Collin Brooks*
12 Ibid.
13 *Daily Mail*, 8 June 1934
14 House of Commons Debate, 14 June 1934
15 Andrew, *The Defence of the Realm*, p. 192
16 Taylor, *The Great Outsiders*, p. 284
17 Letter from Princess Stephanie to Lord Rothermere, 22 August 1934
18 PRO KV2/1696
19 Ibid.

9 Nazi Party Gold
1 Princess Stephanie Hohenlohe Papers (Box 4)
2 Letter from Hitler to Lord Rothermere, 3 May 1935
3 Letter from Hitler to Lord Rothermere, 19 December 1935
4 Letter from Rothermere to Hitler, 16 December 1936
5 Ibid.
6 Martha Schad, *Hitler's Spy Princess*, p. 40
7 Ibid.
8 Ibid., p. 41
9 Letter from Princess Stephanie to Hitler, 12 January 1937
10 Martha Dodd, *My Years in Germany*, pp. 223–4
11 Prince Franz Hohenlohe, *Steph: the Fabulous Princess*, p. 107
12 Letter from Hitler to Lord Rothermere, 20 May 1937
13 Princess Stephanie Hohenlohe Papers (Box 5)
14 Ibid.

10 The Language of Butter
1 *Daily Mail*, 7 October 1929
2 *Daily Mail*, 24 September 1930

3 Princess Stephanie Hohenlohe Papers (Box 1)

4 W.S. Churchill, *Great Contemporaries*, p. 203

5 Christopher Andrew, *The Defence of the Realm: The Authorised History of MI5*, pp. 203–6

6 Letter from Lord Rothermere to Neville Chamberlain, then Chancellor of the Exchequer, 5 October 1934

7 Letter from Lord Rothermere to Lord Tyrrell, British ambassador to France, December 1933

8 Letter from Lord Rothermere to Lady Vansittart, 19 February 1934 (Sir Robert Vansittart was Permanent Under-Secretary at the Foreign Office from 1930 to early 1938. He stood for rearmament and opposition to appeasement more strongly than any other Whitehall mandarin)

9 S.J. Taylor, *The Great Outsiders: Northcliffe, Rothermere & the 'Daily Mail'*, p. 301

10 Princess Stephanie Hohenlohe Papers (Box 1)

11 Ibid.

12 Ibid. (Box 2)

13 Telegram from Lord Rothermere to Churchill, 28 September 1938 (at the time of the Munich Agreement)

14 Princess Stephanie Hohenlohe Papers (Box 2)

15 Letter from Lord Rothermere to Churchill, 30 September 1938

16 Lord Lothian's 29 January 1935 meeting with Hitler was arranged by Leopold von Hoesch, German ambassador in London

17 William E. Dodd and Martha Dodd (eds), *Ambassador Dodd's Diary 1933–38*, p. 411

18 PRO KV2/1696

19 Princess Stephanie Hohenlohe Papers (Box 3)

20 PRO KV2/1696

21 *Durham Chronicle*, 28 February 1936; Ian Kershaw, *Making Friends with Hitler*, p. 141

22 *Manchester Guardian*, 24 February 1936; Kershaw, *Making Friends with Hitler*, p. 142

23 Letter from Lady Londonderry to Hitler, 21 February 1936; Kershaw, *Making Friends with Hitler*, p. 145

24 Lord Londonderry's conversation with Goering, 22 September 1937 – quoted in Marquess of Londonderry, *Ourselves and Germany*; Kershaw, *Making Friends with Hitler*, p. 203

25 Princess Stephanie Hohenlohe Papers (Box 3)

26 N.J. Crowson, *Fleet Street, Press Barons & Politics: The Journals of Collin Brooks*

11 The Princess, the King and Wallis

1 PRO KV2/1696

2 Charles Higham, *Wallis: The Secret Lives of the Duchess of Windsor* (the author notes the source as Mrs Milton E. Miles, whose husband became an admiral in the US Navy. She was among navy wives in China and Hong Kong in 1925. 'It was gossip among Navy wives in Hong Kong. It was an open scandal.' At the time Wallis was in her first marriage to Earl Winfield Spencer, an officer in the US Navy.)

3 Henry Channon, *'Chips': The Diaries of Sir Henry Channon*

4 Higham, *Wallis*, p. 81

5 Channon, *'Chips'*

6 Stephen Dorril, *Blackshirt: Sir Oswald Mosley and British Fascism*

7 *The Diaries of Sir Robert Bruce Lockhart 1938–45*

8 Martha Schad, *Hitler's Spy Princess*, pp. 56–7

9 Princess Stephanie Hohenlohe Papers (Box 3)

10 Ian Kershaw, *Making Friends with Hitler*, p. 213

11 Ibid., p. 247
12 Ibid., p. 144
13 Higham, *Wallis*, p. 84
14 Ibid., pp. 120–1
15 Keith Middlemas & John Barnes, *Baldwin: A Biography*
16 Paul Schwarz, *This Man Ribbentrop: His Life and Times*
17 FBI Report to President Roosevelt, 1939
18 N.J. Crowson, *Fleet Street, Press Barons & Politics: The Journals of Collin Brooks*
19 Dorril, *Blackshirt*, p. 403
20 Ibid.
21 Ibid., p. 404
22 Crowson, *Fleet Street, Press Barons & Politics*
23 Schad, *Hitler's Spy Princess*, p. 63
24 Ibid., p. 64
25 '7 January 1937', in Fred Taylor (ed.), *The Goebbels Diaries 1939–41*
26 Dorril, *Blackshirt*, p. 406
27 Michael Bloch, *Ribbentrop*, p. 123; Kershaw, *Making Friends with Hitler*, p. 189
28 Kershaw, *Making Friends with Hitler*, p. 160
29 Schad, *Hitler's Spy Princess*, p. 53
30 PRO KV2/1696
31 Princess Stephanie Hohenlohe Papers (Box 3)
32 Sûreté Nationale Report, 9 April 1934
33 Charles Higham, *Trading with the Enemy*
34 Fred Taylor (ed.), *The Goebbels Diaries 1939–41*
35 *New York Daily News*, 13 December 1966
36 *New York Times*; Mark Allen, *Hidden Agenda*
37 Allen, *Hidden Agenda*
38 PRO ADM 223/490 Spanish help to the Germans
39 Michael Bloch, *Operation Willi: The Plot to Kidnap the Duke of Windsor, July 1940*, p. 74
40 Philip Ziegler, *Edward VIII*, p. 434
41 King George VI writing to Queen Mary, 7 July 1940
42 Baron von Hoyningen-Huene, German ambassador to Portugal, to Berlin, 10 July 1940
43 Higham, *Wallis*, p. 249
44 Ziegler, *Edward VIII*, p. 435
45 Bloch, *Operation Willi*, pp. 226–7
46 *Liberty*, 22 March 1941
47 FBI Report on Wallis Simpson sent to President Roosevelt, 1939
48 FBI memorandum to Hoover, 13 September 1940
49 Fred Taylor (ed.), *The Goebbels Diaries 1939–41*
50 FBI memorandum to Hoover, 2 May 1941

12 Intrigue in America and London

1 Charles Higham, *Trading with the Enemy: An Expose of the Nazi-American Money Plot 1933–49*
2 Martha Schad, *Hitler's Spy Princess*, p. 71
3 Letter from Hitler to Princess Stephanie, 28 December 1937
4 Princess Stephanie Hohenlohe Papers (Box 3)
5 Memorandum from Ward Price, 30 March 1938; Foreign Office Papers 800/313/54-5
6 'Munich – The 1938 Appeasement Crisis', *The History of the Times Vol. IV 1912–1948*, p. 193
7 Ibid.

8 Princess Stephanie Hohenlohe Papers (Box 3)

9 Ibid.

10 Schad, *Hitler's Spy Princess*, p. 84

11 '11–16 July 1938', in J. Harvey (ed.), *The Diplomatic Diaries of Oliver Harvey 1937–40*, pp. 161–2

12 W. Selby, *Diplomatic Twilight*, p. 72

13 David Faber, *Munich: The Appeasement Crisis*, p. 107

14 Lord Halifax Memorandum, 11 August 1938

15 Faber, *Munich*, p. 198

16 Jan Masaryk, Czechoslovakian ambassador to London, memorandum to Prague, 22 July 1938

17 Sir Walford Selby, British ambassador to Austria, memorandum to British Foreign Office

18 H. Von Dirksen, *Moscow, Tokyo, London: Twenty Years of German Foreign Policy*

19 Fritz Wiedemann's memorandum to Ribbentrop; Documents of German Foreign Policy D/VII Appendix 111(H); Princess Stephanie Hohenlohe Papers (Box 3)

20 Andrew Roberts, *'The Holy Fox': A Biography of Lord Halifax*, p. 103

21 *Daily Express*, 31 July 1938

13 Chatelaine of Schloss Leopoldskron

1 Martha Schad, *Hitler's Spy Princess*, p. 92

2 Document signed by Wiedemann, adjutant to the Führer, 10 June 1938

3 *Time Magazine*, 30 January 1938

4 British and Foreign Newspaper Reports; Princess Stephanie Hohenlohe Papers (Box 4)

5 Telegram from Rothermere to Hitler, 1 October 1938

6 Letter from Princess Stephanie to Hitler, November 1938

7 PRO KV2/1696

14 Comic Opera in the High Court

1 Martha Schad, *Hitler's Spy Princess*, p. 105

2 '24 October 1938', in Fred Taylor (ed.), *The Goebbels Diaries 1939–41*

3 Ibid., 'January 1939'

4 Fritz Wiedemann, *Der Mann, der Feldherr warden wollte – The Man who Wanted to Command: Memoirs of Fritz Wiedemann*

5 Schad, *Hitler's Spy Princess*, p. 108

6 *Time Magazine*, 30 January 1939

7 Ibid.

8 Princess Stephanie Hohenlohe Papers (Box 3)

9 PRO KV2/1696

10 Princess Stephanie Hohenlohe Papers (Box 1); Letter from Rothermere to Princess Stephanie, 19 January 1938

11 Princess Stephanie Hohenlohe Papers (Box 1); Letter from Princess Stephanie to Rothermere, 2 February 1938

12 Letter from Rothermere to Ribbentrop, 7 July 1939

13 PRO KV2/1696

14 Letter from Rothermere to Hitler, 17 June 1939

15 '15 November 1939', in Fred Taylor (ed.), *The Goebbels Diaries 1939–41*

16 PRO KV2/1696

17 Ibid.

18 Ibid.

19 Ibid.

20 Ibid.
21 PRO KV2/1697
22 Ibid.
23 Ibid.
24 Ibid.
25 '15 November 1939', in Fred Taylor (ed.), *The Goebbels Diaries 1939–41*
26 *Eastern Daily Press*, 11 November 1939
27 'Law Report', *The Times*, November 1939
28 Letter from Lady Oxford to Princess Stephanie, 14 November 1939; Princess Stephanie Hohenlohe Papers (Box 3)
29 *Time Magazine*, November 1939
30 PRO KV2/1697

15 Exile

1 Letter from Lord Rothermere to Churchill, summer 1939
2 Quoted as a footnote to N.J. Crowson, *Fleet Street, Press Barons & Politics: The Journals of Collin Brooks*
3 Telegram from Lord Rothermere to Lord Beaverbrook, 4 May 1940
4 Crowson, *Fleet Street, Press Barons & Politics*
5 Ibid.
6 'Review of *My Fight to Rearm Britain*', *The Times*, December 1939
7 Letter from Lord Rothermere to Ribbentrop, 2 August 1939
8 Letter from Ribbentrop to Rothermere, 5 August 1939
9 *Daily Mail*, 4 September 1939

16 Trailed by the FBI

1 *New York World Telegram*, 12 December 1939
2 Princess Stephanie Hohenlohe Papers (Box 2); Letter from Hearst Magazines Inc., 31 July 1941
3 Princess Stephanie Hohenlohe Papers (Box 3); Letter from Wiedemann to Princess Stephanie, 3 March 1940
4 Princess Stephanie Hohenlohe Papers (Box 3); *Time Magazine*, 30 January 1939
5 Memorandum from John Wiley (US Treasury official) to Henry Morgenthau Jnr, 2 January 1940
6 Fred Taylor (ed.), *The Goebbels Diaries 1939–41*
7 Charles Higham, *Trading with the Enemy: An Expose of the Nazi-American Money Plot 1933–49*
8 Ibid.
9 Martha Schad, *Hitler's Spy Princess*, p. 133
10 H. Montgomery Hyde, *The Quiet Canadian: The Secret Service Story of Sir William Stephenson*
11 Morgan Reynolds, *Wilson, Churchill, Roosevelt & Bush: The Banality of Betrayal*
12 President Roosevelt received a thirty-page report from the FBI on the November 1940 meeting in suite 1024–1026 of the Mark Hopkins Hotel in San Francisco
13 Princess Stephanie Hohenlohe Papers (Box 2)
14 Memorandum re Princess Stephanie von Hohenlohe, 24 October 1941: Franklin D. Roosevelt Library
15 Schad, *Hitler's Spy Princess*, pp. 143–4
16 Directive from President Roosevelt to Attorney General Robert Jackson, 7 March 1941
17 Princess Stephanie Hohenlohe Papers (Box 1)

18 Higham, *Trading with the Enemy*
19 Princess Stephanie Hohenlohe Papers (Box 2)
20 Ibid.; Memorandum from Lemuel Schofield to Attorney General Francis Biddle
21 Schad, *Hitler's Spy Princess*, p. 151
22 Higham, *Trading with the Enemy*
23 Princess Stephanie Hohenlohe Papers (Box 1); Report, *New York Journal*, December 1941

17 The President's Anger

1 Paul Atkinson, 'Pearl Harbor and the Nazi Geopolitik Fifth Column', from Ellis Zacharias, *Secret Missions* (1946), www.buzzle.com (accessed 2010)
2 *Time Magazine*, 8 October 1945
3 Martha Schad, *Hitler's Spy Princess*, p. 152
4 Letter from President Roosevelt to J. Edgar Hoover, 17 June 1942
5 Letter from President Roosevelt to Attorney General Biddle, 11 July 1942
6 Charles Higham, *Trading with the Enemy*
7 Princess Stephanie Hohenlohe Papers (Box 1)
8 PRO KV2/1697

18 Just Desserts?

1 N.J. Crowson, *Fleet Street, Press Barons & Politics: The Journals of Collin Brooks*
2 Princess Stephanie Hohenlohe Papers; Letter from Rothermere to Princess Stephanie, 19 January 1938
3 Princess Stephanie Hohenlohe Papers (Box 2); *Yorkshire Post*, November 1939
4 Crowson, *Fleet Street, Press Barons & Politics*
5 '9 January 1940', in Fred Taylor (ed.), *The Goebbels Diaries 1939–41*
6 *San Francisco Examiner*, 13 July 1947
7 'Society Notes', 26 March 1947
8 *Philadelphia Sunday Bulletin*, April 1953
9 *Philadelphia Inquirer*, August 1955
10 Letter from Lemuel Schofield to US Immigration authorities, 15 September 1950
11 Invitation to Presidential inauguration etc.: Princess Stephanie Hohenlohe Papers
12 Princess Stephanie Hohenlohe Papers (Box 6); Letter from Princess Stephanie to Roy Jenkins, 4 December 1966

BIBLIOGRAPHY

Allen, Mark, *Hidden Agenda: How the Duke of Windsor Betrayed the Allies* (London: Macmillan, 2000)

Andrew, Christopher, *The Defence of the Realm: The Authorised History of MI5* (London: Allen Lane, 2009)

Atkinson, Paul, 'Pearl Harbor and the Nazi Geopolitic Fifth Column', from Ellis Zacharias, *Secret Missions* (1946), on www.buzzle.com (accessed 2010)

Bloch, Michael, *Operation Willi: The Plot to Kidnap the Duke of Windsor, July 1940* (London: Weidenfeld & Nicolson, 1984)

———, *Ribbentrop* (London: Bantam Press, 1992)

———, *The Secret File of the Duke of Windsor* (London: Bantam Press, 1988)

Channon, Sir Henry, *'Chips': The Diaries of Sir Henry Channon* (London: Weidenfeld & Nicolson, 1967)

Churchill, Winston S., *Great Contemporaries* (London: Thornton Butterworth, 1937)

Clarke, Tom, 'A Stately Super-car', *The Flying Lady* (Rolls-Royce Owners' Club magazine, Sept/Oct & Nov/Dec 2001)

Crowson, N.J., *Fleet Street, Press Barons & Politics: The Journals of Collin Brooks 1932–1940* (London: Camden Society Fifth Series Cambridge University Press, 1998)

Dodd, Martha, *My Years in Germany* (London: Victor Gollancz, 1939)

Dodd, William E. & Dodd, Martha, *Ambassador Dodd's Diary 1933–38* (New York: Harcourt Brace, 1941)

Dorril, Stephen, *Blackshirt: Sir Oswald Mosley and British Fascism* (London: Viking, 2006)

Faber, David, *Munich: The 1938 Appeasement Crisis* (London: Simon & Schuster, 2008)

Harvey, J., *The Diplomatic Diaries of Oliver Harvey 1937–1940* (London: Collins, 1970)

Higham, Charles, *Wallis: The Secret Lives of the Duchess of Windsor* (London: Sidgwick & Jackson, 1988)

———, *Trading with the Enemy: An Expose of the Nazi-American Money Plot 1933–49* (New York: Delacorte Press, 1983)

Hohenlohe, Prince Franz, *Steph: The Fabulous Princess* (London: New English Library, 1976)

History of the Times Vol. IV 1912–1948: 150th Anniversary and Beyond (London)

Kershaw, Ian, *Making Friends with Hitler: Lord Londonderry & Britain's Road to War* (London: Allen Lane, 2004)

MacDonogh, Giles, *1938: Hitler's Gamble* (London: Constable, 2009)

McLeod, Kirsty, *Battle Royal: Edward VIII & George VI, Brother Against Brother* (London: Constable, 1999)

Middlemas, Keith and Barnes, John, *Baldwin: A Biography* (London: Weidenfeld & Nicolson, 1969)

Montgomery Hyde, H., *The Quiet Canadian: The Secret Service Story of Sir William Stephenson* (London: Hamish Hamilton, 1962)

Neville, Peter, *Hitler and Appeasement* (London: Hambledon Continuum, 2006)

Picknet, Lynn, Prince, Clive and Prior, Stephen, *Double Standards: The Rudolph Hess Cover-Up* (Little, Brown & Co., 2001)

Pugh, Martin, *We Danced All Night: A Social History of Britain Between the Wars* (London: Bodley Head, 2008)

Reynolds, Morgan, 'Wilson, Churchill, Roosevelt & Bush' (2004), www.lewrockwell.com

Roberts, A., *'The Holy Fox': A Biography of Lord Halifax* (London: Weidenfeld & Nicolson, 1991)

Rothermere, Viscount, *Warnings & Predictions* (London: Eyre & Spottiswoode, 1939)

Schad, Martha (trans. A. McGeoch), *Hitler's Spy Princess* (Stroud: Sutton Publishing, 2004)

Schwarz, Paul, *This Man Ribbentrop: His Life and Times* (New York: Julian Messner, 1943)

Selby, W., *Diplomatic Twilight* (London: John Murray, 1953)

Shawcross, William, *Queen Elizabeth, The Queen Mother* (London: Macmillan, 2009)

Taylor, Fred (ed.), *The Goebbels Diaries 1939–41* (London: Hamish Hamilton, 1982)

Taylor, S.J., *The Great Outsiders: Northcliffe, Rothermere & The Daily Mail* (London: Weidenfeld & Nicolson, 1996)

Young, K., *The Diaries of Sir Robert Bruce Lockhart* (London: Macmillan. Vol. 1, 1973; Vol. 2, 1981)

Zeigler, Philip, *The Official Biography of King Edward VIII* (London: Collins, 1990)

INDEX

Other titles published by The History Press

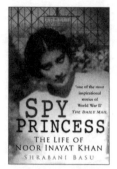

Spy Princess: The Life of Noor Inayat Khan
SHRABANI BASU

This is the riveting story of Noor Inayat Khan, a descendant of an Indian prince, who became a British secret agent for SOE during the Second World War. Noor was one of only three women SOE agents to be awarded the George Cross and, under torture, revealed nothing, not even her own real name. Months after she was captured by the Germans, she was taken to Dachau concentration camp and shot. Her last word was 'Liberté'.

978-0-7509-5056-5

Hitler's Women
GUIDO KNOPP

A focus on the leading women of the Third Reich and the role they played in the Nazi regime. To illustrate this theme, the author paints pen portraits of six famous women who were all bound up with Hitler's regime: Eva Braun; Magda Goebbels; Winifred Wagner; Leni Riefenstahl; Zarah Leander; and the legendary screen goddess Marlene Dietrich.

978-0-7509-4438-0

Odette: World War Two's Darling Spy
PENNY STARNS

Odette Brailly entered the nation's consciousness in the 1950s when her remarkable – and romantic – exploits as an SOE agent first came to light. In the first full biography of this incredible woman for nearly sixty years, historian Penny Starns delves into recently opened SOE personnel files to reveal the true story of this wartime heroine.

978-0-7524-4972-2

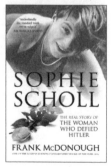

Sophie Scholl: The Real Story of the Woman who Defied Hitler
FRANK MCDONOUGH

Sophie Scholl, a 21-year-old student, was executed by the Nazi regime, along with two fellow students from the White Rose resistance movement. They had fought against Hitler's tyranny, not with bullets and bombs, but with words, in the form of leaflets. This is a shocking but ultimately inspirational biography of a German heroine who defied Hitler and was executed for her beliefs. It is a story that will stand for all time.

978-0-7524-5511-2

Visit our website and discover thousands of other History Press books.

www.thehistorypress.co.uk